Roma and Egyptians in Albania

From Social Exclusion to Social Inclusion

Hermine G. De Soto
Sabine Beddies
Ilir Gedeshi

THE WORLD BANK
Washington, D.C.

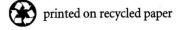
World Bank Working Papers are published to communicate the results of the Bank's work to the development community with the least possible delay. The manuscript of this paper therefore has not been prepared in accordance with the procedures appropriate to formally-edited texts. Some sources cited in this paper may be informal documents that are not readily available.

The findings, interpretations, and conclusions expressed herein are those of the author(s) and do not necessarily reflect the views of the International Bank for Reconstruction and Development/ The World Bank and its affiliated organizations, or those of the Executive Directors of The World Bank or the governments they represent.

The World Bank does not guarantee the accuracy of the data included in this work. The boundaries, colors, denominations, and other information shown on any map in this work do not imply and judgment on the part of The World Bank of the legal status of any territory or the endorsement or acceptance of such boundaries.

ISBN-10: 0-8213-6171-6
ISBN-13: 978-0-8213-6171-9
eISBN: 0-8213-6172-4
ISSN: 1726-5878

Hermine G. De Soto is a Senior Social Scientist in the Environmentally and Socially Sustainable Development Sector Unit of the Europe and Central Asia Region of the World Bank. Sabine Beddies is a Social Scientist in the Social Development Department of the World Bank. Ilir Gedeshi is an Economist at the Center for Economic and Social Studies.

Cover Photo: Roma children from Berat, Albania (by Hermine G. De Soto).

Library of Congress Cataloging-in-Publication Data has been requested.

Contents

LIST OF FIGURES

LIST OF TABLES

Foreword

This Needs Assessment was carried out at the request of the Government Albania, as a first step in addressing the problems of the Roma and Egyptian communities within the context of the new National Strategy for Socio-Economic Development. The study was designed to illuminate the multi-dimensionality of Roma and Evgjit poverty and exclusion in Albania, and to provide recommendations to promote their inclusion over the medium term.

Although the standard of living has improved for the majority of the population in Albania in the process of the country's efforts to create a market economy, the Roma and the Egyptian communities have been negatively affected by the transition. They are now the poorest and most marginalized people in the country. Their skills do not match new labor market requirements, and they suffer from limited access to public service such as health and education. They also lack political voice which renders them unable to participate in or influence decisionmaking that affects their lives. Further, their traditional values of mutual assistance have been eroded as different clans are forced to compete for scarce resources.

To identify as accurately as possible the key issues and dynamics underlying the social exclusion of the two communities, the study was designed and implemented in consultation with Roma and Evgjits across Albania. The findings are based on qualitative and quantitative survey data covering all parts of the country.

The Government of Albania has actively supported the study in particular. The Minister of Labor and Social Affairs provided access to official reports, statistics, and databases. The donor community, and specifically, the Embassy of the United States of America, the Swiss Development Corporation, UNDP and the Soros Foundation provided logistical, technical, and financial support. The participation of these and other dedicated partners has helped to ensure that the study has broad relevance for the Roma and Evgjit communities, and for the policymakers and other actors trying to design effective approaches to assist them.

Shigeo Katsu
Vice President
Europe and Central Asia

Acknowledgments

T he authors dedicate this report to the Roma and Egyptians in Albania. Numerous Roma and Egyptians participated in the study; helped us patiently in the design of the questionnaires; and provided feedback during the fieldwork, during field data analysis, and while we were writing the report.

Many people and organizations contributed to make this study possible. At the World Bank our special thanks go to Alexandre Marc, Sector Manager of the Europe & Central Asia Department of Socially Sustainable Development (ECSSD), Christiaan J. Poortman, former Country Director for Albania, and Orsalia Kalantzopoulos, current Country Director for Albania. We also thank Eugen Scanteie, Resident Manager of Albania, and his staff for their valuable and kind assistance while we were in the country.

Several people reviewed the conceptual framework that guided the study. We are most grateful to the peer reviewers, Conception E. Del Castillo, Dena Ringold. And Kathryn Funk, Albania Country Officer, provided us throughout with useful suggestions and much appreciated assistance.

We extend our thanks to members of the Albanian Parliament, and central and local government officials who supported the Needs Assessment. Special thanks go to Servet Pellumbi, Chairman of the Albanian Parliament; Valentina Leskaj, Minister of Labor and Social Affairs (MoLSA; Ahmet Ceni, Deputy Minister of MoLSA; and Gjergj Murra, of the Regional Initiative and Stability Pact in the Ministry of Foreign Affairs.

Without the financial generosity and collaboration of our National Strategy for Socio-Economic Development (NSSED) partners in Tirana, this study would have been far less comprehensive. We are most grateful for the support of Ana Stjarnenkint of the United Nations Development Programme (UNDP), the American Embassy, the Soros Foundation, the Swiss Development Cooperation, and the Delegation of the European Commission.

Throughout the study, we gained valuable insights from meetings, discussions, and feedback from representatives of international agencies: the European Council, the Swedish International Development Cooperation Agency (SIDA), the Friedrich Ebert Foundation, The United Nation Children's Fund (UNICEF), the Dutch Embassy, the French Embassy, the German Embassy, the Goethe Institute, the European Roma Rights Center (ERRC) in Budapest, and the European Council in Strasbourg, and the Organization for Security and Co-Operation (OSCE) in Europe.

Our very special thanks go to Luca Schio, Country Manager for Albania, the Council of the European Development Bank, Paris. He participated energetically in the preliminary field research, and rapid appraisals. His tireless contributions and encouraging support were inspirational.

During the course of the study, we gained new insights from Marcel Courthiade of the University of Rare Languages in Paris. He enriched our knowledge on Roma history, culture, and language.

The field research was coordinated by the Center of Economic and Social Studies (CESS) under the supervision of Ilir Gedeshi. We are most grateful to the CESS team: Hekuran Mara, Jorida Cila, Eridana Cano, Blendi Ceka, Admir Meko, Edita Fino, Dolores Purova, Pranvera Jahollari, Entela Shehaj, Naxi Mamani, Stella Zoto, Esmeralda Polena,

Irena Nikaj, Sonila Danaj, Nadire Xhaxho, Esmeralda Erindi, Iris Lala, Mira Haxhiu, and Sofia Noti. An outstanding contribution was made by Daniel Perez, who worked tirelessly with the team to finalize the first draft. His knowledge of Albanian has invaluably enriched the report to convey the cross-cultural, linguistic nuances.

Doreen Conrad receives our special thanks for her skillful editorial touches and for much more: her kind assistance in compiling the final version of the report. Daphne Sawyerr-Dunn's continuous assistance and logical support were enormous and our deepest thanks go to her excellent input throughout the study. Finally, our sincerest hope is that voicing the needs of the people in this study will lead to solutions that will help improve their lives and empower their communities.

Acronyms and Abbreviations

B.C.E.	Before Current Era
C.E.	Current Era
CEE	Central and Eastern European
CESS	Center for Economic and Social Studies (Tirana)
EC	European Council
ECRE	European Committee on Romani Emancipation.
ECRI	European Commission against Racism and Intolerance
ECSSD	Europe & Central Asia Department of Socially Sustainable Development
EDA	European Development Bank
ERRC	European Roma Rights Council
EU	European Union
GDP	Gross Domestic Product
INSTAT	Albanian National Institute of Statistics
MOLSA	Ministry of Labor and Social Affairs
NSSED	National Strategy for Socio-Economic Development
NGO	Nongovernmental organization
OSCE	Organization for Security and Co-Operation
QA	Qualitative Assessment
SMEs	Small and medium-size enterprises
UNDP	United Nations Development Programme

Glossary of Terms

Aga: a word with Turkish roots that during Ottoman times was a title given to wealthy landowners.

Bektashi Order: a Sufi Order of Islam whose members adhere to Shi'a Islamic Law.

Commune: a local administrative unit in rural areas, comprising several villages, which is governed by a chief who is elected for three-year terms by commune residents.

Çam: an Albanian population, living mainly in Southern Albania, that originates from northern Greece. They have lived in Albania since the end of World War II.

District: an administrative unit comprising one or more municipalities, communes, and usually a large number of villages.

Drachma (GRD): the currency of Greece now replaced by the euro. The rate of exchange at the time of this study was 1.00 GRD to US$0.003.

Dynym: an area of land comprising 1,000 m². Ten dynyms comprise a hectare.

Endogamy: a rule requiring marriage within a specified social or kinship group.

Erli: a Turkish word that can mean "native inhabitant" or "non-nomadic". Some Roma in Korça refer to themselves as Erli.

Euro (€): The pan-European currency that is legal tender in some European Union countries. The rate of exchange at the time of this study was €1.00 to US$1.10.

Fis (plural = *fise*): A "*fis*" is a clan-type social organization that is based on a unilineal descent group. A unilineal descent group can be based on patrilineal descent (patri-lineage) or matrilineal descent (matrilineage) whose members trace descent from an apical ancestor/ancestress by known genealogical links. The Albania Roma *fis* (as well as the white Albanian *fis*) is based on patrilineal descent. A patrilineal descent traces through a line of ancestors in the male line, whereas a matrilineal descent is a principle of descent from an ancestress through her daughter, her daughter's daughter, and so forth (in the female line).

Gadje: A Roma term that refers to "white" or "non-Roma" persons. It can also refer to para-digms or institutions dominated by white or non-Roma persons.

Kryeplak: the head of a local administrative unit chosen by elections at the village level who serves the village for four-year terms.

Lek (plural = lekë)(L): the currency of Albania. At the time of the study, US$1.00 equaled L130.

Llokum: a gelatinous candy referred to in English as "Turkish delight."

Matrilineage: a lineage whose members trace their genealogies through specified female links to a common female ancestor.

Municipality: the local administrative unit governing a town that is larger than a village and that usually comprises more than 4,000 people and hosts industry.

Ndihmë Ekonomike: an Albanian Government program to provide cash assistance to households that earn insufficient income through employment or other activities. Described in full in Chapter 5 on Economic Assistance.

Omonia: a central location in a city where those looking to find work gather to meet employers, usually for part-time work for a daily wage. Named after the square in Athens where similar employee-employer activity occurs.

Patrilineage: a lineage whose members embrace the genealogies through specified male links to a common male ancestor.

Raki: a traditional Albanian hard liquor.

Segmentary Clan (or *Fis*): a kinship descent system, defining descent categories with reference to more and more remote apical ancestors so that the descent categories form a treelike structure (including successively wider ranges of descendants) (American Anthropological Association).

Vigje: a celebratory dinner held when a child is born.

Village: a small center of families that is led by a *Kryeplak*. Usually, d 5 to 10 villages make up a commune.

A Roma Folk-Tale:
The Cup of Gold Coins[1]

Once upon a time, there was a very poor Roma who had many children. He lived next door to a wealthy white man. Every night, the Roma family would play music and dance and entertain themselves with the few things they had and didn't think about tomorrow. "Let God think about tomorrow," they would say.

One night, hearing the music coming from the Roma house, the wealthy neighbor decided to give the Roma family a cup full of gold coins, so that they could make a better living for themselves. The Roma thanked their neighbor for his generosity and went home.

That day, the Roma family began to argue. The husband wanted to spend the gold coins on one thing and his wife wanted to use them for other purposes. They were so upset that they stopped playing music and dancing; they lost their peace and could barely sleep at night.

Finally, they couldn't take it any longer and decided to return the gold coins to their neighbor. "Those wretched coins took our joy and happiness away. We have done nothing but fight ever since we took them. We Roma are poor but we are happy with our own lives," the husband told the neighbor, as he returned the gold gift.

Soon, the neighbor heard the sounds of music coming from the house next door again.

---

1. Qirici, M. T. (1999). "Gjylbeharja, Përralla dhe legjenda nga Romët e Shqipërisë". STEVLA. Tiranë.

Executive Summary

Objectives of the Study

The Needs Assessment investigated the socioeconomic, cultural, institutional, and historical situation of Roma and Egyptian communities in Albania. Its objectives were to: (a) provide quantitative and qualitative data on these communities that would assist the Albanian government in drafting special programs for these communities; (b) provide insights into potential social exclusion processes that affect these communities that will help the government meet some of the European Union (EU) recommendations on ethnic minorities; and (c) provide advice on the design of concrete actions that facilitate the inclusion of Roma and Egyptians in Albanian society.

Albanian Roma in a Regional Perspective

This study focused on two of the most marginalized groups in Albanian society: the Roma and Egyptians. Albanian Roma have many of the same socioeconomic and transitional problems as Roma in other Southeast European (SEE) and Central and Eastern European (CEE) countries. A 2003 World Bank draft report estimates the Roma population in several of these countries, as shown in Table 1.

The same report (Qirici 1999) states: "Although the Central European countries have indeed avoided violent conflict, ethnic relations between Roma and majority populations has reportedly deteriorated to a significant extent in the last decade. Unlike other minorities, who benefit from psychological, and sometimes material and political, assistance from their "homelands," the estimated seven to nine million Roma who live dispersed throughout Europe and the former Soviet Union, with the largest concentrations in Macedonia, Bulgaria, Slovakia, and Romania, lack this support."

Throughout the region, Roma have difficulty procuring and keeping employment. Their unemployment rate in CEE is estimated at between 50 and 90 percent, resulting in part from the loss of jobs on collective farms during the socialist period. In general, Roma have not been landowners; indeed, most live in abject poverty. In Bulgaria, for example, Roma constitute only 6.5 percent of the population, but 84 percent of these households live under the poverty line. Similarly, in Romania, where Roma make up only 2.3 percent of the total population, more than 78 percent live in dire poverty (Ringold 2002).

Unlike Roma in other CEE and SEE countries, Albanian Roma are able to move freely within the country and beyond its borders, primarily for migratory labor. The migrants generally send remittances back to their families.

Throughout the CEE and SEE, the Roma live on the periphery of towns and cities in neighborhoods that have no sewerage systems, utility connections, or public transportation. Living in such unsanitary conditions, with little health care or basic health information, they generally live 10–15 years less than non-Roma.

Table 1. Distribution of Roma Population 1991–94
　　　　(thousands)

Country	Roma Population	Total Population	% of Roma
Albania	95	3,421	2.0
Bosnia & Herzegovina	45	4,383	1.0
Bulgaria	750	8,459	8.9
Croatia	35	4,788	0.7
Czech Republic	275	10,323	2.7
Hungary	575	10,280	5.6
FYR Macedonia	240	2,191	10.9
Poland	45	38,446	0.1
Romania	2,150	22,761	9.4
Slovak Republic	480	5,345	9.4
Slovenia	10	1,993	0.4
FRYugoslavia	425	10,675	4.0

Note: Roma population estimates are midpoints of ranges.
Source: World Bank (2003). "Draft: Social Development in Europe and Central Asia Region: Issues and Directions." Washington, DC: *Environmentally and Socially Sustainable Development,* Social Development Team, Europe and Central Asia, pp. ix, x (March).

Like the Albanian Roma, few CEE or SEE Roma children move beyond an elementary school education because of poverty, low cultural valuation of education, and often severe discrimination at school.[2] Roma schoolchildren also suffer discrimination and difficulty because they do not speak the majority language. One result is that some are labeled mentally disabled.

Rural Roma in these countries who move to towns do not qualify for unemployment or social assistance because they are not registered as residents of those towns, or at the various levels of government.

Albanian Roma, in contrast to those in other CEE and SEE countries, have a unique form of social organization, the *fis*,[3] the key function of which is to support individuals and communities in sustaining their livelihoods though social cohesion, trust, and solidarity. Extensive *fis* networks played a special role during the socialist period. Social capital[4] held the *fis* together and provided its members with essential connections for finding markets and trade goods in the informal sector.

---

2. World Bank (2003), pp. 30–31.
3. A "*fis*" is a clan-type social organization that is based on a unilineal descent group. A unilineal descent group can be based on patrilineal descent (patrilineage) or matrilineal descent (matrilineage) whose members trace descent from an apical ancestor/ancestress by known genealogical links. The Albania Roma *fis* (as well as the white Albanian *fis*) is based on patrilineal descent. A patrilineal descent traces through a line of ancestors in the male line, while a matrilineal descent is a principle of descent from an ancestress through her daughter, her daughter's daughter, and so forth (in the female line). (Keesing, R. M., *Cultural Anthropology: A Contemporary Perspective*. Chicago: Holt, Rinehart and Winston, 1992).
4. Social capital is discussed fully in Chapter 10.

As a social organization, however, the *fis* has weakened during the transition period, as a result of the downward socioeconomic trend among Roma families, which has worked against the close solidarity that existed between the families under socialism.

Alternative forms of social organization have emerged that exist parallel to the *fis.* Albanian Roma are attempting to invent new civic institutions, such as associations and solidarity networks. In contrast to the *fis,* these alternative organizations are based on trans-local and transregional organizational principles. Nevertheless, Roma continue to use the *fis* and its inherent networks for business activities.

Roma have scarcely any representation in the government. Few are employed at the local, regional, or national administrative level, nor do they have any elected officials at any level. According to the head of a Roma association in Korça, "You won't find any one of us in local administration." Without this representation, they have only limited ability to voice their concerns.

Historical Background

The Origins of Roma and Egyptians

The origins of both Roma and Egyptians are unclear. Based on linguistic evidence, scholars believe that Roma began migrating westward from India beginning in the ninth century C.E. (Silverman 1995). The time of their arrival in the Balkans is also uncertain, but present-day Croatian sources point to a Roma presence there as early as the fourteenth century.[5] One or more Roma *fis* may have settled in Albania by the fifteenth century (Koinova 2000).

In contrast, Albanian Egyptians claim to have originated in Egypt, and at least three distinct theories link them to this alleged homeland: (a) they arrived in the Balkans from Egypt in the third century B.C.E.[6] or arrived in the fourth century C.E. as Coptic migrants (Koinova 2000), (b) they descended from Egyptian slaves in the Ottoman army (Courthiade and Duka 1995), and (c) they are semi-integrated Roma who, much earlier than other Roma, ended their nomadic traditions and lost the Roma language. None of these claims has been substantiated, and despite claiming separate origins, the Albanian Egyptians are now considered a subcategory of the Roma.

The Twentieth Century

During the period between the world wars, the first reliable sources on Egyptians and Roma in Albania describe two peoples who were distinct in terms of traditional occupations, skills, crafts, language, religion, and other anthropological categories. They also depict diversity among Roma *fis.*

---

5. Kolsti, J. (1999). *A History of the Gypsies of Eastern Europe and Russia.*
6. Zemon, R. (2001). "Evërteta mbi Evgjitianët e Shqipërisë," *Papirus* (April).

Relations were distant between Egyptians and Roma, and among Roma, Egyptians, and Albanians. Both Roma and Egyptians rejected the notion of being a single community. According to Hasluck (1938), "nomads regarded sedentary groups [Egyptians] as their inferiors," while these sedentary groups "despised" the Roma. Generally, Egyptians felt that they were "above the Roma" (Mann 1937). Members of the two groups rarely intermarried. Some sources claim that Albanians despised both groups (Kolsti 1999), but sometimes preferred Egyptians over Roma, since the former were "so much the nearer to Albanians" (Hasluck 1938).

World War II

During World War II, Roma suffered great losses at the hands of pro-German occupation regimes across Europe. In Albania, however, the Italian and German occupations were relatively mild (Fisher 1999), and Roma and Egyptians faced fewer hardships than elsewhere. Some Roma joined the Albanian partisan resistance movement.

The socialist government established in Albania following the war was the first organized effort to control the Roma and Egyptian ways of life. The ruling Communist Party sought to suppress their cultural distinctions and forced Roma and Egyptians to conform with the dicta of the socialist Albanian nation. The government had specific social policies to support poor population groups and integrate them into society. As a result, these communities experienced improvements in their general welfare, including improved employment, education, housing, health care, and free access to social services during the socialist period. Thus, the Roma and Egyptian communities made gains in employment and living standards during this period.

Employment

During the socialist period, everyone, including the Roma and Egyptians, was guaranteed lifetime employment. Some were integrated into agricultural cooperatives and state farms. Others were employed in state-owned handicraft and forest enterprises. In the cities, members of both groups worked as unskilled laborers alongside Albanians in street sweeping and cleaning, industrial enterprises, and construction (Taho 2002).

The Roma and Egyptians under the Constitution of 1976

The 1976 Constitution was the apex of the Albanian government's attempts to construct a socialist state. All private business and private property, including livestock, were outlawed, which created hardship for most Albanians. However, many Roma were allowed to continue their involvement in small-scale private enterprises, including trading horses and selling traditional copper, wickerwork, and other products that that they purchased in cities and in villages across Albania.

In effect, the Roma *fis* system helped govern the private sector along with Albanians. Different Roma *fis* members established business connections with other *fis* across Albania and, to a limited extent, served as important intermediaries between Albania's rural and urban economies, providing rural areas with access to goods from the cities that otherwise would not have been available to them (Courthiade and Duka 1995). The Roma *fis* system is one of the few examples of a nongovernmental system that facilitated economic activity in Albania under the socialist regime—a notion that was unheard of among most Albanians after 1976.

The Egyptians, who are generally more educated than the Roma, were better integrated into the state sector during this period. In addition to having workers in various economic sectors, the Egyptian community also produced engineers, doctors, teachers, economists, military officers, and state employees. Egyptian instrumentalists and vocalists contributed to the development of music in Albania.

Transition

The fall of the communist regime in 1991 marked the beginning of the Roma's and Egyptians' decline from relative well-being to extreme poverty (De Soto and others 2002). By 1996, while the country's overall unemployment rate was 18 percent, it was between 80 percent and 90 percent in the Roma communities (Koinova 2002 citing Kovacs). Low employment skills, discrimination, and the collapse of various state-owned industrial and agricultural enterprises contributed to their mass unemployment.

Roma and Egyptians coped with economic insecurity in different ways. Socialist-era trends partly explain these variances. The Albanian-speaking Egyptians worked as skilled laborers in the industrial and service sectors. Roma, on the other hand, continued to be employed in their clan-specific occupations, and those Roma who lived near the Greek border began to migrate.

While market liberalism sparked economic uncertainty, political liberalism during the 1990s allowed the Roma and Egyptian communities to gain some national and international recognition. Shortly after the end of communist rule, a number of local nongovernmental organizations (NGOs) were established in Albania specifically to assist the Roma and Egyptians. These included Amaro Dives, Rromani Baxt, Amaro Drom, Rromani Braxt, Disutni Albania, Alb Rrom, Roma for Integration, Rromani Kham, the Jevg Association, Nefreta, Kabaja, and Vëllazërimi, among others.

Methodology

This study is based on research in 11 districts throughout the country that were chosen to represent: (a) all regions in which large groups of Roma and Egyptians live; (b) urban, rural, and semiurban populations; (c) all Roma *fis*; (d) varying degrees of socioeconomic development, particularly since the start of the transition period; (e) different economic structures; and (f) any existing large-scale coping strategies, such as international and internal migration. The selected districts were Berat, Delvina, Durrës, Elbasan, Fier, Gjirokastra, Korça, Kruja, Shkodra, Tirana, and Vlora.

Table 2 below provides estimates of Roma and Egyptian populations by district in Albania.

Table 2. Estimated Population of Albanian Roma and Egyptians, by District

Regions	Local Government		Roma Association Amaro Drom	Poulton[a]	Bugajski[b]	State Department[c]	Brunër[d]	Egyptian Association Vëllazërimi
	Roma	Egyptian	Roma	Roma	Roma	Roma	Roma	Egyptian
Shkodra	50	4,500	600–1,000	n/a	n/a	n/a	n/a	n/a
Kruja	n/a	n/a	1,500–2,000	n/a	n/a	n/a	n/a	n/a
Tirana	n/a	n/a	10–12,000	n/a	n/a	n/a	n/a	n/a
Elbasan	2,622	8318	9–10,000	n/a	n/a	n/a	n/a	10,000
Durres	n/a	n/a	3–4,000	n/a	n/a	n/a	n/a	20,000
Korça	2,383	n/a	10–11,000	n/a	n/a	n/a	n/a	28,000
Fier	5,323	n/a	17–18,000	n/a	n/a	n/a	n/a	400
Vlora	1,036	3,000	2,000–2,500	n/a	n/a	n/a	n/a	30,000
Berat	n/a	n/a	3–4,000	n/a	n/a	n/a	n/a	10,000
Gjirokastra	1,200	5,000	2,000	n/a	n/a	n/a	n/a	5,000
Delvina	285	2,500	2,000	n/a	n/a	n/a	n/a	1,100
Total	n/a	n/a	120,000–150,000	10,000	10,000	100,000	60,000	Over 200,000

Notes: The official statistics, provided in all the population censuses conducted in Albania since the World War II (2002), do not give separate figures about the Roma and Egyptian communities. These are included in the total Albanian population figures. Meanwhile, in some districts, local governments have made their own estimates of the Roma and Egyptian population. In addition, the Roma and Egyptian associations have also attempted to approximate the numbers of these two communities. The striking differences between these estimates show that these figures must be taken with a grain of salt.

a. Poulton, H (1991). "The Balkans: Minorities and States in Conflict." London: Minority Rights Group.

b. Bugajski, J (1994). "Ethnic Politics in Eastern Europe." Armonk, NY: M. E. Sharp.

c. U.S. Department of State (1995). "Country Reports on Human Rights Practices for 1994." Washington, DC: U.S. Government Printing Office, February.

d. Brunër, G (1995). "Nemzetisegi kerdes es kisebbsegi konfliktusor Kelet-Europaban." Budapest: Teleki Laszl Alapitvany.

Source: ERRC (1997). "No Record of the Case: Roma in Albania," *Country Report Series* No. 5, June.

The analytic work for this study included primary and secondary data analysis. It involved: a desktop review of relevant literature, qualitative and quantitative methods, and Roma and Egyptian community profiles. The research methodology instruments included: (a) focus group discussions with local Roma and Egyptian communities (separate focus group discussions with women, children, and men); (b) semi-structured interviews with key stakeholders and formal and informal male and female leaders in the Roma or Egyptian community and the neighboring Albanian community; (c) eight ethnographic case studies—two women, two men, two girls, two boys per community; and (d) one socioeconomic household survey questionnaire for Roma and Egyptians, comprising 188 questions for 661 households, and another questionnaire for Albanians (non-Roma and non-Egyptians) comprising 10 questions for 440 households.

Findings

The end of socialism marked the beginning of the Roma's and Egyptians' decline from relative well-being to extreme poverty (De Soto and others). Low skills, discrimination, and the collapse of many state-owned industrial and agricultural enterprises during the transition period have contributed to their mass unemployment, along with rising illiteracy rates and deteriorating health, infrastructure, and housing conditions.

Because of high unemployment in the formal labor market, Roma and Egyptians seek employment in the informal labor market. When income from informal labor is insufficient to meet daily needs, Roma and Egyptians seek alternative poverty-coping methods such as international migration and, as a last resort, prostitution and trafficking of children and drugs. Forms of cognitive and structural social capital—such as trust, elastic community solidarity, and Roma and Egyptian associations—have also emerged during transition to assist families in coping with poverty and economic insecurity in the absence of traditional forms of social organization and government programs. However, social capital is fragile and does not pull families out of poverty.

According to collected empirical data, the causes of poverty and social exclusion for Roma and Egyptians in Albania are lack of education, lack of employment, and weak basic infrastructure. The symptoms of poverty and social exclusion are seen in their informal sector activities—migration, dependence on aid, and prostitution—which they employ as coping strategies in their daily lives. Their overall approach is to use social capital, evident in different kinds of relationships, exchanges, and collaboration. These strategies help to sustain their livelihoods at the edges of mainstream society, but also tend to trap them in poverty and social exclusion. Effective policies are needed to address the multiple dimensions of their poverty and social exclusion, and identify the specific social, institutional, and political barriers that need to be overcome. The analytical framework, which guided the study, is illustrated in Figure 1 below.

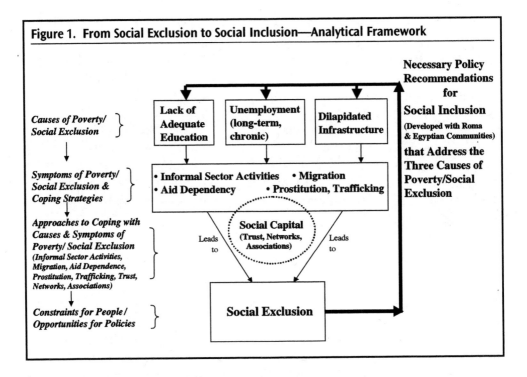

Figure 1. From Social Exclusion to Social Inclusion—Analytical Framework

Findings are based on assessments in the following areas:

Culture

In surveys, Roma have identified distinguishing cultural markers as language (99 percent), music (80 percent), community celebrations (80 percent), family ceremonies (74 percent), wickerwork (67 percent), and women's dress (63 percent). Egyptians have identified metal work (75 percent) and music (45 percent). In interviews, both Roma and Egyptians expressed the importance of supporting culture and identity through the establishment of cultural centers. However, poverty and other socioeconomic changes during the transition period have contributed to the decline of their cultures, particularly in the areas of transmission of folktales, handicrafts, and music.

Marriage and Family Planning

Since the beginning of the transition, ever-earlier ages for marriage and childbearing have become common, and some are beginning to relate these marriage practices directly to increasing poverty. Other consequences of these practices include high illiteracy rates, low levels of education, lack of vocational skills, and separation and divorce, all of which contribute to increased economic insecurity.

The majority do not receive formal family-planning education at school, because family planning in school is provided during higher primary school grades, which the majority do not attend. Only 10 percent of Roma and 8 percent of Egyptian respondents used birth control. Poor birth control use is partly the result of lack of knowledge about and mistrust of birth control methods. One consequence of lack of information is that the average number of children—6.4 for Roma and 5.2 for Egyptians—is larger than the national average of 4.2. Roma women have the lowest average marriage age (15.5 years) of all ethnic groups in Albania.

Income and Living Standards

Both groups have fewer opportunities for formal employment than the majority population. They increasingly rely on income sources such as casual work and self-employment, which are in decline because of increased competition, and in any case offer few prospects for improving living standards. An average of 46 percent of their decreasing household income comes from casual work or self-employment.

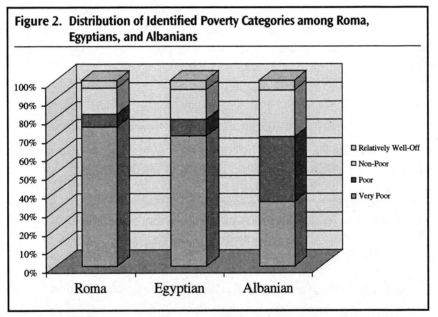

Figure 2. Distribution of Identified Poverty Categories among Roma, Egyptians, and Albanians

Source: Socioeconomic household questionnaires with Roma and Egyptians for the Needs Assessment, 2002/03.

In comparison with the majority of the population of 'white' Albanians, the percentage of the very poor group of households among Roma and Egyptians is apparently much higher (De Soto and others 2002); as seen in the above figure, the Roma and Egyptians fall into lower poverty categories than the "white" Albanians. Very poor and poor families face higher levels of social exclusion, because they are less capable of affording daily needs and less likely to participate in processes that affect their individual livelihoods, such as employment and education.

Roma and Egyptian household incomes are less than half of 'white' Albanian urban household incomes at the national level,[7] and their expenditures are primarily for food.

---

7. Average household income for *urban* households at the national level is 37,232 lekë (US$286) (INSTAT, 2003). Reliable statistical data are unavailable for average household income for all households, urban and nonurban, at the national level.

Based on the socioeconomic survey, the average household income is L16,492 (US$127) for Roma, and L17,769 (US$137) for Egyptians. Average monthly household expenditures are L25,867 (US$199) for Roma and L25,641 (US$197) for Egyptians.

The state's inability to provide infrastructure and public services contributes to the poverty of the Roma and Egyptians. The structures to extend utilities into the areas where most of these populations live have not yet been built. More than 40 percent of Roma and 30 percent of Egyptian families do not have running water in their home, because water connections have not been installed. The majority of these families live in makeshift or dilapidated housing with surface areas much smaller than the national average. They also face difficulties obtaining state assistance and other forms of social assistance.

Much like Albanian households surveyed in 2000, 39 percent of Roma and 45 percent of Egyptian households highlighted that the health of household members has declined over the past five years.[8] Determinants of poor health include malnutrition, limited access to health care facilities—especially for Roma and Egyptians in rural areas—and a weak governing capacity to provide health services. Only 25 percent of Roma and 29 percent of Egyptians said they have enough money to buy medicines.

Education

The educational attainment level of the Albanian population has decreased during transition and is most pronounced among the Roma and Egyptian communities. Sixty-four percent of Roma and 24 percent of Egyptians ages 7–20 are illiterate,[9] while 40 percent of Roma and 11.3 percent of Egyptians ages 20–40 are illiterate.

The biggest barrier to education is poverty. Families cannot afford to pay for school books or supplies, or to feed and clothe children sufficiently for them to attend school. In fact, 67 percent of Roma and 60 percent of Egyptian families cannot afford the costs of books and school supplies.

Many children do not attend school because they are required to contribute to household income by begging or working with parents. Some children migrate abroad to work with their families for several months a year.

Other barriers include limited access to educational facilities. In some areas, the long distance between schools from homes, along with a lack of public safety, prevent children from attending school. Moreover, many Roma children, who speak only Romani at home, have little knowledge of the Albanian language when they begin primary school. Discrimination is also a barrier to education. In some cases, parents and children described forms of frequent mistreatment by teachers in some localities, such as Korça and Tirana.

---

8. De Soto, H., Gordon, P., Gedeshi, I., Sinoimeri, Z. 2001. "A Qualitative Assessment of Poverty in 10 Areas of Albania," Washington, DC: World Bank.

9. Respondents aged 21–40 attended state schools from 1970–1990, and Roma illiteracy rates and educational levels are comparable from as early as 1970. By 1970, all Roma had been settled in permanent localities, which created the appropriate conditions for the state to enforce mandatory school attendance. Prior to the settlement of Roma, school attendance was unenforceable, so education levels prior to 1970 are not comparable to education levels in later periods.

The Labor Market

While the national unemployment rate level was around 16 percent at the end of 2002, the rates for Roma and Egyptians derived from the socioeconomic survey were 71 and 67 percent, respectively, for the working-age population.[10] Further, 88 percent of Roma and 83 percent of Egyptians have been unemployed for more than a year. Many became unemployed when state enterprises began restructuring in 1991.

For 92 percent of Roma and 90 percent of Egyptians, who consider merely finding a job a challenge, getting a job when there is a general lack of employment opportunities in Albania is difficult. Moreover, there is little call for their traditional professions, such as music and handicrafts, which both groups enjoyed during the socialist period.

Because of poverty and exclusion from the formal labor market, both groups work in the informal labor market, mainly in casual work, musical performance, can and metal collection, and begging. This work provides inadequate incomes to their families. However, even these incomes are in decline, which contributes to emotional stress. If viable alternatives are not developed, their future economic welfare is in jeopardy.

Migration and Remittances

When income from formal or informal work is insufficient to meet daily needs, members of both groups try to migrate abroad for short periods, mainly to Greece. Migrants travel to the recipient country in large groups of 30–300 individuals, and in small groups of 10–30 individuals. Most international migration is illegal, since migrants are unable to procure legal visas to recipient countries. Clandestine travel and visas purchased on the black market are expensive, and migrants face risks while traveling.

International migration is a poverty-coping method that allows many families to subsist in the short term. Major forms of migrant labor are agriculture, casual work, begging, can and metal collection, and trade in used clothes, and none produce enough income for migrants' families to escape poverty. Most international migrants send remittances home to their families to purchase basic consumption items. If the remittances are inadequate, families are sometimes extended credit by being put on a "list" by local shop owners.[11] In the end, the migrants' absences from home eventually lead to increased poverty because their indebtedness outruns their income. As a result, few migrants can afford to spend their earnings on investments in local infrastructure or business.

Finally, migration among Roma and Egyptian contributes to divorce, the weakening of cultural traditions, and low educational attainment levels. For example, families separate for long periods of time, resulting in significant emotional stress. Musical traditions are being lost because families of musicians work entire days in agriculture and cannot pass down musical traditions to children. Another drawback of Roma and Egyptian international migration is that it prevents children from attending school, resulting in increased child illiteracy.

---

10. The national unemployment figure is derived from INSTAT, 2002. Roma and Egyptian unemployment data results form the socioeconomic household questionnaires with Roma and Egyptians for the Needs Assessment (2002/03).

11. A "list" refers to informal credit granted by a shop owner to a customer that permits a customer to take goods now and pay later.

Prostitution and Trafficking

Prostitution and trafficking of children or drugs are used as coping mechanisms when other coping methods are unavailable or fail to meet the families' basic needs. However, prostitution and trafficking contribute to increased poverty.

Women in abusive marriages who wish to separate from their husbands regard prostitution as one of the few existing exit strategies available to them, in terms of both life choices and economic survival.

Surprisingly, in relatively prosperous Roma localities, girls or women may be lured into prostitution by Albanian acquaintances who gain the trust of their families by making false marriage proposals, or through business arrangements with family members who might be willing to approve the selling or renting of girls and women. In this way, Albanian traffickers succeed in bringing Roma girls and women into prostitution.

Child trafficking is also practiced by some Roma families. There are essentially three ways that children are trafficked. They are: (a) "rented" to other families for financial gain; (b) sent by families to nearby cities and towns to work; or (c) taken abroad by their families, where they work as informal migrant laborers.

Social Capital

Roma and Egyptians employ social capital to cope with poverty and social exclusion. Both benefit from a wealth of cognitive social capital, but are weak in structural forms of social capital. Cognitive social capital[12] includes a high level of trust, which enables them to purchase food on credit (the "list"); migrants send remittances home with friends or acquaintances, as part of the tradition of collaboration among families and clans.

Roma and Egyptians are both poor in structural social capital, which is particularly crucial in fostering their participation in decisionmaking processes at the local, regional, and national levels.[13] They lack effective political representation, and their associations are fragmented and unable to advocate effectively for their interests and needs. Moreover, 64 percent of Egyptians and 51 percent of Roma do not trust their own associations. They both will remain ill equipped to rise above poverty and social exclusion as long as their structural social capital remains weak.

Social Exclusion

Both groups face social exclusion in different aspects of their lives. These aspects are related to economic restructuring, unemployment, poverty, weak government capacity, and discrimination. The combination of these factors, their linkages, and dynamics increasingly traps their families into poverty, and makes the majority of both Roma and Egyptians "outsiders" to Albanian society. In contrast to mainstream society, both groups are denied participation in, and governance of, numerous aspects that affect their lives.

---

12. Cognitive social capital refers to very intangible values, norms, and attitudes that govern behavior.

13. Structural social capital refers to formal or informal associations or networks that facilitate collective action.

Roma and Egyptians conveyed that poverty and discrimination at the institutional and individual levels were the primary causes of social exclusion. They suggested that social exclusion could be addressed by creating more jobs and opportunities to attend schools and universities, and by hiring them to work in local and state administration offices.

Social Inclusion: Recommendations and Policy Implications

Public options[14] should not be seen in isolation, but as part of a holistic development approach. Policies can be implemented individually, in combination, or in sequence at the local, district, or national level with the support of, and in partnership with, different government organizations, NGOs, Roma and Egyptian community organizations, the private sector, and international partners.

Improved access to public goods and services is one key aspect of promoting the social inclusion of these groups. Policies regarding access to the public education system would help improve the quantity and quality of education facilities and teaching for Roma, Egyptian, and Albanian children alike. Inclusion could be fostered through policies that include specific teacher training, Romani and Albanian language courses, after-school classes, and mentoring programs. Another key aspect is the need to establish confidence that education will improve future livelihoods and development opportunities. There also needs to be improvement in public safety for children going to and from school, and improved protection of citizens and crime victims.

Policies regarding improved access to public water supply, sanitation, and electricity networks should include improved service provision in areas where the utility infrastructure exists, and an expansion of the public utility networks for families living outside the current network systems.

Policies to improve access to health care must include the provision of basic health care services in remote areas, including sufficient medical personnel. Improved access to healthcare also needs to address citizen complaints about extra charges for medical treatment, through built-in measures to discourage overcharges of health care services personnel.

Changes in the eligibility criteria for state assistance, such as making assistance available to designated family members, should replace the current practice of giving benefits only to the male head of household. Modification in the unemployment benefit system would also be useful; benefits could incrementally decrease over time instead of the present one-year provision.

The strategic promotion of market and employment opportunities for Roma and Egyptians is another way to support their social inclusion. Policy options include the expansion of existing and creation of new local, national, and international markets for their traditional handicrafts and music. In areas where Roma and Egyptians have traditional and new skills, support could be provided to help ensure the sustainability of small and medium-size enterprises (SMEs) based on those skills. The current gap between these traditional skills and labor demands could be addressed through vocational skills training and qualifications that

---

14. Public options are part of public choice. Public choice is a policy term that refers to an institutional system that is based on pluralism, in which policymakers can choose between different policy options to meet priorities.

are tailored to employment opportunities. Similar training and counseling could give more choices to women who are currently not included in SME programs.

Access to the justice system and policy options further advance social inclusion of many. Among other legislative remedies are the enactment of legislation that enforces spousal and child support payment, the issuance of birth certificates, and granting the Roma and Egyptians official citizen status. Currently those in, or born from, unregistered marriages do not have formal citizen status.

Humanitarian aid for families should be instituted in the form of food, clothes, and basic amenities that encourage school attendance and the completion of compulsory education. Aid could also be used to encourage trainees' attendance at and completion of vocational training courses.

Strengthening the civic organizations of Roma is important in the process of empowerment. This structural social capital—formal or informal associations or networks—would offer opportunities for both groups to voice their needs and interests, and foster their participation in decisionmaking at all levels.

The creation of cultural centers has been requested by many Roma and Egyptians to support the Romani language, music, history, and handicrafts, and Egyptian music and metalworking traditions. Such centers could also provide services that address the needs that they identify, such as counseling and pre-marriage counseling, help for abused women, family planning support, child care, health and hygiene education, and vocational training relevant to the local market. The development of women's associations should also be encouraged, as they could provide legal advice and counseling and assist women in making decisions that affect their lives.

Cultural centers could help promote community-based development by enabling Roma and Egyptians themselves to develop their communities with the assistance of local, national, and international partners. Finally, such centers could serve as a vehicle for interethnic contact. Through bottom-up social inclusion, Roma, Egyptians, and Albanians would all contribute to social cohesion.

Table 3 below summarizes the possibilities for ameliorating the causes of social exclusion.

(*text continues on page xli*)

Table 3. From Social Exclusion to Social Inclusion Matrix of Exclusion Manifestations and Recommendations for Inclusion Policies and Actions

Roma and Egyptians have been affected particularly negatively by the social changes during transition. For many Roma and Egyptians today, social exclusion has become a part of their daily lives because multiple institutional barriers obstruct their development opportunities in Albania. In the effort to foster social inclusion, tailoring policies for different local problems is key. The following recommendations provide a wide spectrum of possible policies and programs. These could be taken individually, in combination, or in sequence. Implementation is possible at the local, district, and national levels. Realization of recommendations could further draw on the support and partnership of a variety of actors that include different government organizations, NGOs, Roma and Egyptian community organizations, the private sector, and international partners.

Dimensions	Identified Manifestations of Sociocultural, Economic, Political, and Institutional Exclusion	Proposed Inclusion Policies and Actions
Lack of Access to Public Goods and Services		
1. Education		
Particularly acute for Roma	Lack of knowledge of the Albanian language	Preschool: tailored and formal Albanian language training taught by Roma teachers
		Primary school: provision of 2 to 3 hours of class instruction in Romani by a qualified Roma teacher
Particularly acute for Roma and Egyptians	Frequent mistreatment by teachers in some localities: Roma and Egyptian students are made to sit at the back of classrooms and receive punishment from their teachers more frequently than white Albanian students.	Promotion of inclusive and participatory teaching methods, and raising teachers' awareness in public and special-needs schools: tailored teacher training in Roma and Egyptian cultural values and norms to meet the different needs of pupils
		Classes on Roma and Egyptian history and culture for Roma, Egyptian, and Albanian pupils to increase respect for diversity, and raise awareness among children about their respective cultural backgrounds and ways of life.
	Lack of education and vocational skills; lack of recognition of the long-term benefits of education and vocational skills in view of limited employment opportunities in the formal sector	Mentoring program for Roma and Egyptian pupils and their parents to convey the need for formal education and training for the post-transitional labor market Mentors such as students at secondary schools and universities, teachers, trainees, and public and private sector specialists and professionals from all walks of life would act as examples for pupils, sharing their personal educational development, employment, and future aspirations.

(continued)

Table 3. From Social Exclusion to Social Inclusion Matrix of Exclusion Manifestations and Recommendations for Inclusion Policies and Actions (*Continued*)

Dimensions	Identified Manifestations of Sociocultural, Economic, Political, and Institutional Exclusion	Proposed Inclusion Policies and Actions
Relevant for all Albanians and particularly acute for Roma and Egyptians	Lack of enforcement of the eight-year minimum, compulsory education because of weak government capacity	Activities to strengthen existing and build further capacity of government officials at the central and local level. Support to implement the education law.
	Lack of access to education, qualification, and vocational skills as a result of income-poverty	Provision of free access to school services, facilities, and amenities, e.g., schoolbooks, clothes, meals, or the use of education facilities; humanitarian aid in the form of food, clothes, or basic amenities for very poor Roma and Egyptian families, conditional upon their children's regular school attendance.
		Increased accessibility of secondary and higher or university education through specific scholarships, conditional upon central and local government capacity to establish, administer, and monitor scholarship and grant schemes. This could be done with the support of Roma and Egyptian organizations.
	Lack of educational qualifications, due in to lack of parental enforcement of school attendance	Public awareness campaigns and measures to make annual grants or scholarships to parents and pupils conditional on past school attendance
	Lack of vocational skills needed in the formal labor market	Increased and improved formal employment opportunities for all Albanians through a concerted effort between the government, NGOs, and the private sector to promote vocational training, where qualifications are tailored to the demands of the respective geographical or sectoral labor market
	Lack of adequate facilities in schools for physically challenged children; lack of adequate special needs schools and facilities for mentall-challenged children	Creation of facilities and equipment in public schools for physically challenged children; development of special needs schools and facilities for mentally challenged children; creation and improvement of these schools and facilities with geographical dispersion across Albania

2. Health		
Particularly acute for Roma	Multiple and chronic health problems due to lack of knowledge of basic health care and medical conditions requiring formal treatment	Awareness campaigns for basic health care; education in basic health care and medical conditions that call for professional attention in health centers and schools, or by medical personnel who travel to different communities
Particularly acute for Roma and Egyptians	Discrimination by medical personnel who charge extra for treatment or consultations	Clear government policies to identify, monitor, and act upon the misuse of public service provision, including elimination of illegal payments for medical treatment and holding offending personnel accountable for respective activities; partners and project managers with experience in countering offensive practices could assist the government.
Relevant for all Albanians and particularly acute for Roma and Egyptians	Multiple health problems resulting from lack of funds to pay for formal in- and out-patient treatment	Provision of basic medical treatment, such as vaccinations, medical checkups, and treatment for illnesses free of charge
	Remote or isolated location and long distances to the nearest health facility	Outreach activities with provision of basic medical services and treatment, and provision of personnel in remote areas
3. Infrastructure		
Particularly acute for Roma	Lack of access to basic amenities, e.g., potable water, sanitary facilities, electricity, and heating because of inadequate housing in run-down inner-city areas, urban periphery, and rural areas	Concerted efforts of the government, private sector, and international partners to expand the public water supply and sanitation and electricity networks to families who are located outside of the respective service networks; government efforts to increase and/or improve the infrastructure service delivery to families with formal service connection
Particularly acute for Roma and Egyptians	Overcrowded, dilapidated, inadequate housing without basic amenities	Actions to improve housing conditions and provide basic amenities, which could include provision of building material and equipment
Relevant for all Albanians and particularly acute for Roma and Egyptians	Restricted access to potable household-use water, sanitary facilities, electricity, heating, and adequate housing	Concerted efforts of the government, private sector, and international partners to increase and/or improve access to public water supply and sanitation and electricity networks through improved infrastructure service delivery and network expansion.
4. Social Protection		
Relevant for all Albanians and particularly acute for Roma and Egyptians	Inability to claim state assistance; e.g., economic assistance ("*ndihmë ekonomike*"), retirement benefits (pensions), unemployment benefits, and disability payments.	Welfare reforms addressing general eligibility for social protection, its actual provision, and its reliability, e.g., current requirements that make state economic assistance conditional on the actual presence of the male head-of-household at local social security offices to collect monthly benefits; new policies that allow other designated family members to collect benefits regardless of their status as the formal head of the household

(*continued*)

Table 3. From Social Exclusion to Social Inclusion Matrix of Exclusion Manifestations and Recommendations for Inclusion Policies and Actions (*Continued*)

Dimensions	Identified Manifestations of Sociocultural, Economic, Political, and Institutional Exclusion	Proposed Inclusion Policies and Actions
	Lack of long-term unemployment benefits, as state assistance is cut completely after one year without formal employment.	Reforms that extend the duration of eligibility for unemployment benefits and include a time-scaled benefit system, in which benefits would be scaled down over an extended period and cut only after this extended time.
5. Information—Public Sector Governance		
Particularly acute for Roma	Lack of access to information on government policies, decisionmaking processes, the rule of law, and rights and responsibilities because of language difficulties	Translation of key documents and information material into the Romani language and broadcasting over local radio stations as public service announcements (PSAs) This could be realized with the support of Roma organizations.
Particularly acute for Roma and Egyptians	Lack of access to information because of illiteracy	Dissemination of key information through community meetings, village councilors, and information centers where Roma would receive support in obtaining and handling documents, such as service contracts, property rights documents, application forms, and notifications
Relevant for all Albanians and particularly acute for Roma and Egyptians	Lack of access to information because they reside in rural and remote areas	Broadcasting of information on government policies, decisionmaking processes, the rule of law, and rights and responsibilities over local radio stations as PSAs
		Joint efforts of the government, NGOs, community representatives, and international partners to promote vocational training of Roma and Egyptians in the local and national media sector to voice their communities' interests, foster their understanding of governance processes, and promote their participation in decisionmaking processes
6. Law and Justice		
Particularly acute for Roma and Egyptians	Subjective jurisdiction and discrimination	Clear government policies to address the misuse of public office and to hold offending personnel accountable for respective activities; international partners with experience in countering judicial discrimination could assist the government

	Lack of formal marriage registration and denial of citizenship rights for children who are formally unregistered because of unregistered marriages	Public awareness campaigns by Roma and Egyptian associations to highlight the negative effects of early and unregistered marriages and unregistered childbirths
		Government policies that address unregistered Roma and Egyptian marriages and childbirths and allow citizen status to obtain legal access to public goods and services, including the judiciary, formal employment, and mainstream society
	Under the legally nonbinding common law, lack of enforcement of alimony and child support for persons in formally unregistered marriages and for unregistered childbirths	Change in the common law to allow alimony to divorced common-law wives and enforce payments
		Public awareness campaigns by Roma and Egyptian associations to highlight the negative effects of unregistered marriages and the legal accountability of husbands for spousal and child support. Information dissemination in cultural centers.
Relevant for all Albanians and particularly acute for Roma and Egyptians	Lack of understanding of judiciary procedures as a result of unclear laws, rules and regulations, and limited access to lawyers	Improvement in judicial transparency and accountability through dissemination of information on judicial processes and procedures; promotion of legal advice and counseling in community and/or cultural centers
	Lack of use of judiciary system because of ambiguous laws, rules, and regulations	Improved legislation with clear definition of rights, rules, and responsibilities, such as clear land titling, ownership rights, dispute resolution, and compensation for loss of land following the government's land distribution in 1992

Market Opportunities and Employment

7. Labor market

Particularly acute for Roma and Egyptians	Informal sector activities resulting from decreasing value of existing educational qualifications and vocational skills in a labor market with changing demands	Vocational training tailored to sectoral and geographical labor market demands and traditional skills and qualifications, held for instance in cultural centers
	Informal sector activities resulting from discrimination	Tax incentives to the private sector or copayments to social security benefits for Roma and Egyptian private sector employees in extremely poor localities

(continued)

Table 3. From Social Exclusion to Social Inclusion Matrix of Exclusion Manifestations and Recommendations for Inclusion Policies and Actions (Continued)

Dimensions	Identified Manifestations of Sociocultural, Economic, Political, and Institutional Exclusion	Proposed Inclusion Policies and Actions
	Decline in employment opportunities for traditional professions (e.g., handicrafts, music) as a result of restructuring of former state-owned enterprises in handicrafts, and the general decline in demand for these products	Development of existing and creation of new local, national, and international markets for handicrafts; organization of trade fairs and exhibitions through collaboration among the government, the private sector, and international partners
		Advancement of the existing Roma and Egyptian music market at local, national, and international levels, honing in on Roma and Egyptian skilled musical performances
	Prostitution resulting from lack of access to formal market and employment opportunities	Vocational training courses for Roma and Egyptian women forced into prostitution—the poverty-coping mechanism of last resort—with a specific focus on divorced women, who are particularly vulnerable
		Government assistance programs in which divorced women become eligible for state economic assistance
		Partnership with Roma and Egyptian associations to further encourage divorced women to attend vocational training courses in cultural centers
Relevant for all groups and particularly acute for Roma and Egyptians	Limited formal employment opportunities, unemployment, long-term unemployment, or under employment because skills are mismatched in the posttransition labor market	Vocational training tailored to sectoral and geographical labor market demands
		Creation of new employment opportunities through joint efforts of the government and the private sector, with possible assistance from international partners
	Dependence on the informal sector, casual work, self-employment, and/or migration with attendant low wages, job insecurity, and high socioeconomic vulnerability because of lack of formal employment opportunities	Concerted efforts of the government, private sector, and international partners to improve the formal business environment and investment climate that attracts the national or international private sector and increases demand for a steady workforce and supply of employment opportunities, with a focus on specific growth sectors and geographical locations with prospective industries, including the creation of viable and sustainable small- and medium-size enterprises

Safety and Security of Livelihoods

8. Social Risks and Vulnerability		
Particularly acute for Roma and Egyptians	Low school attendance and illiteracy because local governments do not implement safety measures for children traveling the often long distances to the nearest school, and parents' fear of kidnapping of children, particularly girls	Design and implementation of anticrime measures by central and local government to foster local protection of citizens and crime victim.
Relevant for all Albanians and particularly acute for Roma and Egyptians	Insecure livelihoods as a result of financial instability of very poor households	Provision of humanitarian aid for food, clothes, and basic amenities conditional on children's school attendance and completion of compulsory education, or to trainees' attendance and completion of vocational training courses.

Social Capital, Voice, and Participation

9. Social Capital		
Particularly acute for Roma and Egyptians	Limited voice in policy decisionmaking processes because of lack of formal or informal associations or networks that facilitate collective action	Joint efforts by the government and international NGOs to encourage coordination and strengthen cooperation among and between Roma and Egyptian communities and to make funding conditional to such coordination and cooperation
	Limited participation in policy decisionmaking processes because of lack of trust in formal or informal associations or networks	Building trust between Roma and Egyptian communities and associations by including both in the planning and implementation of programs for the community as a whole Increasing trust and rapport between Roma and Egyptian communities and their associations by attaching associations to programs that would benefit both communities
	Unfocused voice and scattered participation in policy decisionmaking processes because of lack of experience with effective interest representation, and respective project interventions	Joint efforts by the government and international NGOs to promote future national and international links between Roma and Egyptian associations in Albania with related associations in other European countries to exchange experiences and assist in replicating workable projects tailored to the local context

(continued)

Table 3. From Social Exclusion to Social Inclusion Matrix of Exclusion Manifestations and Recommendations for Inclusion Policies and Actions (*Continued*)

Dimensions	Identified Manifestations of Sociocultural, Economic, Political, and Institutional Exclusion	Proposed Inclusion Policies and Actions
Cultural Identity and Diversity		
10. Empowerment—CDD Particularly acute for Roma	Discrimination based on cultural identity	Establishment of cultural centers to address the eroding family structure of the Roma *fis*, bringing far-flung Albanian Roma together, supporting expressions and sharing cultural practices, and strengthening their social capital through instruction in Romani, traditional crafts and customs, music, dance, and history
	Low education qualifications and vocational skills	Creation of cultural centers to provide Albanian language classes for Roma children and after-school classes with help for homework from bilingual Roma teachers
		Provision of adult vocational training aimed at the realities of the local job market, including basic accounting and grant proposal writing, and establishing reading centers to remedy high illiteracy
Relevant for all Albanians and particularly acute for Roma and Egyptians	Lack of community and social cohesion, low value of cultural identity and diversity	Establishment of cultural centers to promote community-based development, in which Roma and Egyptians themselves rebuild their communities with the assistance of local, national, and international partners; this would help to promote interaction and foster cultural, social, and institutional inclusion and social cohesion among Roma, Egyptians, and Albanians.
	Isolation and lack of information, low levels of health care	Establishment of cultural centers to provide pre-marriage counseling and legal advice for women, including abused women; assistance in the formation of informal women's groups to help support women in making decisions that affect their lives and by raising awareness of the negative effects of early marriage and its impact on vocational qualifications
		Information on basic health and hygiene, reproductive health, family planning, and parenting, particularly for population groups without access to medical facilities
11. Minority status	Discrimination based on lack of a formal minority status	Government efforts to provide formal minority status to Roma in order to meet the European Union accession criteria calling for the respect for, and protection of, minorities

Summary of Short-Term and Most Urgent Policy Recommendations

The policy recommendations elaborated above include short-, medium-, and long-term measures to foster inclusion. In the short term, the priority areas for policy action are education, infrastructure, cultural identity, and, specifically for Roma, the recognition of formal minority status. The short-term recommendations in these four areas are elaborated below in Table 4.

Table 4. Summary of Short-Term and Most Urgent Policy Recommendations	
1. Education	
Lack of knowledge of Albanian language	Preschool: tailored and formal Albanian language training taught by Roma teachers
	Primary School: provision of 2 to 3 hours of class instruction in Romani by a qualified Roma teacher
Frequent mistreatment by teachers in some localities: Roma and Egyptian students are made to sit at the back of classrooms and receive punishment from their teachers more frequently than white Albanian students	Promotion of inclusive and participatory teaching methods, and raising teachers' awareness in public and special-needs schools: tailored teacher training in Roma and Egyptian cultural values and norms to meet the different needs of pupils; classes on Roma and Egyptian history and culture for Roma, Egyptian, and Albanian pupils to increase respect for diversity and raise awareness among children about their respective cultural backgrounds and ways of life.
Lack of access to education, qualifications, and vocational skills as a result of income-poverty	Provision of free access to school services, facilities, and amenities, e.g., schoolbooks, clothes, meals, or the use of educational facilities; humanitarian aid in the form of food, clothes, or basic amenities for very poor Roma and Egyptian families, conditional upon their children's regular school attendance
	Increased accessibility of secondary and higher or university education through specific scholarships, conditional upon central and local government capacity to establish, administer, and monitor scholarship and grants schemes; this could be done with support of Roma and Egyptian organizations.
2. Infrastructure	
Lack of access or limited access to basic amenities, e.g., potable water, sanitary facilities, electricity, and heating because of inadequate housing in run-down inner-city areas, urban periphery, and rural areas	Concerted efforts of the government, the private sector, and international partners to expand the public water supply and sanitation and electricity networks to families who are located outside the respective service networks; government efforts to increase and/or improve the infrastructure service delivery to families with formal service connection.
3. Cultural Centers	
Discrimination based on cultural identity	Establishment of cultural centers to address the eroding family structure of the Roma *fis,* bring far-flung Albanian Roma together, support expressions and sharing of their cultural practices, and strengthen their social capital through instruction in Romani, traditional crafts and customs, music, dance, and history

(continued)

Table 4. Summary of Short-Term and Most Urgent Policy Recommendations (*Continued*)	
Low education qualifications and vocational skills	Creation of cultural centers to provide Albanian language classes for Roma children and after-school classes with help for homework from bilingual Roma teachers
	Provision of adult vocational training aimed at the realities of the local job market, including basic accounting and grant proposal writing, and establishment of reading centers to remedy high illiteracy
Lack of community and social cohesion; low value of cultural identity and diversity	Establishment of cultural centers to promote community-based development, in which Roma and Egyptians themselves rebuild their communities with the assistance of local, national, and international partners; this would help to promote interaction and foster cultural, social, and institutional inclusion and social cohesion among Roma, Egyptians and Albanians.
4. Minority Status	
Discrimination based on lack of formal minority status	Provision of formal minority status to Roma by the government to meet the European Union accession criteria calling for the respect for, and protection of, minorities

CHAPTER 1

Introduction

In several assessments, Roma and Egyptians have been identified as one of the most marginalized groups in Albania.[15] This Needs Assessment investigated the specific needs of these two communities and the key issues and major constraints that impair their sustainable livelihoods. It suggests respective policy actions the Government of Albania can address in its efforts for poverty reduction and social inclusion.

The assessment first analyzes the most pressing problems that these communities face in Albania's transition to a market economy, such as low educational qualifications and vocational skills, high unemployment, limited access to public goods and services, and social exclusion from Albanian society.

The study employed both qualitative and quantitative techniques and is based on a thorough observation of 11 Albanian districts that have concentrations of Roma and Egyptians. Some of the study findings have already been shared and discussed with representatives of the Roma and, to some extent, Egyptian communities in a series of workshops that were organized in the different study districts across Albania.

The report deriving from the Needs Assessment focuses on the process and methodology employed to determine the extent of the needs of the subject groups. It provides insights into the different dimensions of social exclusion and summarizes the main needs of these communities. It ends with policy recommendations that aim to address the needs and promote the sustainable livelihoods of the Roma and Egyptians.

The report also contains a delineation of Roma and Egyptian history and culture and details the main reasons for poverty and social exclusion that have been identified for each group. It also illustrates several of the strategies that these groups use to cope with poverty and social exclusion, such as migration, prostitution, and trafficking. This is followed by a discussion of the social capital of these groups, which has been identified as both a prerequisite to cope with poverty and social exclusion, and a crucial opportunity to improve livelihoods. The Appendixes contain the profiles of the study sites; working definitions; measuring instruments; statistical data, tables, flowcharts; extensive quotes from Albanians, Roma, and Egyptians; a kinship chart; a list of NGOs; a description of Albania's national minorities; and other relevant materials.

The study team solicited the active participation of Roma and Egyptian communities in the study design, realization, and discussion, as well as dissemination of findings. This study marks the first occasion that the participatory approach was used to study Roma and Egyptian issues in Albania, for the purpose of assessing the needs and proposing policy actions for support of these groups. A first draft report was discussed with Roma and Egyptian leaders in Tirana to get feedback on, and input in, the policy recommendations. For the conference summary, see Appendix M.

The report contributes to existing analyses of Central and Eastern Europe. We believe that this report will contribute to raising awareness of local governments, the private sector, and civil society with respect to the major challenges facing the Roma and Egyptians that have emerged during the structural change of transition. We hope that the assessment will further contribute to improving the capacity building of Roma and Egyptian NGOs to address the problems of their communities. It is hoped that the findings will assist the Albanian government in developing policies and programs that foster the integration of these communities into Albanian society while retaining their cultural identities.

Objectives and Methodology

The Needs Assessment investigated the socioeconomic, cultural, institutional, and historical situation of Roma and Egyptian communities in Albania.

Objectives

The specific objectives of the assessment were:

1) To help the government gather quantitative and qualitative data and information on these groups and the key issues and main constraints that impair their ability to generate sustainable livelihoods
2) To provide insights into potential social exclusion processes that affect these communities in order to help the government meet some of the EU recommendations related to ethnic minorities
3) To provide advice on the design of concrete actions that will facilitate the inclusion of the Roma and Egyptians into Albanian society.

Pursuant to these objectives, the assessment investigated the causes, nature, extent, and perceptions of the Roma and Egyptians in 11 study sites throughout Albania.

Focus

The Needs Assessment focused on several themes that pertain to the welfare of the general population, and pertain specifically to the welfare of Roma and Egyptians. Comparisons were made among Roma, Egyptians, and Albanians with respect to.

- ▨ Unemployment/underemployment
- ▨ Infrastructure
- ▨ Education
- ▨ Health
- ▨ Internal and international migration
- ▨ Social services
- ▨ Social capital and social organization
- ▨ Culture (including expressive culture, e.g., language, music, dress, and art)
- ▨ Handicrafts
- ▨ Gender
- ▨ Children/family planning
- ▨ Security/violence/trafficking
- ▨ Community participation and involvement in local decisionmaking
- ▨ Access to judicial system
- ▨ Exclusion through stereotypes and discrimination
- ▨ Empowerment through participation, transparency, and gaining capital assets.

The analysis gave priority to the following issues:

1) What effects has Albania's transition to a market economy had on these communities?
2) How can Roma and Egyptians actively build upon their culture to improve their inclusion in Albanian society?
3) How do non-Roma and non-Egyptians perceive Roma and Egyptians in their respective localities?
4) How can Roma and Egyptians who are subjected to social exclusion be included in society?
5) What policies need to be formulated to foster their social inclusion and promote community social cohesion and Albania's EU integration?

Methodology

To examine the socioeconomic, cultural, institutional, and historical situation of Roma and Egyptians in several dimensions, the needs Assessment identified emerging areas of concern in 11 districts.

Study Team. The study team was composed primarily of trained researchers and field-workers with previous experience and established trust relationships in their communities. The supervisory staff—composed of senior World Bank staff and local research managers—and the study team jointly determined the research design of the study, selected the study sample, developed the questionnaire for interviews, and received feedback on the questionnaires from the respective local Roma and Egyptian community leaders.

Site Selection. Based on field research undertaken for the Qualitative Poverty Assessment, and on consultation with their community leaders, the research team selected the 11 districts: Berat, Delvina, Durrës, Elbasan, Fier, Gjirokastra, Korça, Kruja, Shkodra, Tirana, and Vlora to acquire a representative sampling of the country's Roma and Egyptian communities. The districts of Korça, Shkodra, Tirana, and Vlora had already been assessed in the framework of qualitative poverty.[16] Selections were made to ensure the representation of: (a) all country regions and topographies in which large groups live; (b) urban, semi-urban, and rural populations; (c) all Roma *fise*;[17] (d) varying degrees of socioeconomic development, particularly since the start of the transition period; (e) different types of economies and industries; and (f) any existing large-scale social processes, such as international and internal migration. For each selected site, the study team collected and analyzed information across a variety of categories such as men, women, children, youth, the disabled, and elderly. The study team was also sensitive to issues of social differentiation, discrimination, age, income, education occupation, social capital, and culture within each district.

Qualitative and Quantitative Research Techniques. The analytic work for this study included primary and secondary data analysis. It involved: a desktop review of relevant literature (including official documents on minorities in Albania), qualitative and quantitative methods (cross-reference), and community profiles. The qualitative and quantitative methods component included: (a) focus group discussions with local Roma and Egyptian communities (separate sessions with women, children, and men); (b) semistructured interviews with key stakeholders and formal and informal male and female leaders in the community and the adjoining Albanian community; (c) eight ethnographic case studies—two women, two men, two girls, and two boys per community; (d) a quantitative socio-economic household survey questionnaire for 661 Roma and Egyptian households, comprising 188 questions; and (e) a socioeconomic household questionnaire of 10 questions for 440 households of non-Roma and non-Egyptian Albanians.[18]

During the fieldwork and data collection, the study team kept fieldwork diaries every evening in which each team member recorded reflections about the idiosyncrasies of fieldwork and themselves. No single family or individual participated in more than one research method. All names that are cited are fictitious, unless otherwise noted. Standard procedures were employed to ensure the confidentiality of participants' input.

1. *Desktop Review.* The research team reviewed literature on the history, politics, economics, and cultures of these communities in Albania and other Central and Eastern European countries. All sources used are listed in the bibliography.

2. *Focus Group Discussions.* Members of the research team facilitated focus group discussions using semistructured questions compiled by the research team in consultation with community representatives. These discussions allowed for broader, more open-ended discussion and (a) collected information on the impact that Albania's transition to a market economy has had on communities; (b) assessed

---

16. De Soto and others (2001).

17. A "*fis*" is a clan-type social organization that is based on a unilineal descent group. This group can be based on patrineal descent (patrilineage) or matrilineal descent (matrilineage) whose members trace descent from an apical ancestor/ancestress by known genealogical links. The Albania Roma fis (as well as the white Albanian *fis*) is based on patrilineage that traces through a male line of ancestors, while a matrilineal descent traces from an ancestress through her daughter, her daughter's daughter, etc. (Keesing, R. M. *Cultural Anthropology: A Contemporary Perspective.* Chicago: Holt, Rinehart and Winston, 1992.)

18. For the measuring instruments and extensive statistical data, see Appendixes.

the needs of and major impediments to sustainable livelihoods; (c) discussed their coping mechanisms and responses to different forms of inequality; and (d) determined how Albanians perceive these minorities. All focus group discussions were recorded, and a verbatim transcription was prepared.

Four focus group sessions with members of both communities, and two focus group sessions with non-Roma and non-Egyptians, were conducted in each selected district. Focus groups were designed to include residents of urban, semiurban, and rural areas as participants. Separate focus groups were held with women, men, and children. Each group was composed of 7–12 participants of different ages and socioeconomic levels.

3. *Semistructured Key Informant Interviews.* Semistructured interviews were conducted with community representatives; local, regional, and national government; and EU officials. Interviews were designed to allow for a comprehensive understanding of the key issues, main constraints, and opportunities to improve the livelihoods of Albanian Roma and Egyptians. These interviews (a) collected information on the perceived impacts of Albania's transition to a market economy on Roma and Egyptian communities; (b) identified perceptions of Roma and Egyptians by non-Roma throughout the country; (c) explored ways to include the socially excluded in society; and (d) helped determine which policies needed to be formulated to foster the social inclusion of both groups and facilitate Albania's integration into the EU. These interviews further identified the different interests and incentives of national minorities and of those groups that can directly affect these groups by supporting, opposing, or slowing down potential positive changes.

4. *Interviews with Albanian, Egyptian, and Roma Local Leaders and Experts.* The research team recruited more than 110 local experts, community leaders, school principals, teachers, and doctors who informed the team on qualitative aspects of their communities. The team interviewed this group on the topics of education, employment, infrastructure, economic assistance, and health in the central and local government, NGOs, and the private sector.

5. *Interviews with Albanian Citizens.* Furthermore, 33 interviews were held with non-Roma and non-Egyptian Albanians of different ages, genders, educational attainment, professions, and socioeconomic levels who live in close proximity to Roma or Egyptians. Interview questions were intended to acquire an understanding of the relationships among the different ethnic groups in areas inhabited by Roma or Egyptians, and of the perceptions that these groups have about each other. Interviewees were selected through purposive sampling.

6. *Ethnographic Case Studies.* The research team undertook eight ethnographic case studies (two each of men, women, girls, and boys, for a total of 16 case studies). Through open-ended questions, the research team aimed to acquire detailed insights into the life histories of the respondents.

7. *Socioeconomic Household Questionnaires.* To cross-reference the qualitative information, and to obtain quantitative data, the research team used household questionnaires, with Roma and Egyptians, and with Albanians.

Socioeconomic Household Questionnaires with Roma and Egyptian. The research team conducted 661 door-to-door surveys of Roma and Egyptian households (331 Roma and 330 Egyptian households) throughout the 11 districts. The surveys contained 188 questions that were intended to produce quantitative data concerning needs of these households, particularly in the areas of employment, education, health, infrastructure, economic assistance, violence and trafficking, and family planning, as well as information on formal and informal institutions.

The number of surveys collected from both communities in each district was proportional to the size of their local populations in the selected district. The quantitative method is as follows: (a) before fieldwork began, population and family estimates were determined; (b) to guarantee reliability of these population estimates, two to three independent sources, such as directors of Roma and Egyptian associations, local government representatives, or local representatives of the Organization for Security and Co-Operation (OSCE) were consulted, and the mean of these estimates was used; (c) according to the number of families identified, a percentage of the total was calculated; and (d) the resulting figure indicated the number of questionnaires per site. A lack of sufficient data on Roma rendered purposive sampling difficult, but these families were selected through a combination of purposive sampling that aimed at representing different levels of affluence. In general, more affluent Roma households live outside Roma quarters, making purposive sampling possible. Households at each identified level of affluence were selected through purposive sampling. Local Roma associations assisted in the family selection process.

Surveys conducted in the village of Levan in the district of Fier were conducted to accommodate the residing two Roma *fise,* namely, the Meçkar *fis* and the Cergar *fis.* Because each has separate economic and cultural characteristics, surveys were conducted to include an equal representation of both. Within each, purposive sampling characterized the selection of survey respondents.

Selection of Egyptian respondents was particularly difficult. In contrast to Roma, they live scattered throughout the city, and city records do not distinguish Egyptian households from Albanian ones. Consequently, it was more difficult to identify these households. Egyptian associations, or local *kryeplak*s were helpful in this capacity and, on some occasions, led the research team to individual Egyptian households. However, Egyptian associations did not have offices in every district and so were not able to assist in every district where surveys were conducted. The research team encountered another difficulty while conducting surveys with Egyptians in that some families, particularly in Tirana, Fier, Elbasan, and Durrës, denied affiliation with the Egyptian community and refused to be surveyed. Consequently, for some sites, information about local Egyptians is less comprehensive than for other sites where people openly identified themselves as Egyptians.

Socioeconomic Household Questionnaires with Albanians. Surveys were conducted with 440 Albanians in the 11 districts. The number of surveys conducted in each district depended on the size of the general population in the locality where surveys were conducted and the number of sites selected for study within each district. The research team purposively selected individuals of various ages and gender who lived and worked in close proximity to Roma and Egyptians. Respondents were selected on the street or in local businesses. Surveys contained questions about perceptions, behaviors, and relations among various ethnic groups, and between Roma and Egyptians.

CHAPTER 2

Historical Background

The Diversity of Roma and Egyptians

Historical and contemporary sources depict Roma and Egyptian communities as different with regard language, history, professions, and nomadic or stationary residence practices. Despite these differences, these communities are commonly grouped together simply as Roma, and their cultural divergences are rarely recognized. To understand these two groups in context, a brief history of Albania follows.

During Albania's socialist period, which began in 1944, several Roma *fise* and Egyptians practiced different types of formal and informal work and accumulated distinct forms of social and financial capital that would not only influence their post-communist experiences, but also the poverty-coping mechanisms that they have used since the start of transition in 1991.

The Origins of Roma and Egyptians

The origins of both Roma and Egyptians are unclear. However, based on linguistic evidence, scholars believe that Roma began migrating westward from India beginning in the ninth century C.E. The time of their arrival in the Balkans is also uncertain, but present-day Croatian sources point to a Roma presence there as early as the fourteenth century. One or more Roma *fise* may have settled in Albania by the fifteenth century.

In contrast, Albanian Egyptians claim to originate in Egypt, and at least three distinct theories link them to this alleged homeland. The first connects Albanian Egyptians to ancient Egypt. Secondary sources suggest that they arrived in the Balkans from Egypt in the third century B.C.E. or in fourth century C.E. as Coptic migrants. A second major theory posits that Albanian Egyptians descend from Egyptian slaves in the Ottoman army. A third suggests that Albanian Egyptians are semi-integrated Roma who, much earlier than other Roma, ended their nomadic traditions and lost the Roma language. Despite these claims, none is based on any substantial evidence. Egyptian associations in other Balkan countries that have appealed to respective Egyptian embassies for even the lowest level of recognition as one of Egypt's "lost tribes" have been unsuccessful.

Despite claiming separate origins, Albanian Egyptians' place in history has fallen under the Roma category. While most sources do distinguish Egyptian from Roma communities, the latter are considered a Roma *fis*, or what some would call today a national minority.

A Brief History of Albania

It is believed by many linguists, archaeologists, and anthropologists that part of what is now Albania was first inhabited by the ancient Illyrians around 1225 B.C.E. Modern-day Albanians speak a derivative of Illyrian.

From its beginning, Albania was a target for occupation, annexation, absorption, and acquisition by its contiguous neighbors as well as those across the Adriatic and marauders like the Goths, the Huns, and others who swept across the continent. Empire builders like the centuries-old Roman and Ottoman empires and, later, the Third Reich and its Italian ally also tried to impose their will upon the small country. However, none could completely obliterate its spirit and will to survive as a separate entity.

The Interwar Period

From the end of World War I in 1918 until the commencement of the European conflict of World War II in 1939, Albania fought to maintain its geographical presence and identity. After receiving recognition as a sovereign state by the League of Nations in 1920, Albania became a republic. However, amid bitter disagreement between a liberal faction dedicated to making Albania a Western-style democracy and a more conservative group, an armed conflict resulted in a coup. In 1928, Ahmed Bey Zogu, a chieftain from the Mat region of north-central Albania, who had been president of the country since 1925, declared himself King Zog I, and immediately signed a treaty with Italy that promised financial aid. However, in 1939, Italian premier Benito Mussolini invaded Albania as a first step toward expanding Italian territory, and the king fled to Greece.

During this period, the first reliable sources on Egyptians and Roma in Albania describe two peoples that are distinct according to traditional occupations, skills and crafts, language, religion, and other anthropological categories. Moreover, they also depict diversity among Roma *fise*.

Language, Residence Patterns, Social Organization, and Religion

The languages of Roma, Egyptians, and Albanians varied. Egyptians spoke only Albanian, while Roma spoke Romani, a completely different language. Moreover, separate Roma *fise* spoke different Romani dialects. The Meçkar *Fis*, for example, had adopted many "Albanianisms" into their Roma dialect. Many Roma also spoke languages that were commonly used in the towns near their communities, such as Greek.

Egyptians were settled, while Roma were traditionally nomadic. In 1938, Hasluck estimated that out of a total Roma and Egyptian population of 20,000, only 2,000 Roma were still nomads. Both Roma and Egyptians lived in separate urban or rural areas and in quarters that were very modest by most accounts.

Religious affiliations also vary among some Roma *fise* and Egyptians. Foreign accounts describe Shkodra and Korça Roma as Muslim, with their own local mosques. Muslim Roma in Durrës built their own mosque in 1923 (Hasluck 1938). Some Roma even joined the ranks of the Bektashi Order.[19] However, Swire (1937) describes animistic beliefs prevailing among some nomadic Roma, as Milaj (1944) claimed about the Egyptians: "They superficially practice the Muslim faith, but in reality they have a system of beliefs that are related to nature. Every year, a group of Egyptians gather on a Leskovik mountain to slaughter an animal as a sacrifice and to pray to their gods." There were Albanian Orthodox Egyptians in the Kato Varosh quarter of Korça and in Gjirokastra, who worshipped along with Albanians (Hasluck 1938).

Relations Between and Among Roma, Egyptians, and Albanians

By some standards, relations were distant between Egyptians and Roma, and among Roma, Egyptians, and Albanians. Both minority groups rejected the notion of being a single community. According to Hasluck (1938), "nomads regard sedentary groups [Egyptians] as their inferiors," while these sedentary groups "despised" the Roma. Generally, Egyptians felt that they were "above the Roma" (Mann 1937). Members of the two groups rarely intermarried. Regarding Albanians' attitudes, some sources claim that Albanians despised both groups (Kolsti 1999), but sometimes preferred Egyptians over Roma, since the former were "so much the nearer to Albanians" (Hasluck 1938). Describing Egyptians in Tirana, Swire (1937) writes: "Their intelligence is average, but they keep their horses much cleaner than the lowland Albanians. Nevertheless the latter despise them. . . ."[20]

Roma and Egyptian Socioeconomic Occupations, Skills, and Crafts

Traditional Roma and Egyptian skills and crafts varied. Most Egyptian men were blacksmiths or tinsmiths, while a small percentage were shoemakers. Some Egyptian women were house servants for wealthy families. Egyptians were particularly known for their skill at playing music at weddings and other festive ceremonies held by Albanian families (Milaj 1943). They worked mainly in towns, but in some cases also in larger villages located off major roads.

Other traditional Roma occupations and skills were (and still are) more diverse and vary among the different Roma *fise*.[21] Meçkars Roma worked in livestock and agriculture (Milaj 1943); a small number were landowners who dealt in small-scale agriculture. The nomadic Karbuxhinj Roma were horse dealers, willow basket weavers, and handicrafts producers who also belonged to Albania's class of small-scale merchants. Roma in Shkodra were horse

---

19. *Bektashi Order:* a Sufi Order of Islam whose members adhere to Shi'ia Islamic law.
20. This historian's racist observations on the Roma were typical of the period.
21. In Albania, there are four Roma patrilineal organizations called "*fise*" namely, Meçkar, Karbuxhinj, Bamill, and Cergar.

dealers, as were the Rupane Roma of central Albania. The latter were also known for their crafts and as coppersmiths. The Bamill Roma were tinsmiths who also made coffee roasters, kettles, and pots. Both the Meçkars and the Karbuxhinj were popular musicians at weddings and other ceremonies.

Not only did Roma and Egyptians fulfill social and economic roles the importance of which was recognized by Albanians, valued as musicians and experts in handicrafts, they also served as important intermediaries between city and rural markets, selling goods made by townspeople to villagers.

The Roma and Egyptians performed necessary low-skilled jobs that were rarely performed by Albanians. Describing Egyptians in Tirana, Swire wrote: ". . . it is the Gypsy who drowns the stray dog and carts away the refuse—tasks to which the Albanian will not stoop." Also, most Albanians relegated both Roma and Egyptians to the category of "the black hand," as opposed to "the white hand," the latter being bestowed only upon Albanians, Greeks, and Slavs (Courthiade and Duka). Thus, Albanians labeled both simply as "Gypsy."

Despite differences, both shared important common elements. They were both identified as "poor" by Albanians—a commonality that provided the basis for many Albanians to overlook the substantive cultural diversities between them.

World War II

During World War II, Roma suffered great losses through pro-German or occupation regimes across Europe. In Albania, however, the Italian and German occupations were relatively mild (Fischer 1999). Roma and Egyptians faced fewer hardships in Albania than elsewhere. Some Roma and Egyptians participated in the Albanian Partisan resistance movement.

The Socialist Era

In November 1944, when the Germans withdraw from Tirana, exiled Albanian Communist Party members returned to Tirana. They were led by an anti-fascist former teacher named Enver Hoxha. By December, the party had formed a provisional government, with Hoxha serving both as prime minister and minister of foreign affairs. By 1946, under Hoxha, who had also assumed the roles of defense minister and commander-in-chief, one-party elections had brought to power the People's Assembly that proclaimed Albania "a people's republic." In 1948, the Communist Party renamed itself the Party of Labor, signaling a governmental turn. Hoxha's turbulent reign was to last until his death in 1985.

Impacts on Roma and Egyptian Culture

The socialist government that was established in Albania following the war was the first organized movement to successfully impose intentional, lasting effects on Roma and Egyptian ways of life. In its quest for total control of the country, the ruling Communist Party sought to eliminate the influence of all non-party institutions. Cultural distinctions were suppressed to conform with the socialist Albanian nation, but even so, some Roma and Egyptian communities made gains in employment and living standards.

The suppression of cultural distinctions among the country's minorities was in accordance with the construction of the socialist Albanian nation, in which cultural identities were subjugated to a greater Albanian identity. Describing the country's Egyptians, president Hoxha (1981) wrote: "Now, under socialism, there are no distinctions between them and the others. There is no segregation among us, nor racism or apartheid against them; they have cast off their roots completely, they have learned, they have struggled . . . They have produced 'Heroes of the Socialist Order,' party secretaries, officers, doctors." According to party and orthodox Marxist theory, the distinct features of minority populations, if they hadn't already, would eventually wither away.

The Albanian government employed coercive measures and "paternalistic" incentives to assimilate Roma and Egyptians into socialist society. A policy of forced migration or settlement was implemented during the 1960s, intended to end Roma nomadism and expedite their assimilation. Pursuant to this policy, some Roma populations from towns and villages such as Llakatund and Delvina were settled in concentrated neighborhoods that were segregated from neighboring Albanian towns and villages. Nevertheless, they retained their language and distinct Roma identities. Others who lived in the villages around Delvina were forced to settle in the district's administrative capital next to Albanians. They lost some aspects of their cultural identities as a result of this forced integration.

While harmful to the country's cultural diversity, Communist Party rule was beneficial for its poorest and most marginalized communities, including some Roma and Egyptians. The government had specific social policies to support poor population groups and integrate them into society. As a result, both communities experienced improvements in their general welfare that included improved employment, education, housing, health care, and free access to social services during the socialist period.

Employment

During the socialist period, everyone, including the Roma and Egyptians, was guaranteed lifetime employment. Members of the Meçkar *fis*, working traditionally in agriculture, were integrated into agricultural cooperatives and state farms. Some Roma—including many in Gjirokastra, Berat, and Korça—were employed in state-owned handicraft and forest enterprises, while continuing to practice their traditional production of willow crafts. In the cities, both were employed alongside Albanians in public street sweeping and cleaning, industrial enterprises, and construction, where they worked as unskilled laborers (Taho 2002).

The Roma and Egyptians under the 1976 Constitution of Albania

The 1976 Constitution was the apex of the Albanian government's attempts to construct a "truly" Marxist-Leninist state. It brought socialism to new heights, when all private business and private property, including livestock, were outlawed throughout Albania. Most Albanians remember this period as a time of incredible difficulty. However, many Roma, mainly from the Karbuxhinj, Cergar, and Bamill *fise*, were allowed to continue their engagements in small-scale private enterprises, including dealing horses, and selling traditional copper and wickerwork products and other articles that they purchased in cities and in villages across Albania.

However, some Roma had an advantage over other Roma and Albanians. Bujar, a well-to-do Roma from Elbasan, recalled that, "During the socialist period, we worked in the public sector. But the system did not stop us from engaging in the small informal market. We worked in the horse market, where we would sell to villagers and cooperatives . . . , our women went to the villages and sold clothing and textiles." As before, Roma musicians continued to practice their music at weddings and other occasions. Participation in these informal activities provided supplementary income and gave them advantages over other minority and majority groups. A Cergar Roma from Fier remembered that: "We were the most privileged group, because we were the only businessmen at that time, selling old kettles, when other villagers were not allowed to sell anything." Some Roma were able to accumulate savings of up to US$15,000 during this period.

In effect, the Roma *fis* system helped govern the private sector along with Albanians. Different Roma *fis* members established business connections with other *fise* across Albania. To a limited extent, these Roma *fise* continued to serve as important intermediaries between Albania's rural and urban economies. They provided isolated rural villages with access to goods from the cities that would have been unavailable to them otherwise (Courthiade and Duka 1995). The Roma *fis* system is one of the few examples of a nongovernmental system that facilitated economic activity in Albania under the socialist regime—a notion that was unheard of among Albanians after 1976.

Differences in work experience had further repercussions; for instance, the Meçkars generally had more interaction with Albanians as "working-class proletariats." They worked side by side mainly in agriculture, and rarely participated in the informal employment sector. However, the Karbuxhinj and Cergars often worked segregated from Albanians in low-skilled state jobs and frequently engaged in informal private sector activities.

At the same time, Egyptians, who were more highly educated than the Roma, were better integrated into the state sector. In addition to having workers in various economic sectors, the Egyptian community also produced engineers, doctors, teachers, economists, military officers, and state employees. Then, too, Egyptian instrumentalists and vocalists contributed to the development of music in Albania.

Although the period was far from prosperous for Roma and Egyptians, their status, compared to ethnic Albanians, seemed to improve for those who engaged in private enterprise. It also improved in terms of health and education compared to the interwar period.

Transition

Beginning in 1990, during the general uprisings by all sectors of Albanian society against the post-Hoxha socialist regime, the Party of Labor of Albania allowed political pluralism and a market economy. The government gave in and relinquished its monopoly on foreign commerce and opened Albania to foreign investment.

By 1991, the first multiparty elections were held. Soon after, the Assembly passed a series of laws that provided fundamental human rights and separation of powers. Most tellingly, it invalidated the Constitution of 1976. In this way, in the midst of economic freefall and social chaos, the new government of Albania embarked upon a universal program of encouraging a market economy.

In contrast to the health, education, housing, and other benefits they were given during the socialist period, the transition period brought significant decline in the standards of living for Roma and Egyptians. But it also brought with it a re-emergence of many aspects of their cultural identities, and Roma and Egyptian diversity described in interwar historical sources still exists today.

The end of socialism marked the beginning of both groups' decline from relative well-being to extreme poverty (De Soto and others 2002). By 1996, while the country's overall unemployment rate was 18 percent, it was between 80 percent and 90 percent in the Roma communities (Koinova 2002 citing Kovacs). Unemployment among Roma in Gjirokastra and Delvina reached levels close to 100 percent.[22] Low employment skills, discrimination, and the collapse of various state-owned industrial and agricultural enterprises contributed to their mass unemployment. Low-skilled workers in mono-industrial districts, such as Delvina, where the closure of the agricultural industry led to massive job layoffs, were especially vulnerable.

They coped with economic insecurity in different ways. Socialist-era trends partly explain these variances. Many Meçkars and other southern district Roma who had worked in agriculture during socialism—and thus had developed relatively good relations with Albanians—began migrating to Greece soon after the Albanian border's opening in 1991. Then Meçkars and Roma in southern districts, although extremely poor, began migrating to neighboring countries. Karbuxhinj, Cergars, and other Roma who had accumulated savings during socialism sold used clothes or other high-demand goods purchased abroad.

Other Roma, particularly in Shkodra and Fushë Kruja, were more disadvantaged. They were not financially able to migrate to prosperous neighboring countries like Greece, nor did they have the financial means to engage in small-scale business. Although Roma who engaged in the used clothes business were relatively well-off during the early transition period, Roma in Shkodra and Fushë Kruja—as well as most Egyptians—experienced extreme poverty.

While market liberalism sparked economic uncertainty, political liberalism during the 1990s allowed these communities to achieve some gains in national and international recognition. Throughout Eastern Europe, in fact, Roma and Egyptian communities established political parties, nongovernmental NGOs, and newspapers, with such aims as cultural awareness, economic development, and political representation. Shortly after the end of communist rule, several NGOs were established in Albania, including Amaro Dives, Rromani Baxt, Amaro Drom, Rromani Braxt, Disutni Albania, Alb Rrom, Roma for Integration, Rromani Kham, the Jevg Association, Nefreta, Kabaja, and Vëllazërimi.

Conclusion

Lack of cultural recognition and political representation in Albania remains a continuing challenge to Roma and Egyptians. Roma are represented in Albania by the United Party for Human Rights, led by the country's Greek minority, and some experts claim that the party mainly represents the interests of the Albanian-Greek community (Koinova 2002). Moreover, Roma are not recognized as an ethnic minority, but as a second-tier, "linguistic minority."

---

22. According to the Labor Office in Gjirokastra, the Roma represent 30 percent with 4,500 persons who have registered as unemployed (OSCE, 2000, p. 2).

In Albania, these groups rarely face the open discrimination by Albanian politicians or society that is visible in many Eastern European countries (Kolsti 1999, Silverman 1995). However, they reportedly face more covert, institutional discrimination and social exclusion (Koinova 2002). One report claimed discrimination and social exclusion from municipal and school personnel, as well as arbitrary police harassment (Koinova 2002 citing ERRC Report). Roma interviewed in 1996 claimed that although discrimination is not overt, Albanians "act" as if Roma were inferior, viewing Roma as "poor" and "dirty." Both continue to face discrimination by local authorities and resistance from lawmakers to recognize Roma and Egyptians as ethnic minorities.

They also face continuing declines in welfare. For instance, Cergars, Karbuxhinj and other Roma who, at the beginning of the transition period, engaged in small-scale business, were forced to seek other poverty-coping strategies, despite their initial advantage over Albanians. In the late 1990s, increasing numbers of Roma began migrating temporarily to Greece, where there were more employment opportunities. Today, short-term, seasonal migration to Greece is the most sought-after poverty-coping method among them. This is an example of a structural change during Albania's transition that enabled some groups to benefit from economic growth, while other groups sustained severe declines in welfare. As poverty increases for some groups, they are forced to move into the businesses that were previously held by poor groups, who themselves are pushed out of the respective business into deeper poverty.

CHAPTER 3

Culture

Roma and Egyptian cultures are distinct from the culture of the majority Albanian community. Roma culture has a larger number of easily distinguishable elements than the Egyptians' and is more pronounced and recognizable (Figure 3.1).

Roma and Egyptians in 11 districts described the major cultural elements that distinguish them from Albanians. Most Roma listed language (99 percent), music (80 percent), community celebrations (80 percent), family ceremonies[23] (74 percent), wickerwork (67 percent), and women's dress (63 percent) as distinguishing their own culture from Albanian. Egyptians responded that metal work (75 percent) and music (45 percent) are distinguishing aspects of their own culture. Figure 3.1 depicts the percentages.

Because of its traditional structure and diverse functions, the social organization of the Roma *fis* is another important distinguishing characteristic of the Roma culture.

An attempt to include both minorities in Albanian society requires that respect be paid to supporting the cultural elements that Roma and Egyptians value. Next, it is important to identify ways to ensure social inclusion that do not conflict with Roma identity and social organization.

Language

The Romani language has been a fundamental factor in the cohesion of Roma identity and its distinct difference from the majority culture. At home, 65 percent of Roma families speak Romani, 29 percent speak both Romani and Albanian, and only 6 percent speak

---

23. "Family ceremonies" are those held for births, deaths, weddings, and circumcisions.

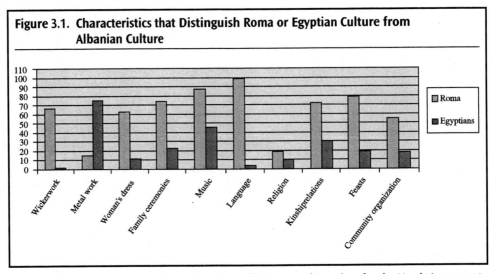

Figure 3.1. Characteristics that Distinguish Roma or Egyptian Culture from Albanian Culture

Source: Socioeconomic household questionnaires with Roma and Egyptians for the Needs Assessment (2002/03).

Albanian. Those that speak only Albanian at home are families of mixed marriages between Roma and Albanians or Roma and Egyptians. A formal Roma leader in Elbasan stated: "We have preserved our old traditions. We speak our language in the house. Until the age of three, [our] children speak only Romani."

In Albania, Romani is divided into separate dialects that were adopted by different *fise* in regions where they lived before they arrived and settled permanently in Albania. Although Romani is spoken and transmitted orally, written Romani is still rare.

In contrast, having lost their original tongue, Egyptians speak only Albanian. An Albanian grammar teacher who teaches Egyptians in Shkodra stated: "They don't have original words of their own, but they use some Turkish words, as all our people do."

Expressions of Culture and Identity

Distinguishing markers of both cultures are expressions of culture, such as women's dress, handicrafts, music, and folktales. Of those, handicrafts and folk-tale traditions are in the most serious decline.

Women's Dress

Roma women's dress is distinguishable by vibrant colors such as cherry red, long dresses, and pleated skirts. A Roma woman explained: "The Roma woman's style of dress is completely different from the 'white hand's' style", a term which Roma often use to describe 'white' Albanians. Even if there were 500 women of the white hand and only one Roma among them, the Roma woman would still stand out because of her dress. Roma women usually wear blouses with printed flowers and embroidered gold threads. . . . , at weddings, men and women dress up in very beautiful clothes. Women wear dresses decorated with roses and gold threads, while men wear dark red suits. Young men wear flower-printed shirts."

Handicrafts

Making handicrafts is another important expression of both of the cultures or both Roma and Egyptians; 15 percent of Roma and 10 percent of Egyptians produce them. Traditional Roma handicrafts include wicker objects such as baskets, while Egyptian handicrafts are decorative metalwork, such as railings, balconies, and window bars. Skënder, a formal Egyptian leader in Tirana, said: "We've done studies which have shown that in Gjirokastra, Korça, and Elbasan, there were masters of making iron handicrafts, such as a man named Qato and his son." Family knowledge of handicraft making is passed down from generation to generation.

During the socialist period, some Roma in Gjirokastra, Korça, Tirana, and Berat worked in handicraft enterprises. However, the demand for handicrafts has declined, and these enterprises were shut down during the early years of the transition period. Continuation of this tradition is doubtful.

Many other aspects of both cultures have been negatively affected by declining socio-economic conditions. Specifically, poverty has made it difficult for extended families to transmit traditions such as folktales, handicrafts, and even music. Traditional *fis* roles have also changed because of widespread poverty.

Music and Dance

Music and dance are highly valued by both Roma and Egyptian cultures; 79 percent of Roma and 69 percent of Egyptians indicated that there were Roma or Egyptian musicians in their neighborhood. Their most popular instruments are the keyboard, accordion, clarinet, saxophone, violin, and guitar. Ervehe, a Roma informal leader, explained: "Roma have their own music that has been preserved and passed down from generation to generation . . . our grandparents and great grandparents came from Greece and Turkey, and we are very familiar with the music of these countries. Roma music is different from the others." As a result, they have also contributed to Albanian music by introducing musical elements derived from Roma and Egyptian music.

Although traditional music is still an important element of their cultures, knowledge of their indigenous music may be in decline in certain localities. For example, one Roma, familiar with his culture, stated that musical traditions are being lost among Albanian Roma migrant families because musicians' families work long days in agriculture and have neither time nor energy to pass down their musical traditions to their children. An OSCE Report on Roma in Gjirokastra added: "Regular migration to Greece and ubiquitous Greek pop [music] are eroding Roma musical traditions."[24]

Although 69 percent of Roma know folk dances that accompany their traditional music, Egyptian folk dancing is in more serious decline, with only 28 percent knowing the folk dances that accompany their traditional music.

---

24. OSCE Special Report 39.

Folktales

Most Roma (67 percent) and Egyptians (66 percent) learned folktales as children from their grandparents. Since transmission of oral history by the family represents the first form of enculturation[25] that children receive, many are concerned that the traditional telling of folktales is now in decline. Today, only 27 percent of Roma and 11 percent of Egyptians know folktales.

The decline of the telling of folktales began during the late twentieth century, and some Roma attribute this decline to poverty. Hilmi, a Roma from Delvina, added: "Both my grandfathers lived to be more than 80 and they knew many folktales." In an effort to stem the tide, some Roma folktales have recently been published in Albanian but not in Romani.[26] Thus, Roma are unable to read their own folktales.

Family Ceremonies

Roma and some Egyptian customs and ceremonies for marriages, births, deaths, and weddings are distinct from Albanian customs and ceremonies.

Marriages

Most marriages, especially among Roma, are intra-ethnic and arranged through matchmakers. In fact, 95 percent of Roma and 74 percent of Egyptians preferred members of their own ethnic group as marriage partners.

Traditional Marriage Partners. Most Roma and Egyptians still marry within their own ethnic group. More Egyptians than Roma would accept a marriage between a family member and an Albanian.

Among many Roma families, moreover, marriage partners must be members of their own primary *fis.* Many Cergar and Bamill Roma in Delvina, Gjirokastra, Levan, Fier, Fushë Kruja, and Korça arrange marriages between first and second cousins. Endogamy[27] is practiced by some Roma in isolated localities, or by Roma that recently migrated from the country, and is explained by the limited access to available eligible marriage partners there. Roma explain endogamy through such metaphors as "The good horse should be sold within the village" and "Why should the good apple get eaten by someone else?"

The tradition of marrying members of one's own primary *fis* is, however, undergoing change. One Roma leader in Tirana explained: "Many marriages happen nowadays between members of different Roma *fise,* whereas before they didn't. Everyone wanted [to marry someone] from his own *fis.* My father and my wife's father belong to the same *fis;* therefore

---

25. Enculturation is the process by which a human being adapts to his/her culture and learns to fulfill the function of his/her status and role.

26. See Qirici (2002, 2001, and 1999).

27. "Endogamy" is a rule requiring marriage within a specified social or kinship group. (http://www.anth.ucsb.edu/glossary/index.html)

my wife and I married . . . Today, however, the youth don't care about this tradition, and they've even started marrying whites, Egyptians, or Roma from other *fise.*"

Marriage with a member of another ethnic group is sometimes punished with ostracism. Bujar, a member of a well-to-do Roma family, stated: "One of my sisters married out of love with a man of the white hand, and our father was not at all pleased because he was not Roma. The man came from a good family, and his father worked as an officer in the army. But we refused to accept both my sister and her husband into our family. Only after two years, when my sister had given birth, did our father tell us that we should accept my sister and her husband [back] into the family."

Marriages are often arranged between females ages 13–15 and males ages 16–18. Refik, a Roma *kryeplak*[28] in Elbasan, explained: "Marriages happen at early ages. This is a bad thing, but it's a tradition that we haven't changed because if a [single] girl gets to be 20 years old, we say that she'll be left at home unmarried. We see early marriages as something good, because when you marry early, then you have children quick and they become a support to their family. Another reason is that if the girl reaches a later age, then she is likely to sin . . . I myself am opposed to this tradition, but no one really cares. It will take many years and a lot of work to undo it."

Matchmaking Customs. Most Roma and some Egyptian marriages are arranged by matchmakers and are carried out without the consent of potential mates. Most matchmakers are male members of the groom's family or close friends of the families.

Matchmaking, especially for Roma, is conducted with the assistance of an intermediary, who is usually a close family friend who is also experienced in matchmaking. According to Roma, the intermediary adds credibility and seriousness to the proposed arrangement.

When an arrangement is sought, the father of the male marriage candidate, and the intermediary, approach the family of the female marriage candidate. When the father meets the girl's parents, he announces: "We have come to seek a piece of bread,"[29] and the response given by the girl's parents indicates their interest in the proposed marriage. In some cases, the prospective groom is present during this process, and the fathers of both families allow him to meet his proposed wife. Seiti, a Roma from Delvina, explained: "My aunt who lives in Vlora told me about a girl. . . . I went with my father to the girl's house . . . and we asked for her hand in marriage. The girl's family consented and we were engaged. I saw the girl when she brought us *llokums*[30] to entertain us and I liked her. If I had not, . . . I would have told the girl's father that we would give our final response later. With this, it would have been understood that I had refused. The girl also told her parents that if they liked me, then she would be fine with it. I stayed in Vlora for four or five days, and then we married."

Parents of both families often make marriage decisions without the bride-to-be's consent, and often, but less frequently, without the groom's consent. Arben, a Roma parent from Elbasan, explained: "We consider it to be a great shame if a girl falls in love with a boy.

---

28. *Kryeplak:* the head of a local administrative unit chosen by elections at the village level who serves the village for four-year terms.

29. The Albanian translation, from which the English translation is derived, is "Kemi ardhur për të kërkuar një copë bukë."

30. A gelatinous candy referred to in English as "Turkish delight."

In general, marriages are arranged, but when a boy loves a girl, then we discuss it immediately in the family and afterwards give our decision. We do not ask the girl when we 'engage' her. Only in very rare cases is she asked for her opinion."

If both families consent to the marriage, the groom presents gifts to his chosen bride, and the wedding date is set between a week to several months after the engagement. If the future bride or groom's family cannot afford wedding expenses, both families agree for the bride to be "kidnapped," that is, for the couple to cohabit before the wedding ceremony.

Weddings

Traditional Roma wedding ceremonies last three days and include feasts, music, and dancing on Saturday and Sunday.

The bride's family hosts a wedding party on Saturday, followed by a Sunday party hosted by the groom's family. On that morning, the groom picks up his bride from her family's home, and guests throw candy and rice over their heads. Her uncle and brother escort her to the entrance of the groom's home. At the entrance, her uncle says to the groom: "Present to me your tribute."[31] The groom presents the tribute to him and states: "That's what I have in my pocket."[32] The uncle responds: "May you have good fortune."[33] The couple enters the home and initiates the Sunday celebration. Festivities include a traditional dinner and dances.

The paramountcy of female virginity governs many forms of public interaction with unmarried females. Therefore, the most important event of the three-day wedding ceremony takes place on Monday morning, following the couple's first night together, when experienced female members of the groom's family conduct the virginity "sheet" test. A Roma woman explained: "We have a tradition that on Sunday night, when the newly married couple goes to the bedroom, we put a sheet on their bed. On Monday morning, the sheet is displayed to family members. . . . When the bride is proven to be a virgin, then a lunch is served . . . , because she honored her family and me as her mother-in-law."

The repercussions of noncompliance are strong if they determine that the bride was not a virgin before marriage. Then the marriage is called off and the bride is returned to her family's home. In rare cases, couples are reconciled and the marriage proceeds.

Some marriages are certified by the local municipality, at which time the bride adopts her husband's surname. In many cases, however, marriages are not officially recognized because one or both of the spouses are below the legal age. Weddings are seldom carried out by religious authorities.

Births and Deaths

Relatives often celebrate the birth of a child with a ritual called *"vigje"*[34] The guests bring gifts or money to the new parents.

---

31. The Albanian translation, from which the English translation is derived, is: "Më jep haraçin." Tribute amounts are negotiated before the wedding.
32. The Albanian translation, from which the English translation is derived, is: "Këto kam në xhep."
33. The Albanian translation, from which the English translation is derived, is: "Mirë, qoftë për hajër."
34. *Vigje:* a celebratory dinner held when a child is born.

When a family member dies, a funeral and a series of commemorative dinners are held. A Roma woman described: "Before, when we were nomadic, and a relative died, we would bury him. Now we have communal cemeteries just like the rest. The day he dies, we have a dinner, then we have a dinner three days after, then seven days, and so on. *Fis* members and neighbors take part in these ceremonies. When people come to express their condolences, they either give a contribution in cash, or bring sugar, rice, or anything else, depending on their income."

Religion

Most Roma are Muslim, whereas Egyptians are either Muslim or Eastern Orthodox. Religious beliefs or affiliations are expressed through celebrations or commemorations, such as Bajram for Muslims and Easter for Orthodox, or through joint celebrations such as the festival of Saint George. The festival of Saint George, celebrated on May 6, is the primary religious holiday for Roma.

The Festival of Saint George

"We have celebrated the festival of Saint George for centuries. But not only do Muslims celebrate it, but also those who have converted to other religions in other European countries. Saint George is the symbol of Roma. It is a special day when [traditionally] each Roma family sacrifices a sheep or bird, goes to a river to get some water, gathers flowers, and cuts their hair for good fortune. In the morning, we clean the yard to avoid being caught by witchcraft. We stay up all night with our family. The women, men, and children sit separately, and they eat and drink and enjoy the band. At 3:30 or 4.00 in the morning, everyone gets up, and with the band there, too, we head for the river.

We have gone through the entire winter; and we have survived many problems like cold and illnesses. All these things went away; the river took them away." Quoted by a Roma women respondend.

The Roma *Fis*

Structure of the Fis

Roma social organization is based on the *fis*. Members of one *fis* are usually persons who patrilineally descend from a common male *fis* name. The main branches of the *fis*—large families—serve as the bases for the creation of new *fise*.

Arben, a Roma who enjoys a high standing within his *fis*, explained: "My *fis* is made up of all cousins [first, second] that have my last name, Demir." When a *fis* extends for several generations into a few dozen families, *fis* membership can reach into the hundreds. Now into its third generation, the Demir *fis* is composed of approximately 70 families and several hundred individuals. (For a full description, see Appendix E.)

Fis structures can take several forms. Many Roma only consider persons with a common last name as *fis* members. But some Roma think that the children of female *fis* members can still be considered *fis* members although they have different last names. The concept of the *fis* is relative and dependent upon the outlook of *fis* members and the point in the family tree from which the *fis* begins. Patrilineage indicates an ongoing social change. But while patrilineage has, up to now, been a rather stable form of kinship social organization of the Roma *fis*, forms of matrilineage have become less common.

Structure of Arben's *Fis* in Korça

"My grandfather's name is Shaziman. He was born about 100 years ago in Kostur, Greece, as the son of Demir Demirit, and he had two wives. My grandfather had four children with his first wife—two boys [Arshin and Dajlan] and two girls [Makbule and Xhuliana]. He had four children with his second wife—three boys [Demir, Ali, Sali] and one girl [Shubeqare]. The oldest son from his first wife, Arshin, had nine children, while the other son, Dajlan, had four children. The oldest daughter, Makbule, was married in Korça and had eight children. The other daughter from his first wife, Xhuliana, was married in a village in Fier [Zhupan] and had 14 children.

My father, Demir, had his grandfather's name. He was the first son from my grandfather's second wife and had nine children—three boys and six girls. The second son, Ali, had three boys and four girls. So, just taking the first cousins from my father's side, we have over 60 people. Each one of them is married and has three or four children. Just from my father Demir's side, there are 94 of us, whereas Makbule with her grandchildren numbered 120. So, starting with my grandfather, Shaziman, there are a few hundred of us. The *fis* is made up of all cousins that have my last name, Demir." Quoted from a male Roma respondend.

Function of the Roma Fis

An extensive network of relations exists within every *fis*, based on connections between families within the *fis*, arranged marriages, and close friendships. At the center of this network is one family or designated person with authority that defends and strengthens the *fis*'s continuity. This figure (or family) distinguishes himself over time through abilities and ethical qualities, and thus enjoys the respect and trust of *fis* members. The members of one *fis* can meet to advise one another on different problems. *Fis* members convene when one family or individual within the *fis* is in conflict with one another, in cases of misfortune such as an illness or death, when a *fis* member is in a difficult financial situation and requires assistance, and when two families want to arrange a marriage.

Function of Arben's *Fis* in Korça

"They say that my grandfather, Shaziman, was very well-off and had a lot of influence with other Roma. In King Zog's time, if someone was arrested by the police without cause, he would intervene and have the man freed. He resolved many conflicts between Roma families and because of this, he was referred to by all as Shaziman *Aga*.[35] He was the only Roma from Korça to have gone to America three times as a migrant. He worked there in metallurgy, but in addition to this he was involved in horse dealing. My grandfather had two brothers from different mothers and one of them lived in the village of Çuka in Saranda. The other migrated to America and later returned to Greece, where he died. Shaziman was half-Karbuxh Roma on his father's side, and half-Cergar Roma on his mother's side, but he lived among the Karbuxh *fis* of Korça.

My father, Demir, was a very able person and had a lot of influence within the Roma community. He maintained relations with the local government authorities, arranged marriages, and resolved conflicts. He inherited this influence partly from his father and partly from his own achievement. He was involved in private business, and he continued to do business during the socialist period, when private enterprise was strictly forbidden." Quoted from a male Roma respondend.

Under extreme circumstances, the *fis* can expel one of its members from the family circle. "One of our cousins," described Kujtim from Korça, "did some things that were immoral. So then we got together and expelled him from the *fis*. Whenever we have weddings, engagements, marriages, or other ceremonies involving families within our *fis*, we no longer invite him."

Specific Roles of the *Fis* Leader

By providing outstanding leadership, a *fis* leader can earn respect and authority from a large number of Roma *fise*, and gain the title of "Barorom" [Great Roma]. This leader usually comes from a large and well-known family, is better off than most Roma, has connections with state representatives, and maintains relations with many Albanian and Roma informal leaders. Ilmi, a leader of a large Roma *fis*, explained: "My father was the second son . . . By talking to Roma in homes throughout the country, he carried on the tradition that my grandfather had built during his lifetime. He was very tolerant, generous, insightful, and hard-working. This person, in addition to providing assistance to everyday Roma, also resolved disputes between Roma *fise*." (For a narrative on the Great Roma [Barorom], see Appendix E, More Voices of Albania.)

---

35. A word with Turkish roots that during Ottoman times was a title given to wealthy landowners. In this context, "aga" refers to a man with great authority and respect.

Changes in the Social Organization of the Roma *Fis* over Time

Key functions of the Roma *fis* are the support of individuals and communities in sustaining their livelihoods though social cohesion, trust, and solidarity. As a social organization, however, the *fis* is subject to socioeconomic and structural change in both structure and function. This affects individual Roma as well as the community as a whole.

Strong Structures and Specific Functions of Roma Fise *during Socialism*

Extensive *fis* networks played a special role during the socialist period. Social capital[36] held the *fis* together and provided its members with essential connections for finding markets and trade goods in the informal sector.

During this period, some Roma community leaders served as intermediaries between government authorities and the local Roma population. Bujar described his father's role during socialism: "For every problem that the government or local authorities had with the Roma community, they would come and consult my father—that's how much respect they had for him. At the same time, there were also Roma who were very poor, and my father used his connections with people from the state to find work for those poor Roma."

Weakening Structures and Diminishing Functions of Roma Fise *during Transition*

The significance of the *fis,* however, weakened during the transition period. Dramatic socioeconomic downward trends that have occurred in Roma families have weakened the fiss' social organization and have worked against the close solidarity that existed between the families under socialism. Bujar, a Roma from Elbasan, explained: "We helped each other before, whereas now the tradition is fractured because of poverty."

Another factor that has weakened Roma *fis* structures and functions is migration, which inhibits its members from maintaining close contact with one another.

Alternative forms of social organization that have emerged exist parallel to the *fis.* Albanian Roma are attempting to invent new civic institutions, such as associations and solidarity networks. In contrast to the *fis,* these alternative organizations are based on trans-local and transregional organizational principles. Nevertheless, Roma continue to use the *fis* and its inherent networks for business activities.

Conclusion

Both Roma and Egyptian cultures are distinct both from one another and from the majority Albanian culture. Both groups expressed the need to maintain support for their cultures.

---

36. Social capital is discussed fully in Chapter 10.

Culture is fluid and inherently changes. Poverty and other socioeconomic changes of the transition period have strongly affected certain elements of both cultures and have contributed to strong declines in the transmission of folktales, handicraft making, and possibly music. Moreover, Roma *fis* structures and functions have weakened or diminished.

Social inclusion of Roma and Egyptians depends largely on the accordance of policies with Roma identity, unique cultural aspects, and forms of social organization. Language, marriage, the Roma *fis,* and the importance of female virginity will considerably influence the effectiveness of these policies.

CHAPTER 4

Marriage and Family Planning

Between 1993 and 2001, Albanians' ages at marriage rose steadily. At the national level, men married at 27.2 years and women at 22.6 years in 1993, but in 2001, men were 29.3 years and women, 24.1 years. During that period, the average Albanian family size decreased, and in 2001, the average size was 4.2 (INSTAT 2002). However, running counter to this national trend, Roma and Egyptian marriage ages were considerably lower, and families were increasingly larger.

- The current minimum ages for state-recognized marriage are 16 years old for women and 18 years old for men.
- Average marriage ages for Roma men (18.2 years) are nine years lower than marriage ages at the national level (27.2 years).
- Roma women marry at the youngest average age (15.5 years) of all ethnic groups.
- Approximate marriage ages for Egyptians (17.2 years for women, and 19.4 years for men) are still far lower than the national level (27.2 for men, and 22.6 for women)
- Average family sizes are 6.4 for Roma and 5.2 for Egyptians.

Early marriage and child bearing reflect Roma and Egyptian traditions of marriage and gender roles. Both expect women to be wives and mothers. Additionally, few of both receive formal family-planning instruction. As a result, the use of birth control methods is low among Roma (10 percent) and Egyptians (8 percent), and abortion rates are high.

The main side effects of early marriage and young childbearing ages include low education levels and high divorce rates. For Egyptians, and especially for Roma, divorce rates are higher than for Albanians. For women, divorce leads to increased poverty and social exclusion for themselves, their families, and their children. This may result in a retreat into prostitution as a strategy for survival and a coping mechanism for poverty.

Early Marriage and Young Childbearing Ages

There is a paucity of quantitative data on either group's marriage ages because many occur under the legal age and therefore are not formally registered. Both claim that most couples have their first child after one year of marriage. Because many Roma women marry early in their teens (13–14 years), their ages can be approximated by subtracting one to two years from their first confinement.

Table 4.1. Marriage Ages for Roma, Egyptians, and Total Albanian Population during Transition

Approximate Marriage Ages during the Transition Period, by Gender and Ethnicity			
	Roma	Egyptians	Total Population[a]
Males	18.2	19.4	28.3
Females	15.5	17.2	23.3

a. INSTAT (2003).
Source: Socioeconomic household questionnaires with Roma and Egyptians for the Needs Assessment (2002/03).

In general, Roma and Egyptians are younger when they have their first child.

Table 4.2. Ages of Roma and Egyptians at Birth of Their First Child

By Gender and Time Period			
Roma		Egyptians	
pre-1990	post-1990	pre-1990	post-1990
Males	21.4	19.2	24.6	20.4
Females	18.9	16.9	20.1	18.2

Source: Socioeconomic household questionnaires with Roma and Egyptians for the Needs Assessment (2002/03).

Reasons for Early Marriage and Childbearing

Early marriage ages stem from the adherence to cultural norms and traditional gender roles, poverty, parents' fear of kidnapping and prostitution, and little family-planning knowledge. The influence of these norms and values on marital ages is especially strong for women.

Cultural Norms and Values

Roma and Egyptian women are expected to marry early and have children. Parents feel that their daughters' "eligibility" for marriage declines with age. Fejzi, a Roma from the city of Korça, mentioned: "Here, if a girl grows up and she ages, they say that no one will take her, and this shames us." Eri, a Roma from Levan (Fier), illustrates: "When the girl is 18–19 years old, we say that she's unmarried because there's something wrong with her."

The most important cause of early marriage is the emphasis on the sanctity of female virginity. According to Elida, a Roma woman from Lapardha, virginity "indicates the bride's loyalty to her husband." Roma and Egyptians said that early marriages were preferable to the "shame" that single women brought on the family if they remained single into their late teens. In numerous cases, this "shame" was related to the commonly held belief that unmarried girls are vulnerable to becoming sexually active before marriage. Ana, a Roma in Durrës, explained: "I married my daughter [off] at 13 so that she wouldn't shame us, so that she would be a proper girl."

A second strong influence on women is the family pressure to reconcile women separated from their husbands. Even those in abusive marriages are frequently encouraged by family members to endure abuse rather than separate. In fact, family members intervene and reconcile the couples, even when women in abusive marriages attempt to leave their husbands. Ervehe, a Roma from Pojan, explained: "There are separations, especially in cases where the man drinks and she breaks up with him. I have a sister in Korça; she has separated from her husband two or three times. . . . I have gone about two times to reconcile them. But just now I heard that she has left him again, and I told my sister that there's nothing more I can do. . . . He beats her when he drinks."

In contrast to Roma, Albanian cultural norms and values were subject to more change during the same period. Xhoanna, a Roma mother in Tirana, explained: "The white hand is more modern, they are better off, because they aren't as fanatic as we are. They go out with short skirts . . . whereas we aren't allowed to by our men."

Poverty

In many cases, early marriage is another poverty-coping mechanism. Many poor parents are forced to marry off their daughters at an early age to ease their own economic difficulties. Because married women live with their husbands, and frequently their husbands' families, marriage decreases the numbers of dependents within the woman's family. Arben, a Roma father, stated: "I will be forced to marry my daughter very soon, the sooner the better, because I don't have the means to keep her myself. . . ."

Parents' Fear of Kidnapping and Prostitution

The threat of kidnapping and possible subsequent prostitution also makes early marriage especially desirable. Parents feel that unmarried, unaccompanied women are more easily approached by strangers or are more inclined to talk to strangers. The perceived link between prostitution and early marriage is especially high in Fushë Kruja and other areas that may be considered unsafe, such as Levan. Eni, a Roma woman from Fushë Kruja, stated: "We Roma marry young. For us it's a good thing, because times now are bad. You raise them [children] and somebody takes them from you."

Limited Education for Marriage and Family Planning

Among both groups, early marriage and childbearing is not reinforced by even basic training in marriage skills and family-planning techniques. As a result, their families are larger than those of the majority.

Formal and Informal Family-Planning Education

Both Roma and Egyptian girls receive limited informal marriage and family-planning training through various family members. Mothers teach their daughters basic household chores but generally do not provide sex or pregnancy information. This is the responsibility of mothers-in-law. Makbule, a Roma in Levan, described how she raised her own daughter: "We got her involved in small chores, like washing and ironing. . . . Her mother-in-law tells her all the other things. We don't tell the girl ourselves." If their daughters-in-law are extremely young, the mothers-in-law also teach them more difficult household chores. Most fathers do not contribute to this informal education.

Some reported that husbands provide sex education to their young wives. Dajlan, a Roma from Korça, explained: "The husband teaches his wife. [Parents] don't talk with the girls about these things."

Birth Control and Abortion

Birth control use is rare among these groups. Reportedly, only 10 percent of Roma and 8 percent of Egyptians used birth control. Low birth control use is partly the result of mistrust of, and lack of knowledge about, birth control methods. Drita, a Roma woman in Delvina, explained: "I don't know about birth control methods. I just recently found out that there are pills, but they say that they do bad things to you." Ultimately, only 46 percent of Roma and 49 percent of Egyptians knew of a standard birth control method, but use is also low because of the husbands' refusal to use contraceptives. A Roma woman in Tirana, Anida, illustrates: "I have had a lot of abortions, but my husband still does not want to use contraceptives."

It is usually the role of women to take care of unwanted pregnancies through abortions. Among Roma women, 56 percent have had an abortion, while 77 percent have had two or more abortions. Among Egyptian women, 44 percent have had an abortion and 60 percent have had two or more. While a doctor performs the majority of abortions, 17 percent of Roma and 15 percent of Egyptians perform them themselves.

In addition, family sizes vary according to zone. Roma in peri-urban zones have the highest average family size in comparison with Roma and Egyptians living in urban or rural areas.

Table 4.3. Average Roma and Egyptian Family Sizes, by Zone		
Zone	Roma	Egyptians
Urban	6.1	5.16
Rural	6.4	5.59
Periphery	6.5	5.21

Note: Data on Albanian family sizes are available for rural (4.5) and urban (3.9) zones only. Sources or Albanian family sizes do not indicate how "periphery" zones would be categorized, so data on Albanian family sizes and data acquired from household questionnaires with Roma and Egyptians are not comparable.
Source: Socioeconomic household questionnaires with Roma and Egyptians for the Needs Assessment (2002/03).

Effects of Early Marriage and Childbearing

Early marriage and childbearing have implications for women regarding education levels and child care.

Low Education Levels

Early marriage leads to poor education skills, since girls and young women generally drop out of school to care for their husbands and children. While many Roma and Egyptian girls and young women do not attend school at all, those who do go to school drop out to perform family duties when they get engaged or married. In many cases, the simple expectation of early marriage caused women to leave school early to remain at home and prepare for their forthcoming duties as wives and mothers. Some of the consequences of these choices are high illiteracy rates, low qualifications, and few, if any, useful vocational skills.

Poor Child Care

When women marry young and have children early, the quality of child care tends to be lower than for older women. Many young mothers are still children themselves and lack any understanding of the demands of child care. It seems that mothers-in-law are also responsible for teaching their young daughters-in-law basic child care. Blerta, a Roma woman from Delvina, stated: "When the child has a temperature, I have to take him to the hospital . . . I take care of him because my daughter-in-law is young and doesn't know how."

Increasing Divorce Rates

While both Roma and Egyptians both display traditional attitudes toward marriage, their divorce rates appear to be higher than Albanians. At the national level in 2001, there were 9.6 divorces per 100 marriages (INSTAT 2003). Egyptians, and particularly the Roma, appeared to have even higher divorce rates. In fact, 45 percent of Roma indicated that divorce was very common in their community.

Major causes of divorce are spousal abuse and coerced early marriage. Others are poverty and international migration, which often exacerbate marital problems.

Causes of Divorce

Spousal Abuse. Many of Roma and Egyptians identify spousal abuse as a major cause of divorce. In most cases, abuse is a result of alcoholism, into which Roma men retreat to cope with their poor economic prospects and hopelessness for a better future. Liria, a Roma from Korça, stated: "I married at 13, my husband drank, and I left him. . . . He used to beat me and leave me without food."

Arranged and Early Marriage. Some Roma identified arranged marriages as a cause of divorce, because spouses know little about each other before embarking on marriage. Blendi, a Roma from Llakatund, explained: "My son was not in support of this marriage, but he accepted it anyway. Later he and his wife separated because the marriage had been imposed. The marriage wasn't based on knowing one another. It [divorce/separation] comes from a lack of acquaintance."

It is probable that the earlier the marriage, the more likely the divorce. Arben, a Roma physician from Korça, explained: "The problem is *when* marriages happen, because they are very young and completely immature." However, some Roma believe that marriages improve for couples who remained together as they grow older. Sali, a Roma from Delvina, explained the advantages of marrying later: "The wife will stay quiet [when abused by her husband] because she can't complain to anyone. However, as she gets older, she becomes more equal to the husband. [This happens] from the point when the wife begins to understand herself, when she reaches 25, and the children are older. For example, here in Delvina, if a woman sees that her husband still beats her, she goes to the authorities. . . . Democracy in the family begins after both sides mature–when maturity comes, then democracy begins."

Migration. Both groups also associate migration, especially international migration, with divorce. High unemployment and poverty rates force many Roma and Egyptian men to migrate to neighboring countries for employment. International migrants are often required to stay abroad for extended periods because of visa restrictions, low income levels in the destination countries, and high transportation costs in terms of travel expenses, safety in passage, and the risk of being arrested for illegal entry. When husbands migrate abroad, couples can be separated for long periods. Gëzim, a Roma from Baltëz, described international migration's impact on marriages: "Here most marriages end, because there are those who go abroad and stay for months or even years without coming back. . . . About 20 families here have this problem."

Changing Attitudes Towards Divorce. Divorce is more accepted among Roma and Egyptians than among Albanians, possibly because the problems of early marriage, the resultant poverty, the necessity of international migration, and other factors have made divorce more common during transition. Divorce is no longer a taboo for women and, in many cases, women request divorce from their husbands. Moreover, divorce does not render women ineligible for future marriage. Most divorced women can remarry, but eligible marriage candidates must be men who themselves have been married and divorced. Sonja, an Egyptian divorcée from Korça, still receives visits from matchmakers with marriage offers: "Yes, they come, it isn't a problem. . . . When both the man and woman have been married, it isn't a problem. When only the man hasn't been married, then it's a problem."

The Effects of Divorce. The direct effect of divorce is the increasing poverty of divorcées and their families. In general, divorced women return to their own families, and in 70 percent of cases, the maternal families care for the couple's children. Although some receive financial support from their husband's or their own families, ex-husbands seldom provide spousal or child support. There are several reasons: Frequently, when a marriage is contracted between spouses below the legal marriage age, men can refuse to pay alimony since the marriage was never formally registered, leaving their former common-law wives without legal standing. Other reasons include the husband's remarriage and the refusal of the new wife to permit financial support to the first wife and children. Mira, a Roma woman from Zinxhiraj, explained: "The wife keeps the children. He doesn't help at all, because his new wife doesn't let him and he ends up having children with the other wife."

Many divorced women with children, especially the poor and those who frequently interact with Albanians, may be forced to enter prostitution to survive and support their families.

Conclusion

Early marriage is a coping mechanism for poverty and social exclusion. During transition, marriage ages for both groups have lowered and family sizes have increased. Increasing poverty and social exclusion are the main reasons for these trends.

In addition, socioeconomic and institutional changes have resulted in high poverty rates, high and long-term unemployment, and uncertainty of making a living among all Albanians, but particularly among Roma and Egyptians. Marriages between teenagers and having children early have become even more common and are associated by both as leading to more poverty. Other factors include cultural norms and values, concern for the protection of young girls from kidnapping and prostitution, and lack of family-planning knowledge and marriage counseling. As a result, those who marry at younger ages and have children early also have higher levels of abortions and divorces.

Other aftereffects of early marriage and childbearing on women include high illiteracy, low educational qualifications, lack of vocational skills, high dependence on their husband and his family, spousal abuse, and poverty after separation and divorce. For the families, the economic effects are initially decreased levels of poverty when their daughters marry and join the husband's family, and heightened respect in the community for their adherence to traditional norms and values. On the other hand, the the loss of a daughter through early marriage causes emotional stress and trauma for many families But families' poverty levels increase when their daughters return home with their children after a separation or divorce, as this puts the families' economic situation under additional stress.

In many cases, women are forced to enter into prostitution to survive and feed their families. Their lack of educational qualifications and vocational skills gives them few alternative poverty-coping mechanisms and traps them in a continuing cycle of poverty.

CHAPTER 5

Income and Living Standards

According to government statistics, approximately 20 percent of the country's population receives state economic assistance. This percentage has not decreased significantly during the transition period, despite the improvement in macroeconomic indicators from 1994 to 2001. In all districts, Roma and Egyptian households represented a higher percentage of all households receiving state economic assistance than the percentage of the total population.

Roma and Egyptians confirmed that their incomes and living standards have declined during transition. They have fewer opportunities for formal employment than the majority population and increasingly rely on income sources such as casual work and self-employment.[37] As a result, their household incomes are less than half of national urban household incomes.[38]

- The average monthly household income is L16,492 for Roma, and L17,769 for Egyptians, but average monthly household expenditures are L25,867 for Roma and L25,641 for Egyptians.
- Of total household expenditures, food constitutes 71 percent for Egyptians and 64 percent for Roma.

---

37. Self-employment refers to the used clothes trade and can and metal collecting.

38. Average household income for *urban* households at the national level is L37,232 [US$286] (INSTAT, 2003). Reliable statistical data are unavailable for average household income for all urban and nonurban households at the national level. Because most Egyptians live in urban areas, quantitative data at the national level for urban households are comparable to quantitative data for Egyptian households.

Because of low incomes and limited access to public services, many households suffer from poor sanitation and infrastructure, which hinders these groups from participating fully in public life. Few families have a shower or bath in their home, which makes personal cleanliness problematic and impedes school attendance. These families possess fewer long-term-use items than the national average. For example, 74 percent of Albanian families own a refrigerator, whereas only 36 percent of Roma and 59 percent of Egyptians do.

For all these reasons, many suffer from poor health but have only limited access to health care. Because health care services have decreased in rural areas, Roma there are particularly vulnerable to declining health care.

As incomes decline, the two groups will be less able to afford public services—such as water and electricity—and infrastructure, sanitation, and health will continue to deteriorate.

Household Income

A typical Roma or Egyptian household earns only enough income to afford daily necessities. However, underreporting household income in socioeconomic surveys is common, because respondents have difficulty remembering income amounts and sources during the past month, or fear disclosing their actual income to strangers. Generally, surveys did not count nonmonetary income such as benefits from barter in food or items produced in the home.

Main Income Sources

Major income sources for Roma families are trade in used clothes, can collection, musical performance, and informal and casual work—mainly in construction and portage —, and formal business; together these constitute almost 60 percent of total income. Other income sources are begging and state disability assistance. Income from pensions and economic and unemployment assistance constitutes 13.6 percent of total income, while international migration income is 8.1 percent. At a mere 1.4 percent, monetary income from agriculture is very poor and indicates its increasingly insignificant role.

For Egyptian households, the structure of major income sources is slightly different. These are casual work, such as construction and portage, and private and state-sector wages and self-employment, which represent 64 percent of total income. Retirement pensions, economic assistance, and unemployment benefits count as 17.4 percent of total income, and remittances, 3.6 percent. Another income source for Egyptian families is private business, which produces 8.3 percent of total income. Under the "other" category (4.9 percent), income sources include begging, blood donations, and disability insurance. One Egyptian association leader in Tirana explained that "currently, 70 percent of those that donate blood are from the Egyptian community."

Alternative Income Sources

When they are unable to secure sufficient means through stable employment in cities, or agricultural production from their own land, they cope with their economic situation with alternative income sources.

Informal Work. When income from stable, formal employment is insufficient for meeting basic needs, a number of these families seek income through casual work, self-employment, or begging in the informal labor market.

In the 1990s, in the city of Berat, Egyptians lost their jobs when its largest industrial enterprise closed. They immediately sought income through casual work, mostly in construction. When the demand for local casual labor declined, they sought work in other cities where the demand was still high. Some young Egyptian men turned to short-term international migration, mainly to Greece and Italy. Others, lacking such opportunities, migrated within Albania to urban centers or became dependent on state assistance.

State Assistance

The state's social security fund is comprises four components: (a) state economic assistance, called *"ndihmë ekonomike,"* (b) retirement benefits, (c) unemployment assistance, and (d) disability payments.

The origin of that assistance is shown below in Table 5.1.[39]

Table 5.1. Average Income through State Assistance for Roma and Egyptian Households (in percentages)		
	Roma	Egyptians
Type of State Assistance	Income via State Assistance (%)	Income via State Assistance (%)
Retirement benefits (pensions)	9	11
Ndihmë ekonomike (economic)	4	6
Unemployment benefits	1	1
Total	14	18

Source: Socioeconomic household questionnaires with Roma and Egyptians for the Needs Assessment (2002/03).

Economic State Assistance: Ndihmë ekonomike

Near the beginning of transition, Law 7710 on Economic Assistance (ndihmë ekonomike) (hereafter "the law"), which went into effect in 1993, authorizes the government to pay cash assistance to poor families with temporarily inadequate income. Parliament later enacted laws to add assistance for various vulnerable groups (De Soto and others 2001). Law 8008, for example, covers disabled persons. The law designates two levels of state economic assistance—partial and full. Partial assistance is provided to households that own land or other production means, but whose monthly income is less than L2,400. Full assistance is provided to landless households and those with no employed members.

---

39. Approximately 9 percent of Roma and Egyptian households also receive food assistance from international NGOs and religious organizations. (*Source:* Socioeconomic household questionnaires with Roma and Egyptians for the Needs Assessment (2002/03)).

Albanians, Roma, and Egyptians all report that they never receive the full amount of state economic assistance that they should receive under the law. An official of the Berat State Economic Assistance Office confirmed this: "State economic funds coming from the government are never 100 percent. Something between 75 percent and 85 percent of the funds are given out."

However, some also complained about discrimination by state employees when they attempt to resolve these problems. In fact, 52 percent of Roma and 44 percent of Egyptian households indicated that they have experienced difficulties in qualifying for state economic assistance.

A Roma in Elbasan explained that his local commune "gets a lot of assistance, but they don't give it to us." The local *kryeplak* who was present at the interview added: "I go to the commune . . . to deal with the issue, and they tell me to 'get out of here, you're a Gypsy.' "

This is borne out statistically. According to the Fushë Kruja State Economic Assistance office, 395 (or 7.5 percent) of 5,300 total households receive state economic assistance, but only 25 (or 33 percent) of 76 Roma households do.[40] In the city of Berat, out of 3,070 households that receive assistance, only 70 are Roma and 770 Egyptian.

Most of that income is used for food and clothing, which are the two largest expenditures for Roma (66 percent) and Egyptian (74 percent) households. Village-dwelling Roma have lower food and clothing expenditures because they have access to sufficient food through subsistence agricultural production or barter.[41] However, state assistance covers only a small fraction of daily food requirement purchases. Vjollca, a Roma woman from Delvina, stated that: "There are seven people in my family: me, my husband, and five children. We are jobless. With the money I get from state economic assistance, I buy flour and beans."

In some districts, the number of Roma and Egyptian households that receive state economic assistance has declined because of international migration. The *kryeplak* of Driza stated: "Almost half of Roma families living here receive state economic assistance. Those who have migrated are excluded from receiving state assistance, even if they still have family members here. Most important of all, the commune has issued an order demanding that all family members be present when the family applies for state assistance. Before, it was enough if the head of the family, either the father or the mother, was present . . . But now, they demand that all of the family be there to be able to get it."

Some Roma and Egyptians stated that, despite being eligible, their local State Economic Assistance Office denies them state assistance benefits by claiming that they engage in the used clothes market or other forms of informal labor. Mimoza, a Roma woman from a very poor family in Bregu i Lumit, explained: "I am 70 years old and I am going through very hard times. . . . I don't receive economic assistance. I have gone everywhere to ask for it but nobody will help me. They tell me that 'you Roma sell used clothes.' "

Many families said that because of poor written language skills it was difficult for them to prepare the applications required to receive state economic assistance. However, some state employees assist them in preparing the necessary documentation. An employee at the

---

40. The estimated number of Roma households in Fushë Kruja was provided by managerial-level employees of the State Economic Assistance Office.

41. In rural areas, 128 interviews were conducted with Roma households and 27 with Egyptian households.

Delvina State Economic Assistance Office, Luljeta, confirmed this, stating: "Some Roma families need consulting since they do not know what documents they need to prepare. We help them with this, and they only have to sign with their finger, since they don't know how to write their own names."

Finally, in a classic bind, some families do not receive state economic assistance because the law stipulates that households registered in a given municipality must have been registered there since 1993. Consequently, some Roma households in Shkodra are ineligible to receive that assistance.

Retirement Benefits (Pensions)

Retirement pensions represent a major source of income for Roma and Egyptian households. However, some described how difficult it was for them to qualify for their pensions. One of the main impediments was their inability to obtain the documents that are required to apply, because employee records from some former state-owned enterprises have not been preserved. Esat, a Roma in Gjirokastra, is unable to travel to districts where he has previously worked: "I do not get a pension since I don't have the necessary documentation. . . . I have worked in state-owned agricultural farms, in a forestry enterprise, and in the diesel refinery plant in Cërrik, so I have worked for many years. I had my employment record, but I lost it when my house caught fire. It is difficult for me to collect the required documentation."

Unemployment Benefits

Few households receive income from unemployment benefits. As a result of government policy that the maximum period for provision of benefits is one year, many are no longer entitled to them. This poses a widespread problem, as approximately 88 percent of Roma and 83 percent of Egyptians have been unemployed for much longer.

Disability Payments

Disability payments are cash benefits given monthly to individuals with mental, physical, or sensory disabilities (INSTAT 2003). Out of those households surveyed, only 27 Roma and 21 Egyptian households had applied for this type of assistance, because many families face difficulties in preparing and submitting the required documents.

Household Expenditures

Besides food, Roma and Egyptian households spend what little is left of their income on health, debt repayment, utilities, and transportation (Table 5.2).

Food

A large number of households do not have enough food to meet their daily needs. A typical household's diet is poor and unbalanced. On average, Roma and Egyptian eat bread daily; rice, pasta, and vegetables four to five times per week; cheese and eggs twice a week; and

Table 5.2. Average Monthly Household Expenditures for Roma and Egyptians
(in US$)

Expenditure Type	Roma		Egyptians	
	Expenditure (US$)	Expenditure (%)	Expenditure (US$)	Expenditure (%)
Food	126.62	63.6	140.18	71.1
Clothes	4.80	2.4	5.75	2.9
Electricity, water, heat, rent	10.80	5.4	12.02	6.1
Education and culture	2.29	1.2	2.17	1.1
Transportation	7.79	3.9	2.68	1.4
Paying with use of shop "lists"	19.18	9.6	16.12	8.2
Health care/medicines	22.29	11.2	14.62	7.4
Other	5.21	2.6	3.71	1.9
Total	198.98	100	197.24	100

Note: Data should be interpreted with caution as they are based on statistical averages for 331 Roma and 330 Egyptian families in 11 districts and represent self-evaluations of families. *Source:* Socioeconomic household questionnaires with Roma and Egyptians for the Needs Assessment (2002/03).

meat, milk, butter, and fruit once a week. Makbule, a Roma woman from Pojan, described her family's diet: "During the week, we eat white beans, cabbage, and potatoes. All these foods make up our main food diet. For supper, we drink a little milk or yogurt, and for breakfast, tea and cheese. When we don't have these things, we give our children bread with oil and sugar. We buy meat when we have money to afford it. . . ."

Health

According to a survey conducted in 2002, the average monthly household health expenditure was 3.8 percent for Albanians (De Soto and others 2001). However, for households with lower per capita incomes, averaging 11.2 percent of total Roma expenditures and 7.4 percent for Egyptians spent on health care, these costs are relatively high. These higher expenditures are caused by a lack of preventive care, generally poor health and diet, and larger families, which lead to a higher incidence of illness but insufficient means to pay for necessary treatment.

Another cause of high health expenditures for these households is that many Albanians perceive Roma and Egyptians stereotypically as being "wealthy," despite evidence to the contrary. As a result, most predominantly Albanian doctors or nurses often charge additional informal payments for treatment. In addition, many either have to pay these informal charges, in addition to other costs, or receive no medical treatment at all.

Typical additional charges cited by 28 Roma and Egyptian families ranged from L10,000 to L150,000 for an operation, birth, or simply a medical examination. In urban areas such as Tirana and Durrës, where living standards are higher, informal prices are higher than in other towns. Fatmira, a Roma from Bilisht, described an experience involving informal payments: "My brother had a bad appendix, so I brought him to Korça. At the hospital, I had to pay L37,000 to the doctors. Three doctors took L4,500 each, and then the nurses took money. I paid most of the fee myself, but a few relatives also helped out."

Repayment of Debt Incurred from the Use of the Shop "List"

Another high expenditure is "list"[42] debt repayment, which constitutes 9.6 percent of total expenditures for Roma families and 8.2 percent for Egyptians. Indeed, purchasing "with list" has become common in the economic life of the country. Most debts are from grocery shop owners. It is estimated that 80.3 percent of Roma families and 76.9 percent of Egyptian families purchase food with list to meet daily food consumption needs. The percentage of households that purchase this way is especially high in the districts of Berat, Fushë Kruja, and Tirana. In the city of Berat, many Egyptian households rely on the list because of extreme poverty, while in other areas in the district, Egyptians use the list because household heads are away as short-term migrants in Italy or Greece. In Fushë Kruja and Tirana, high list use is caused by extreme poverty in most areas and limited access to alternative income sources and state assistance. In Tirana, some Roma had been on the list for three months because of the late arrival of pensions.

Utilities and Transportation

Electricity, water, and heat expenditures make up approximately 6 percent of the total for these families. The percentage is slightly lower for Roma families, especially those living in periphery areas, because most do not pay for these services. Another expense is transportation, which represents 3.9 percent of total expenditures for Roma families and 1.4 percent for Egyptians. The higher percentage for Roma stems from a greater frequency of travel between villages and districts to sell used clothes and handicrafts.

Education and Cultural Expenses

More than 272 Roma and 274 Egyptians responded to questions about their expenditures for education and culture (literature and music) in a given month. They reported that these constitute a relatively small item on a household's total monthly expense list: 1.2 percent of total expenditures for Roma families and 1.1 percent for Egyptians. Many chose the option "other expenses," for example, tobacco, alcoholic beverages, and family events.

Living Conditions

Many families live in very poor conditions. In fact, 70 percent of Roma and Egyptian households consider poor housing their second greatest problem, after food. They also have little furniture, such as beds for each family member, and lack even the infrastructure for water supply, sanitation, and roads.

---

42. The "list" is an interest-free credit system kept by store owners, usually grocers, that allows customers to "buy now, pay later." (For an example of a typical "list," see Appendix K.)

Forms of Housing Arrangements

Most Roma (88 percent) and Egyptian (80 percent) households indicated that they own the homes they currently live in, acquired through housing privatization, inheritance, or new and often illegal construction.

Renting is also an option used by 3.6 percent of Roma and 5.2 percent Egyptians. Ilmi, a Roma from Shkodra, described the housing situation in his community: "There are about 13 to 15 families. They live in homes made of concrete blocks. We pay a daily rent of L100, so, L3,000 per month to the landlord, who treats us well."

Among Roma, 2.7 percent, and among Egyptians, 6.1 percent live in flats that are owned by the local municipality or commune. In the Kthesa e Ariut quarter in Sukthi, some Cergar Roma families live on property owned by a former poultry farm. Astrit, an Albanian carpenter, stated: "This used to be the poultry farm, and these Roma families were settled around here by force, because they were in very bad condition. They used to live in huts made of plastic. I have helped them even for free. They have nothing and so you can't get anything from them. . . . They are human beings and they deserve to be equal with us."

In Korça, some Egyptian families live in former state-owned clothing stores. Dija, an Egyptian woman who lives together with 12 other families, stated: "We need to be given housing, because the premises we now live in [are] not at all livable."

Old and Dilapidated Housing

In almost all districts, poor housing is a serious problem. Though home ownership is an important safety net, many owner-occupied flats are old and dilapidated. Conditions have worsened during the transition period for many families for a number of reasons. For some, poor housing conditions are the result of an increase in the size of their family. Agroni, a Roma man living in a makeshift home near Breg i Lumit, said: ". . . I have three children. We have been staying for two or three years at my mother-in-law's house. My father had his own home, but there were seven of us children in the family, so we had to move out." Other families have moved from their villages to the peri-urban areas in the hope of a better life. There, they have built makeshift shelters that lack even basic necessities and infrastructure. Ervehe, a Roma woman from Fushë Kruja, said: "Here we don't have electricity, water, or indoor plumbing. This is the poorest neighborhood in town."

Discontent over housing conditions is evident in both urban and rural areas. Some Roma families who sold their flats during 1994–1996, and then invested and lost their money in the country's pyramid schemes,[43] now live in makeshift housing. Along the Lana River in Kombinat, 70–100 Roma and Egyptian families live in housing made of wood and plastic.

---

43. From 1993 to 1996, pyramid schemes were formed and spread throughout the country through associations, foundations, and individuals. Because they offered high interest rates for deposits, about 1 million people invested their savings into these firms. By the end of 1996, it was estimated that Albanians had invested approximately US$1.2 billion. Starting at the end of 1996, one by one, these firms went bankrupt, and most creditors lost their money. The collapse of these pyramid schemes was one of the main causes of the political and social chaos that overtook the country during the first half of 1997.

Land Distribution, Subsistence Farming, and Housing

Many Roma (42 percent) and Egyptians (39 percent) do not own the land on which their homes are built; these figures also include cases where home ownership rights are still undetermined.

Many households never received land because they took the government's option to receive state economic assistance instead. In some cases, state economic assistance, however, was terminated shortly after it began. Other Roma, mainly from the Cergar, Karbuxhinji, and Bamill *fise,* were pressured by Albanians to take state assistance instead of land, since they were not traditionally engaged in agriculture.

Some northern district Roma and Egyptian households never received land because of land distribution problems. Multiple households experienced these problems in several localities, such as Fushë Kruja and Delvina. In some areas, land was distributed through informal village consensus and, while illegal, the process was accepted by government authorities. In several cases, however, the distributed land was seized by pre-World War II owners, who left the dispossessed Roma and Egyptians without compensation.

Families who own land are unable to derive significant income from agriculture. In many cases, they sold or rented the land that they had received through land distribution because of the lack of agricultural knowledge, and poverty. Twenty-four of the 60 Karbuxhinj Roma families in Pojan (Korça) who received land in 1992 have sold their property. Property rental and sale was also common among Meçkars in Llakatund and Egyptians in Risili.

Available Building Materials

Materials used for home construction indicate the quality of the home. Some homes are made of brick (36.9 percent Roma and 51.9 percent Egyptians), stone (5.5 percent Roma, 13.5 percent Egyptians), or concrete blocks (30.5 percent Roma, 23.9 percent Egyptians). Other homes are built with mud-brick (14.5 percent Roma, 9.4 percent Egyptians) or wood (6.2 percent for Roma, while the research did not discover Egyptians using wood). Based on chosen construction materials, homes for Roma and Egyptians are of poorer quality than the Albanian national average. A general population and housing census for 2001 established that 88.3 percent of homes in Albania are made of brick and stone, 4.5 percent from prefabricated material, and 7.2 percent from other material, such as wood (INSTAT 2002).

Living Space per Capita

Information concerning the number of rooms and total surface area per capita also indicates the quality of their homes. Approximately 75 percent of Roma and Egyptian families live in one- or two-room homes, with an average of 6.04 (Roma) and 5.05 (Egyptians) family members. In these cases, 60 percent of Roma homes and 73 percent Egyptian, are occupied by one married couple. But for 30 percent of Roma and 21 percent of Egyptians, two couples live in the same home, and 10.6 percent of Roma and 5.4 percent of Egyptians live in three-couple homes. Arben from Korça explained: "There are 12 people in my family — my wife, me, my daughter and her son, my son with his wife, and the other children. We all live in one room. Our major problem is housing, given that we all sleep in one room." In Table 5.3, Roma and Egyptian living space is compared to the national average.

Table 5.3. Surface Area of Homes, by Ethnicity			
Surface Area of Homes, by Ethnicity (in percentages)			
Surface Area	**National Average[a]**	**Roma**	**Egyptians**
< 40m²	20.6	52.9	46.1
40–69m²	40	19.1	27.7
70–99m²	28.7	13.7	16.4
100–130m²	8.7	7.3	5
> 130m²	2	7	4.7
Total	**100**	**100**	**100**

a. INSTAT (2003).
Source: Socioeconomic household questionnaires with Roma and Egyptians for the Needs Assessment (2002/03).

Most Roma and Egyptian families live in a home that is smaller than the national average.[44]

Basic Amenities

Possession of long-term-use items, such as furnishings and appliances, is uncommon, especially among Roma families (Table 12). A small number of Roma families own washing machines (15.2 percent), refrigerators (36 percent), radios (14.5 percent), and furniture (35.5 percent). Only 41 percent of Roma families own a bed for each family member; in 59 percent of Roma families, members sleep on the floor, or two or three persons share a bed. Approximately 72 percent of families own a television, and 25 percent a cellular telephone. Only 12.4 percent own a bicycle or motorcycle, and 6 percent own an automobile. Skënderi, a Roma from Zinxhiraj, stated: "OSCE donated a car to me. I work together with my son, collecting cans or scrap iron."

For Egyptian families, owning long-term-use items is more common. Among Egyptian families, 83.3 percent own a television, 58.8 percent own a refrigerator, 68.5 percent own a stove, and 52.6 percent own sitting room furniture. Roughly 53 percent of families own one bed per family member.

Possession of long-term-use items is not necessarily a sign of rising income. Some families had purchased these items before the transition period, or with migrant remittances. In other cases, goods were gifts.

Infrastructure

The availability of basic amenities necessary for daily life—such as drinking water, sanitation, showers, electricity, and roads—serves as an indicator for measuring living conditions.

---

44. Based on the classification of groups above, the average space per capita is 3.14m²for Roma families who live in dwellings with surface areas of up to 39m².

Table 5.4. Type of Appliance/Furnishing Available to Roma and Egyptians,
by Amount (quantity), and Ownership
(percentage)

Appliance/Furnishing	Roma		Egyptians	
	% that own	Average Quantity	% that own	Average Quantity
Telephone	6.9	1.05	17	1.02
Radio	14.5	1.02	26.1	1.06
Wall Clock	44.4	1.06	70.3	1.05
Refrigerator	36.1	1.01	58.8	1.00
Stove	70.9	1.05	68.5	1.06
Television	71.5	1.04	83.3	1.04
Automobile	6.3	1.00	4.5	1.20
Bicycle/Motorcycle	12.4	1.08	11.8	1.08
Tape Recorder	39.9	1.01	48.8	1.02
Satellite Dish/Antenna	13	1.05	13	1.00
Cellular Phone	25.7	1.04	18.8	1.11
Washing Machine	15.2	1.02	29.7	1.00
Shower/Bath	13	1.03	20.3	1.00
WC/Toilet	36.5	1.03	65.5	1.00
Bed for Each Family Member	41	3.49	53.3	3.43
Living Room Furniture	35.5	N/A	52.6	N/A
Other	4.5	1.01	3.6	1.02

Note: Data should be interpreted with caution. Data are based on statistical averages for 331 Roma
and 330 Egyptian families in 11 districts and represent self-evaluations of families.
Source: Socioeconomic household questionnaires with Roma and Egyptians, 2002.

Water Supply

The percentage of families with running water in their homes is 55.5 for Roma and 68.1
for Egyptians. However, because of broken water systems and supply connections, Roma
families with running water have water only 14 hours a day, whereas Egyptian families are
supplied only 10 hours a day. The *kryeplak* of Driza, where many Roma families live,
explained: "Most houses in the village have running water, but the supply has been reduced
to a few hours a day." This situation is more critical, particularly for Roma families living
in periphery areas.

Approximately 48 percent of Roma and Egyptians reported that the lack of drinking
water is an urgent problem for their family. Bujar, a Roma from Fushë Kruja, described
drinking water facilities for most of the families in this community: "There is no drinking
water supply here, so we have drilled a few wells. But the water coming out from these wells
isn't any good because it's mixed with sand and dirt."

A resident of Pojan, where Albanian, Roma, and Egyptian families live, explained: "The
main problem in our village is drinking water, because there is none. We have gone through
periods of eight or nine months with no water at all. The entire village goes and fills up [with]

water in neighboring villages." The head of the "Liria" quarter in Shkodra on the east side of Buna River sees another facet of the problem: "Whoever has money gets water; whoever doesn't have money doesn't get water."

Yet, the situation seems to have improved in some Roma and Egyptian homes in the Liria quarter where about 30 Egyptian families live, because of investments made by religious institutions, international NGOs, and donor agencies. According to a local community leader, "Wherever you go, this quarter is poor, but the church has helped us a lot. It has supplied us with water, because we never had water before." In Zinxhiraj, international donor investments brought drinking water to Roma families.

Sanitation

Living conditions for many households have also become worse because their homes are not connected to a sewage system. About 56 percent of Roma and 36 percent of Egyptian households consider this to be a serious problem, becoming worse. In Fushë Kruja, one Roma responded: "There's no sewage system here worth mentioning." Some families, mainly those living in villages or periphery areas, have constructed septic tanks.

The number of bathrooms per home is another indicator of living conditions. Only 25.3 percent of Roma and 56.2 percent of Egyptian families have a bathroom in their home. This low percentage is explained by the fact that many Roma families live in makeshift homes in periphery areas, while a considerable number of Egyptians live in flats. Those who live in relatively rural areas own outhouses (52.5 percent of Roma, 31 percent, Egyptians). Some own neither. Myrteza, an Egyptian from Korça, described living conditions for his family: ". . . There is no water, and no bathroom. We use the public bathroom in the bazaar."

The lack of bathrooms in many localities prevents Roma and Egyptians from maintaining personal hygiene. In Fushë Kruja, a Roma woman stated: "There are two families living under this one shelter. . . . For bathing, we use a basin in the middle of the room." This is another cause of the spread of infections, and low school attendance. A Roma mother said, "How can I send my child to school unclean? I don't have the means to wash him. He washes his feet only once every few months."

Health problems caused by a lack of hygiene and potable drinking water are further aggravated by lack of sanitation. It is most felt among Roma and Egyptian families living in villages or in periphery areas. The *kryeplak* of Driza reported, "We don't have a sewage system here. A while ago, we requested wastewater and sewage collection facilities, but nothing has been done so far. Up until now, we've built septic tanks."

Electricity

Lack of electricity ranks right after lack of water and sanitation. The lack of electricity is considered one of the most serious problems by 45.3 percent of Roma and 55 percent of Egyptian families. For many, electricity service grew worse during the 1990s. Although almost 96 percent of Roma and 97 percent of Egyptian households are connected to an electricity grid, the average number of hours of electricity service in much of Albania is limited to 4 to 20 hours daily. In many areas, the power voltage is low, not even enough to run a television or other household appliances.

Another critical problem is paying electric bills. Many Roma (55 percent) and Egyptian (48 percent) families cannot pay their bills. In some cases, nonpayment has resulted in the complete interruption of electricity service.

Roads

In many localities, the lack or poor quality of roads is very apparent. Poor roads were cited by 48 percent of Roma and 44 percent of Egyptian households and this percentage is higher in rural and periphery areas, such as in Fushë Kruja. Few roads where Roma and large concentrations of Egyptians live are paved. In some areas, roads become impassible during winters, which present difficulties for those who must travel between towns for informal or formal work. "The roads are full of holes, and so in winters they aren't passable," explained the *kryeplak* of Pojan.

Communications

Although these families do not consider telephone service a major priority compared to other utilities, lack of telephone access is nonetheless another serious problem. This lack particularly affects those families living in rural areas. Only 7 percent of city-dwelling Roma and 17 percent of Egyptian families have telephone service in their homes.[45] The lack of landline telephone service has led many families to use cellular phones. Though 26 percent of Roma and 19 percent of Egyptian households own a cellular phone, in many cases, the possession of a cellular phone is not an indicator of a family's standard of living. Shube, a Roma mother from the Pojan, stated: "We have a mobile phone, which our daughter sent us from Bilisht. We receive only incoming calls from her, because we don't have money to call people."[46] Those families use a neighborhood public telephone (45 percent Roma, 48 percent Egyptians) or a neighbor's telephone (30 percent Roma, 27 percent Egyptians).

Health and Health Care

Levels of health and health care have declined in Albania since 1991. A recent poverty assessment in Albania described an increase in illness, declining health care delivery, and health care personnel and facilities shortages in 10 country districts. With 41 percent of Albanian households concerned that the health standard of household members had declined since 1990, about a third felt that an inability to obtain health care was a major problem in daily life (De Soto and others 2001).

While health and health care are declining countrywide, an analysis of the health and health care status of Roma and Egyptians is even more limited.[47]

---

45. This percentage is higher for Egyptian families in Delvina, Gjirokastra, Korça, and Elbasan.

46. In Albania, all incoming calls on cellular phones are free of charge. Charges apply only to outgoing calls.

47. Studies on Roma in East and Central Europe describe similar problems in monitoring the health status of Roma. See, for example, "Avoiding the Dependency Trap," (UNDP, 2002, p. 63); "Towards Diversity with a Human Face (Draft)," (UNDP-RSC/ILO, 2002, p. 43).

Roma and Egyptians' Perceptions of Health and Health Care Standards

While self-assessments are restricted in determining actual health and health care conditions, they are important indicators of perceptions of care.

Echoing the comments of Albanian households in 2000 (De Soto and others 2001), 39 percent of Roma and 45 percent of Egyptian households agreed that the health of household members has declined over the past five years. Many Roma (26 percent) and Egyptians (23 percent) believe that malnutrition is the most common cause of their declining health. However, many Roma (17 percent) and Egyptians (15 percent) also perceive psychological stress stemming from bad economic conditions to be a major cause of their declining health,[48] as well as poor living conditions and lack of necessary medical treatments.

Nearly 19 percent of Roma and 22 percent of Egyptians suffer from a chronic illness. Both chronic and infectious illnesses include: bronchitis, liver and heart disease, hypertension, asthma, diabetes, jaundice, epilepsy, mental disabilities, and numerous cases of birth defects. Notably, smoking is related to many chronic and infectious illnesses described in self-assessments. However, smoking's effects on health in these households are difficult to assess. Many Roma link birth defects with endogamy, which is practiced by many Karbuxhinj and Cergar Roma, who generally live in isolated, rural areas. However, birth defects are more likely to be associated with malnutrition, poor living conditions, and a lack of prenatal and preventive health care than endogamy. However, children born with physical disabilities are sometimes referred to as "*raki* babies," indicating parental alcohol abuse.[49]

Reasons for Poor Health

While many illnesses identified by Roma and Egyptians are multifactorial, clear links to poor health include malnutrition, poor living conditions, and limited access to health care services and facilities.[50] As a physician in Gjirokastra stated, "Diseases occur mostly among the families of the Roma community because of low resistance among children and from their very difficult living conditions."

Malnutrition. Malnutrition is associated with many chronic illnesses identified by Roma and Egyptians in self-assessments, and is likely to be a contributing factor. Their diets consist mainly of starches and vegetables. Moreover, 28 percent of Roma and 38 percent of Egyptians responded that they "continually" did not have food to eat during the previous year.

Poor Sanitation. As described earlier, water and sewage infrastructure is deteriorating or nonexistent in many localities, and many households drink unfiltered water from nearby rivers or wells. Poor health is a likely consequence.

Limited Access to Health Care Facilities. Roma are particularly affected by limited health care access because most live in rural areas, and rural health care has drastically declined.

---

48. Statistics are based on information provided by survey respondents who mentioned having declining health.

49. "*Raki*" is the local Albanian hard liquor.

50. A report published by the UNDP(2002) identified "poor sanitation levels due to inadequate basic infrastructure," and limited access to health services as major determinants of poor health status among Roma in Central and Eastern Europe.

Many medical personnel have migrated to urban areas, seeking higher pay and living standards (De Soto and others 2002). Without sufficient medical staff, some facilities have closed down, while the quality and types of services being offered in existing facilities have decreased. A Roma woman from the city of Korça explained that in villages, births are sometimes assisted by female family members because village residents lack the necessary transportation for travel to hospitals, and doctors "are not around like in the city."

For most, preventive health care is nonexistent, and many complain of ailments for which they have received no medical attention. They seek medical attention usually only when health difficulties reach late stages.

Weak Government Capacity to Provide Health Care Services. Although also a problem for many Albanians, the two groups are especially affected by limited access to health care because of discrimination, poverty, and demographics.

Cost was the primary barrier to medical treatment in almost all of these cases. Only 25 percent of Roma and 29 percent of Egyptians said they have enough money to buy medicines. Fifty percent of Roma families and 34 percent of Egyptian families mentioned that they do not seek medical attention when necessary. Sania, a mother from Korça, stated: "Last night, my baby had a high fever, I didn't have enough yogurt to feed him. I didn't go to a doctor at the hospital because I didn't have money to pay for the serum."

Albanian doctors earn low salaries and frequently charge patients informal "under-the-table" fees. As a doctor noted, "In Korça, especially during the transition period, you haven't been able to enter the operation room without paying under the table. . . ."

As mentioned earlier, Roma and Egyptians are vulnerable to discrimination during informal payment processes because they are stereotyped as being wealthy. Some doctors who are aware that most cannot afford to pay high informal fees, refuse to treat them. Twenty-two percent of Roma and 12 percent of Egyptians responded that a doctor did not provide proper medical service because of their ethnicity.

Perceptions of Improving Living Conditions and Health Care

According to Roma and Egyptians, to improve housing and living conditions, local governments should provide families with shelter or financial assistance for home construction. A leader of a Roma association in Tirana said that "Those families that now live along the Lana River live in shacks, but when they [the local municipality] tear those down, as they say they will, I don't know where they'll go. . . . The government should invest in shelter for them, because they themselves don't have the financial means. . . ."

During the floods of 2002, many Roma and Egyptian homes were destroyed, since many live on riverbanks. These families expressed a need for financial assistance from the local government to build new homes. Makbule, a Roma woman in Berat, asked: "I just want some assistance to build a home, because I have three children who are ill. I lived in a shack before, but the river flooded over and took [our home]. Now I'm out on the street. The local government doesn't help us. . . . My main problem is housing, because I need to keep my children together. Just one room, that's all I want."

Another Roma leader from Tirana suggested that living conditions would improve for Roma and Egyptians if the government provided equal services to all residents: "In these areas, the living conditions for Roma families are extremely poor, because there are some families that, with six or seven people, live in one shelter. These difficulties are made worse if you add the lack of roads, potable water, sewage network, and other aspects of infrastructure where Roma live. Therefore, as a solution to these problems, the relevant government organs should pay more attention [to these families], by not allowing stereotypes or discrimination, be it even indirect."

Some suggested that one possible way to improve health and health care for them was to provide free or low-cost medicines. While some can afford to see a doctor, many cannot afford prescribed treatments. A leader of a Roma association in Tirana explained that: "In most cases, poor health among Roma families results from their low economic level, which keeps them from being able to purchase the medical treatments prescribed by doctors. To solve this problem, we propose that there be a way to help Roma, particularly with purchasing medicines that are most required in the case of illness, even if it means giving the medicines to some of them for free."

Conclusions

According to income and living standards indicators, many Roma and Egyptians experience daily life in a different way from the majority. Income and living standards have declined during transition, and because income for these households is increasingly unstable, more families are unable to afford public services and infrastructure available to others. Without basic health care, and services and infrastructure such as electricity, running water, and telephones, many face higher levels of social exclusion in the future.

Household incomes for them are less than half the national average urban household income, and main income sources are based on unstable and insecure forms of labor, including casual work and self-employment. Roma who rely on the used clothes trade have experienced a decrease in incomes because of competition from Albanian sellers and a decline in market demand. Consequently, Roma are increasingly dependent on other income sources such as begging and can and metal collecting. In some districts, Egyptians who rely on casual work in construction also face fluctuations in market demand that have forced some families or household heads to migrate to other Albanian districts in search of work.

Because income from self-employment and casual work has declined, they must rely on other alternative income sources, such as *ndihmë ekonomike* and other forms of state assistance. However, these income sources represent only a small percentage of total household incomes for both groups. Some households do not qualify for state assistance. Because of poor educational skills, many are unable to fill out application forms.

They are further at a disadvantage because some state assistance offices require that all household members be present in home districts to qualify. Many households have members who work abroad or in other districts as migrants, but nonetheless do not earn enough income to pull families out of poverty. For these families, state assistance is necessary for coping with poverty.

Most Roma (64 percent) and Egyptian (71 percent) household expenditures are spent on food. Consequently, most families are unable to afford investments in housing infrastructure, pay for public services, or send children to school. Only 1 percent of expenditures goes to education and culture (literature and music).

As a result of poverty, an increase in family sizes, and dilapidated housing, living conditions have become worse during the transition period, which leads directly to the social exclusion of the two groups. The inability of the state to provide some public services also contributes.

For similar reasons, many Roma and Egyptians, along with very poor Albanians, suffer from poor health. Poor infrastructure and sanitation, the inability to afford health care, malnutrition, and limited access to health care were identified in self-assessments as major determinants of poor health. And because health care services have decreased in rural areas, where one part of Roma live, they are particularly vulnerable to declining health.

To improve living conditions and health in these communities, their families should be provided with shelter or financial assistance for home construction, and free or low-cost medicines. Additionally, local government organizations should ensure that equal treatment and services are provided to all local residents.

CHAPTER 6

Education

By the end of World War II, the younger generation of the Albanian population was largely illiterate. When the socialist government took power, it enacted mandatory school attendance laws and launched anti-illiteracy campaigns. These efforts succeeded in substantially improving literacy rates. By the mid-1980s, almost 90 percent of Albanians had completed the compulsory eight-year primary school education. Of those, 74 percent had progressed to four-year secondary school education. By 1989, 93 percent of all Albanians and almost 100 percent of Albanians ages 39 years and younger were literate (INSTAT 2002).

Since the advent of transition in 1991, however, education levels in Albania have rapidly declined. In 1992, the average number of school years completed by Albanians age 25 and older was 6.2 (UNDP 2000b). School attendance has fallen, dropout rates have increased, and widespread illiteracy, especially in poor, rural areas, has reappeared (De Soto and others 2002, Dudwick and Shahriari 2000). This is especially pronounced among Roma and, to a lesser extent, among Egyptians, the two most marginalized groups of Albanian society.

Both groups face the same problems associated with decreasing education, such as economic hardship and the necessity of international migration, and they both suffer from higher poverty and unemployment rates.

Barriers to education are varied but are predominantly linked to poverty. Parents have reported that their inability to purchase books, school supplies, and proper clothing are the biggest barriers to primary education. Internal and international migration, poor living conditions, and insufficient infrastructure were also cited. Other barriers include institutional issues—such as weak government capacity, limited access to educational facilities, safety concerns, and exclusion and discrimination. Finally, other impediments are language difficulties, traditional perceptions of gender roles, nomadic traditions, and poor perceptions of educational benefits, based on parents' low education levels.

Decreasing Education Levels

Although the national illiteracy rate was less than 2 percent in 2001 (INSTAT 2002), it is much higher for these two groups in absolute terms and has also increased considerably in relative terms since 1991. Ermir, a young Roma from Shkodra, said "I am 15 years old but I haven't gone to school. We, the Roma youth who live here, do not know how to read and write, but those older than us know." As Figure 6.1 illustrates, the countrywide decline in education levels has been particularly dire for Roma and, to a lesser extent, Egyptians.

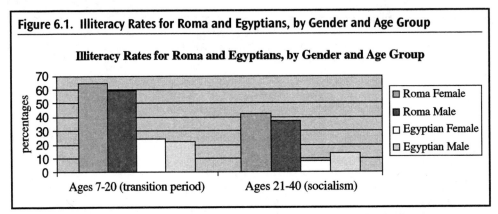

Figure 6.1. Illiteracy Rates for Roma and Egyptians, by Gender and Age Group

Source: Socioeconomic household questionnaires with Roma and Egyptians for the Needs Assessment (2002/03).

Low school attendance is only part of the problem. Some older Roma and Egyptians attend classes with younger Albanian students, because the need to contribute to the household income, security issues, or lack of interest prevented them from attending school when younger. Other students, while being passed through several school grades, have failed to master basic reading and writing skills. Monika, a 14-year-old Egyptian girl from Pojan, stated: "I have finished four grades of school, but I still don't know how to read because I didn't attend classes regularly."

Education levels for both also vary between districts and areas. According to a survey conducted by a Roma association in Levan, only 62 out of 256 (24 percent) children ages 6–15 years are enrolled in school in Levan, and only 36 (14 percent) of those enrolled actually attend school. In Fushë Kruja, only 11 Roma children are enrolled in school,[51] out of a community of approximately 150 households. As a result, illiteracy rates for Roma are extremely high in Shkodra and Fushë Kruja.[52]

Illiteracy rates for Egyptians are also high in Shkodra, Durrës, Berat, and some Tirana neighborhoods. One Egyptian association conducted a survey and found that out of 90 school-age children, only 43 were enrolled in school, while only 20 actually attended. According to this source, "Their poor economic conditions didn't allow them to attend

---

51. "The voice of the children is appealing," Union "Amaro Drom," Tirana 2003.

52. Extremely high illiteracy rates for Roma exist in Shkodra; Fushë Kruja; Rrapishta (Elbasan); Berat; some Tirana neighborhoods such as Bregu i Lumit and Kombinat, Levan (Fier); Kthesa e Ariut (Durrës); Cuka (Saranda); and Pojan (Korça).

school." Another Egyptian association in Tirana concluded that "There are two main problems that our community is facing: education and employment. I believe it is better that people have less to eat and still send their children to school. But very poor families need to send their children out to collect tins and scrap metal, because they do not have sufficient income to live."

In Gjirokastra and Vlora, where Egyptians are more integrated with Albanians, illiteracy rates for those ages 7–20 years are comparatively low, at 5.6 percent (Gjirokastra), and 4.3 percent (Vlora). Table 6.1 below shows illiteracy rates and school years completed for both groups by district.

Table 6.1. Illiteracy Rates and School Years Completed for Roma and Egyptians Ages 7–20, by District

	Roma		Egyptians	
Districts	Illiteracy (percentage)	Number of school years completed	Illiteracy (percentage)	Number of school years completed
Shkodra	100	0	67.5	2.0
Fushë Kruja	97.9	3	27.7	3.9
Durrës	60.4	4.05	30.6	3.47
Tirana	61.9	3.36	32.5	4.6
Elbasan	86.9	2.18	13.4	5.6
Fier	66.2	4.67	30.0	6.7
Vlora	38.0	5.16	4.3	6.7
Berat	59.7	3.81	28.4	5.05
Korça	41.7	3.78	8.3	5.03
Gjirokastra	36.0	3.56	5.6	5.68
Saranda/Delvina	51.6	4.6	0	6.11
Total	62.2	4.02	23.5	5.05

Source: Socioeconomic household questionnaires with Roma and Egyptians for the Needs Assessment (2002/03).

During the socialist period, Roma attended an average of 6.215 years of school (6.20 females, 6.23 males) while Egyptians, an average of 7.37 years of school (7.49 females, 7.25 males). Since transition, however, Roma have attended only 4.02 years of school (3.96 females, 4.07 males), while Egyptians have attended an average of 5.06 years (5.13 females; 4.98 males).[53] In fact, many in each group have either never attended school or have dropped out of primary school after completing just one grade.[54]

Not surprisingly, few go on to secondary and higher education. Only 1.3 percent of Roma and 4.8 percent of Egyptians ages 7–20 have secondary education, while 0.3 percent

53. Data for the socialist period refer to the years 1970 to 1990.
54. Sixty-two percent of Roma (65 percent females; 60 percent males) and 24 percent of Egyptians (25 percent females; 22 percent males) ages 7–20 years have never attended school. Also, 53 percent of Roma (57 percent females; 48 percent males) and 16 percent of Egyptians (16 percent females; 15 percent males) over 6 years old have not finished the first grade.

of Roma and 0.2 percent of Egyptians of the same age group have higher education. These percentages are higher for the age group 21–40 years, among which 4.6 percent of Roma and 10.8 percent of Egyptians attained secondary education, and 0.6 percent of Roma and 1.7 percent of Egyptians have higher education.

There are, of course, exceptions. Nure, a 19-year-old young woman from Delvina, identifies herself as a member of both communities. Her father is a Roma, and her mother Egyptian. Nure's parents both studied to become teachers. Her mother teaches literature and the English and Albanian languages, and her father is a teacher of history and geography. She is a rare of example of either community with high educational qualifications (for the case history of Nure, see Appendix E).

Barriers to Education

Poverty is the greatest determinant of low education levels. It also helps to explain disparities in education levels between and within districts. There are additional barriers to education, including institutional issues, culture, low perceptions of educational benefits, and and parents' education levels.[55]

Poverty-Related Barriers to Education

Barriers to education based on poverty comprise the dimensions of income, internal and international migration, and malnutrition.

Income Poverty. More than 67 percent of Roma families and 60 percent of Egyptians' cannot afford the costs of books and school supplies. Agim, an Albanian teacher in Bradashesh who is familiar with issues affecting local Egyptians, explained: "Most Egyptian families don't have a penny to buy books. For this very reason, about 20 Egyptian children here do not attend school. This year, there were five children who didn't enroll in the first grade. The sole problem is books, as the school is near and the conditions are good."

In some areas, international NGOs have provided funds to purchase books for children of poor families. Mimoza, a second grade teacher in Akërni (Vlora): "The parents of the children who do not attend school complain that they don't have enough money to buy books. An Italian association financed the purchasing of books for some of these children, and they are now attending school."

In addition to books and school supplies, many Roma (57 percent) and Egyptian (55 percent) parents cannot afford to buy their children proper clothes for school. The mayor of Delvina stated, for example, "Some Roma families do not send their children to kindergarten because they are barefooted."

Furthermore, children are required to contribute to the household income. In fact, 25.4 percent of Roma families that have one or several boys, and 15.4 percent of Roma fam-

---

55. To identify barriers to education for Roma and Egyptians, parents whose school-aged children did not attend school, were given a list of 14 possible barriers to school attendance, plus the option of "other." Parents were asked to select the barriers that contributed to their children's nonattendance, according to gender. Families who selected a given barrier are listed in percentage figures in the text, with a distinction by gender if differentials where significant.

ilies that have one or more girls do not send their children to school for this reason. Likewise, 33.5 percent of Egyptian families with one or more boys, and 9 percent with one or several girls require their children to work.

Genci, a Cergar Roma from Levan

"I am 14 years old and I have never gone to school. There are four people in my family . . . Every day I go to Fier to beg and I earn L400 [US$3.08], even up to L500 [US$3.85]. Six years ago, I was begging in Athens with a Roma couple from Fier . . . I want to go to school even at this age, perhaps in afternoon classes. It wouldn't matter how far the school was. There are other Roma children besides me who want to attend school."

Internal and International Migration. The internal and international migration of parents during the school year is also a major impediment to school attendance that can lead to some children dropping out. In the districts of Gjirokastra and Delvina, entire families migrate short term to Greece during the May–October agricultural season. Roma from Elbasan also migrate to Greece short term, where Roma women and children either beg or trade in used clothes. Children who migrate abroad with families do not attend schools in the destination countries for several reasons: lack of a good command of the language, the necessity of working with their parents, poor living conditions, and the temporary character of migration.

Additionally, some Roma families who sell used clothes and wicker products migrate throughout the country for brief periods. When families leave their home communities to migrate, they frequently take their children, who are thus removed from school.

Malnourishment. Hunger, malnourishment, and poor diet commonly affect school performance and force children to drop out of school without attaining a degree.

Institutional Issues. Institutional barriers to education include weak government capacity, limited access to school facilities, lack of child care facilities, and economic uncertainty and safety concerns, as well as discrimination and social exclusion.

Weak Government Capacity. National and local governments do not enforce the compulsory education law that requires Albanians to attend school a minimum of eight years. Weak local government capacity and poor economic conditions among Roma and Egyptians prevent the actual implementation of the law. An inspector of education in Fier said: "This law is unenforceable. First, because the fines we delegate for enforcement to the local authorities never get collected. Second, the penalized families are rather poor. . . . what fine can the state get from them? . . . A child doesn't go to school to simply fulfill an obligation towards the state, but above all, for his own good. We can apply fines whenever we want, but this will serve for nothing."

Limited Access to Education Facilities. In some areas, the long distance between homes and schools prevents children from attending school. During transition, many schools in rural areas have been closed down, because many communities have migrated to urban areas in the hope of improving their livelihoods. As a result, those who stayed have been left without a school. In Shkodra, a school located near the Egyptian community was closed in 1992. Because no alternative school was available in the vicinity, almost no children had one to attend until a new school opened in 1998. Consequently, many young Egyptian adults are illiterate.

Lack of Child Care Facilities. Many children need to take care of their younger siblings, as child care facilities are limited, too expensive, or too far away from their communities. Girls are most often asked to leave school to help in child care. Hyseni, a single Roma father of three children from Akërni, explained: "I leave the house early every morning and return late in the evening. My oldest daughter completed two grades of school, then I pulled her out because she had to care for the other children."

Safety Concerns. Often, security risks within a local community cause many Roma and Egyptian parents to remove children from school at early ages. Parents especially fear that girls will be kidnapped and sent into prostitution. Particularly in Levan, some Roma children do not attend school because the school is three or four kilometers away, and parents are concerned about their children's safety while walking to and from school.

Discrimination and Social Exclusion. Many parents describe an unusually high frequency of mental and physical disabilities among children. Two state-funded boarding schools for disabled children exist in Tirana. There are other schools only in select towns in the nine country districts.[56] Nevertheless, only 2 percent of Roma and Egyptian households have children who attend specific schools for disabled children. Special education schools are unavailable to the children of all groups living in rural areas, and so most do not attend school at all.[57]

The quality of education in schools for the disabled is also problematic. In some cases, children with physical disabilities are placed in the same class with children who suffer mental disabilities.

Some feel that teacher discrimination of children is a further barrier to education. Approximately 5 percent of Roma families and approximately 4.5 percent of Egyptian families have referred to this issue. This is further verified by a report published by the European Roma Rights Center in 1997: "They don't try to teach our kids. Roma kids are put in the back of the classroom, and the teachers don't care about them. The result is that our kids never make it to the end of school." Yet, apart from certain localities, most parents asserted that teachers treated all students equally.

Culture

Cultural constraints to gaining education include the Albanian language, traditional gender roles, and nomadic traditions.

---

56. Schools for the disabled are in Durrës, Shkodra, Vlora, Korça and Elbasan, Fier, Pogradec, Librazhd, and Laç.

57. Children with physical or mental disabilities who do not attend school are used for begging.

As mentioned earlier, most Roma families speak only Romani at home. Most of their children learn Albanian mainly through association with Albanians. Overall, language is a small barrier among Roma, but it becomes a major constraint to attending school for those in isolated communities. An Albanian teacher in a Roma kindergarten in Shkozet asserted that Roma children under the age of six do not speak Albanian.

More than 86 percent of Roma children attend school where the classes are taught in Albanian, the language that the majority of students speak. Lacking Albanian language skills, many of their children perform poorly in school, lose interest, and drop out.

Majlinda, an Albanian teacher in Bilisht, asserted: "Egyptians seem to be more integrated in every day life because they don't have a language of their own, while the Roma community has its own language . . . They are all intelligent children. To overcome this difficulty, I had to learn how to count in their language so that I could teach them the equivalent in Albanian."

Traditional Gender Roles. There are strong gender disparities in school attendance and illiteracy rates. Girls, particularly, are less likely than boys to complete primary school. Parents expect the girls to help with housework and to learn to become wives and mothers, while boys are expected to be the breadwinners for their future families.

In fact, many Roma and Egyptian girls drop out of school because of early marriage. A primary school principal in Baltëz added: "In our school, there are 70 Roma students from the first grade to the ninth grade. . . . But starting in the fifth grade, families keep their daughters at home because they want to marry them off. . . . Boys' attendance also goes down because their parents take them to help with work."

To ensure that absolute propriety be observed, Roma parents discourage girls from associating with boys after the age of 10 (fifth grade), which contributes to girls dropping out of school prematurely. In the village of Morava, a Roma girl explained: "I am 11 years old and in the third grade. . . . She says she is afraid about me being teased by boys. She says 'If rumors spread that boys are teasing you, then the neighbors will think you are not a decent girl.' "

Nomadic Traditions. Low educational levels and nomadic traditions are linked. Few nomadic Roma attended school before their forced settlement by the state in the 1960s. "My oldest daughter," explained a Cergar Roma woman in Levan, "never went to school. We wandered from village to village, so we couldn't send the children to school." On the other hand, Meçkar Roma, who settled during the first half of the twentieth century, gained higher levels of education and integration with Albanians during the socialist era. Sedentary traditions possibly allowed for higher levels of familiarity with and acceptance of formal education. Today, although Meçkars migrate more often than other Roma, their children complete more years of school, and have lower illiteracy rates than children of any other Roma *fise.*

Low Perceptions of Educational Benefits. Many people in Albania share the belief that there are few positive outcomes in giving children an education. One Roma parent stated that his children "must only know how to read and write, because economic conditions do not permit them to continue school any further." They think that the lack of opportunities for formal employment does not merit the costs. As long as education cannot significantly improve chances for employment, parents will consider education as limited in improving their children's opportunities in life. One Roma teacher from Llakatund confirmed "the mentality of their parents, who don't see any good in going to school." So it is not surprising that these parents also fail to perceive the benefits to the lives of their children. Five percent of Roma parents with boys, and 10 percent with girls believe that their children "learn all they need in life at home." Respective Egyptian figures are 3 percent for boys, and 6 percent for girls.

As a result, incentives to acquire educational qualifications are very low, among both parents and children.[58] To reinforce this belief, structural problems, and associated increases in poverty levels during transition tend to make people discount the value of education.

Parents' Education Levels. The low education levels reached by Roma parents and, to a lesser extent, Egyptians, also has a negative effect on children's school performance. For instance, parents with little education are unable to assist children with schoolwork, compared to the parental help received by Albanian students. Xhevrija, a Roma from Pojan, explained: "We have a nephew who is attending the first grade and we cannot help him. We've bought the books, and he has a great desire to learn but we cannot give him a hand with homework."

This attitude toward education obviously has a direct impact on children's attendance. One is the children's attitude toward "gadje"[59] education and state institutions. A UNDP study (2002) suggested that oral learning traditions "may produce different attitudes towards books, learning, and knowledge acquired from books," and that perhaps "this pattern of knowledge acquisition has become identified with gadje culture as something alien that is promoted by the official education system." This may explain the mentality of parents who undervalue existing public education, particularly in segregated communities.

Parents' Suggestions for Improving Education for Roma Children

When parents were asked how education for Roma children could be improved, suggestions centered on state financial aid, assistance with the Albanian language, and, in some localities, constructing schools closer to their neighborhoods and providing special schools taught in Romani.

A large percentage of parents (67 percent) responded that the state could "provide amenities[60] to assist Roma children in their schooling," while 41 percent of parents said that the state could "help facilitate admission into universities." In addition, 30 percent of parents thought that after-school Albanian language lessons would improve education for Roma children.

While many parents supported integrated schools and classrooms taught in Albanian, 34 percent of parents proposed that setting up schools where classes are taught in Romani

---

58. Low demand for education among Roma families was cited as an impediment to education for Roma in Spain: "As a basic education does not guarantee a Roma student a job upon completion, many Roma students view few incentives to stay in school." (Ringold, 2002, p. 156).

59. "Gadje" is a Roma term that refers to "white" or often "non-Roma" persons. It can also refer to paradigms or institutions dominated by "white" or "non-Roma" persons.

60. "Amenities" refers to books and school supplies.

would help improve education for Roma children. Thirty-one percent of parents were certain that hiring more Roma teachers would improve education for their children. This response was especially common in districts with large Roma populations, such as Korça, Elbasan, Tirana, Fier, and Berat.

Additionally, 16 percent of parents, mainly in Levan, Berat, Fushë Kruja, and Tirana, responded that schools located closer to home would increase school attendance.

Skënder, a Roma teacher in Delvina, offered a possible solution to the problem of low education levels among these parents: "[Parents] cannot help their children to advance in their classes along with their classmates. But if after-school lessons could be set up, where Roma students could get help, if there were a special classroom at their disposal, and some heating, this would be very helpful for them."

Conclusions

One of the biggest barriers to education for these groups is the cost of books, school supplies, and clothes. Other barriers to education were poverty-related, such as malnourishment. Then, too, many children are required to earn income for their family or to care for younger siblings.

Albanians, especially in rural areas, face many of the barriers to education that the others face. In some rural areas where Albanians live, the nearest school is several kilometers away, Albanian parents also cannot afford to purchase school supplies or books, and many children suffer from malnourishment (De Soto and others 2002). Thus, improving education levels for all groups in the long term requires solutions that address the entire country's education system and that provide greater employment opportunities for all Albanians.

Improving education levels for both groups also requires solutions that cater to local conditions, and to unique barriers to education that Roma face, such as discrimination and language. Roma parents identified some possible solutions, such as after-school Albanian language tutoring for Roma children and state-funded assistance for books and school supplies.

However, in the eyes of Roma and many Egyptian parents, the long-term benefits of education (beyond the fifth grade) are uncertain compared to the immediate benefits of removing children from school to work or to fulfill family duties.

Parents will continue to choose short-term benefits over education as long as formal employment opportunities are limited, child informal labor provides short-term benefits to families, and certain barriers to education persist.

CHAPTER 7

The Labor Market

One of the particular characteristics of Roma and Egyptian communities is their occupational identity. Pre-socialist-era Roma occupations were agriculture, horse trading, handicrafts, and music. For Egyptians, they were mainly metal work and music, and some manual labor as porters and dock workers.

During the socialist period, both were employed in agriculture and state-owned handicraft enterprises, but also in public service jobs such as street cleaning and gardening. Both, particularly the Egyptians, learned new, more modern skills. Apart from state-sector employment, some were engaged in the informal trade with textiles and dye, and established relations with rural Albanian villagers.

In the postsocialist transition, the restructuring of state-owned enterprises into a market economy resulted in high rates of long-term unemployment. Both groups were disproportionately affected for several reasons. Many met difficulty in adapting to the demands of the labor market in Albania because they lacked many of the required educational and vocational qualifications and expertise. Furthermore, Roma and some Egyptians have low levels of social capital with Albanians, and thus face discrimination and social exclusion.

Faced with these realities, they developed several coping mechanisms. They are now primarily engaged in subsistence agriculture, trade with used clothes, music, casual work—mainly in construction—handicraft trade, and begging.

In their perceptions, the main reasons for their unemployment include: lack of job opportunities, ethnicity, poor educational skills, and lack of vocational ones. Their increasing poverty creates a vicious circle for them: The poorer they become, the more difficult it is to find formal and informal employment.

Traditional Socio-Occupational Identities

Egyptians and Roma of different *fise* still practice several occupations in which they were already engaged before World War II.

A Roma tale about Roma, Egyptians, and Albanian socio-occupational identities

"God gave the white man the pen; the Egyptian, the hammer for metalwork. Whereas us, the Roma, he gave the willow stick for making baskets. When our ancestors went before God, he asked them: 'What took you so long?' 'We were dancing, oh God,' they answered. 'That is why we are late.' 'Then, take the willow stick,' answered God. 'As this is your fate.' "

As for Egyptians, they are also ironworkers, coppersmiths, tinsmiths, shoemakers, and butchers (Dino 2001), and were considered experts in these fields.

During the socialist period, both of their socio-occupational identities underwent significant change. These changes were conditioned by the development of new sectors within the Albanian economy, the imposition of compulsory education, and specific social policies pursued by the state.

Under socialism, like all Albanians, they were assured of full employment in state enterprises and cooperatives. As agricultural workers by tradition, Meçkars were integrated into agricultural cooperatives and state farms, where they learned new agricultural skills. Some Karbuxhinj—mainly in Gjirokastra, Berat, Korça, and Tirana—were employed in the forestry sector and handicraft enterprises owned by the state. Karbuxhinj in the villages of Halilaj, the communes of Sukth, Pojan, and Delvina worked as coachmen, storeroom managers, and watchmen. In most urban areas, however, the majority of Roma remained in unskilled occupations, employed in street sweeping and cleaning, transportation, and industrial plants and as day laborers in construction.

Although the socialist system gradually banned private sector activities, many Karbuxhinj, Cergar, and Bamill Roma continued to ply their trades as private horse dealers, and traditional copper and willow craftsmen, or used clothes traders in the informal sector. Bujar, a prosperous Roma from Elbasan, remembered: "During the socialist system we worked in state sector enterprises. However, the system did not hinder us in exercising small informal trade activities. We were horse dealers and sold horses to the villagers and cooperatives, while our women sold clothing and textiles to the villages. Roma musicians, on the other hand, continued this profession at weddings and other festive ceremonies. These informal activities provided them with supplementary income that made them privileged in comparison to other ethnic groups." These private sector activities were practiced until the 1976 Constitution completely banned them.

Skënder, a Cergar from Fshati Rom, illustrates that: "We (as Roma) have been the most advantaged group, because we did business by trading old pans at a time when the other ethnic groups were not allowed to sell even one egg. . . ."

Figure 7.1 depicts the various employment sectors for Roma during the socialist era, by gender.

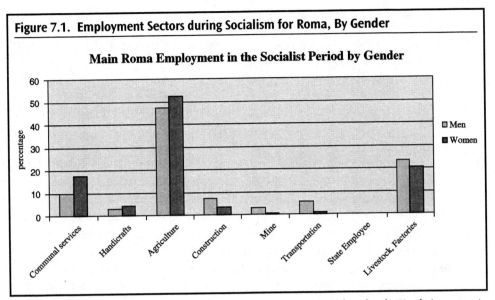

Figure 7.1. Employment Sectors during Socialism for Roma, By Gender

Source: Socioeconomic household questionnaires with Roma and Egyptians for the Needs Assessment (2002/03).

In contrast to Roma, the sedentary Egyptians were better educated and more integrated in Albanian society. They also enjoyed higher integration in state enterprises. Although they continued to practice their traditional occupations, they were also trained in several modern skills and were employed as qualified workers in various sectors of the economy. Some even became engineers, doctors, teachers, economists, military officers, and state employees. Egyptian musicians contributed to musical development in Albania. Many bands and orchestras throughout the country have Egyptian musicians (Kamberi 2001).

Figure 7.2 depicts the various employment sector for Egyptians under socialism, by gender.

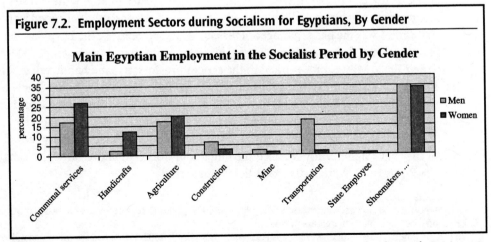

Figure 7.2. Employment Sectors during Socialism for Egyptians, By Gender

Source: Socioeconomic household questionnaires with Roma and Egyptians for the Needs Assessment (2002/03).

The Effects of the Transition Period on Employment

Structural changes from socialism to a market economy have resulted in high unemployment rates, geographical pockets of poverty, and limited social security schemes resulting from weak government capacity.

Restructuring and Unemployment

At the beginning of the transition period in 1991, most state-owned enterprises were closed down or downsized as a result of restructuring and privatization. This led to immediate, massive unemployment. By the end of 1992, unemployment in Albania had ballooned to 26.5 percent of the working-age population between 16 and 60 years old.[61] Unemployment primarily affected population groups with limited vocational skills and low levels of education and other qualifications. Thus, these minorities were disproportionately affected by the restructuring. Most of them had more difficulty in finding alternative employment, had less social capital, and encountered discrimination and social exclusion.

While the unemployment rate at the national level was around 16 percent at the end of 2002, the unemployment rate for Roma was 71 percent, and for Egyptians 67 percent of the working-age population.[62] Most of them were working without employment contracts in small businesses (93 percent Roma and 82 percent, Egyptians).

Geographic Pockets of Poverty

Their unemployment rate is disturbingly high in some districts. According to the Labor Office in Gjirokastra, for example, 30 percent of the officially registered unemployed people are Roma and Egyptians (OSCE 2000). These groups, however, represent only 3.4 percent of Gjirokastra's population.

Of those unemployed, 83 percent of both groups have been without full-time work for more than one year. In fact, many have not had a full-time job since the state-owned enterprises were closed down in 1990–1991. This was confirmed by Mimoza, an inspector at the Labor Office in the city of Berat, who summarized their recent unemployment history: "When the textile factory opened, Egyptians were employed here and were very good workers. At that time, I was the head manager of the entire factory. Some of the Egyptians who worked here also attended secondary school. This not only improved their education level but also their skills. Most Roma worked in the agriculture, forestry, and handicraft enterprises. Eighty percent of the employees of city cleaning enterprises were either Roma or Egyptians. . . . However, during 1991–1994, these enterprises were downsized and then gradually shut down. The local agriculture enterprise was closed in 1991, the willow enterprise in 1992, and the textile factory in 1994. The forestry and city cleaning enterprises still exist, but they have significantly reduced the number of workers. As a result, only a small part of the Roma and Egyptian communities is employed."

---

61. According to Vjetari Statistikor i Shqipërisë (1992), 294,000 people (out of a population of 3.1 million) lost their jobs during this period.

62. The national unemployment figure is derived from INSTAT, 2002. Roma and Egyptian unemployment data results form the socioeconomic household questionnaires with Roma and Egyptians for the Needs Assessment (2002/03).

Limited Provision of Social Security Schemes

Only 2 percent of Roma and 3.3 percent of Egyptians receive unemployment benefits. As a result of government policy, many are no longer entitled to unemployment benefits, having been unemployed for more than one year, the government's maximum allowable term for provision of benefits. As a result, 95 percent of Roma and 91 percent of Egyptians who are unemployed or work informally do not contribute to their social security plans, because they cannot afford to make this investment. This could lead to future economic uncertainties.

Skills Mismatch for the New Labor Market Demands

In spite of these structural changes generated by transition policies, members of both groups continue to practice their traditional occupations to make a living. As a result, most Roma and some Egyptians are now ill-equipped to meet the new demands of the formal labor market. Their educational and vocational qualifications have decreased in value during transition, and generally remain low in comparison to those of Albanians. As an example, Admir, a Roma from Gjirokastra said: "Now it is more difficult to sell our baskets to Albanians, because they use plastic buckets instead. So we have lost our market, and we no longer produce baskets since nobody wants to buy them."

Limited Social Capital

Because most Roma live in isolated mono-ethnic communities in rural or semi-urban areas, they have few opportunities to establish networks with Albanians. This lack of social capital[63] with mainstream society limits their opportunities to find alternative employment. Living in urban areas among Albanians, Egyptians, who have frequent contact with them and are generally more integrated in society, find it easier to gain new employment after job loss.

Within Roma communities and particularly the *fise*, some social capital still exists. However, isolation from mainstream society limits the opportunities of Roma to use these networks beyond community and *fise* boundaries. As a Roma textile trader from Elbasan mentioned: "The white hand is privileged because he has friends in central government, the parliament, and other state institutions. This helps him to pass his imported goods through customs and excise. We Roma do not have such relations, and are discriminated against in regard to trade."

Discrimination and Social Exclusion

Many face discrimination and social exclusion in the formal labor market. For 30 percent of Roma, and 32 percent of Egyptians, ethnicity is the main reason for their unemployment. One leader of a Roma association in Tirana stated: "Before the transition, there was no discrimination against Roma by the state—neither regarding wages for those who were employed, nor in finding employment in state enterprises for those who were unemployed. Today, however, when it comes to hiring Roma, the private sector prefers Albanians to Roma, because of some stereotypes that Roma, for instance, are not honest, or are not qualified to do the job properly."

---

63. For a full description of social capital, see Chapter 10.

Their suspicions of discrimination are not unfounded. In the city of Berat, two foreign-owned textile enterprises refused to hire either Roma or Egyptians. Sonila, an expert at the Berat Labor Office, confirmed this: "This is discrimination because many Egyptians are qualified to work there, since they used to work in the textile factory under state ownership."

Perceptions Regarding Reasons for Unemployment

There are several factors that both groups regard as main reasons for their unemployment.

- Ninety-two percent of Roma and 90 percent of Egyptians perceive that the difficulties in finding employment results from a general lack of employment opportunities in Albania.
- Thirty percent of Roma and 32 percent of Egyptians associate their unemployment with their ethnicity.
- With Roma unemployment at 27 percent and Egyptians, 18 percent, 27 percent of Roma and 22 percent of Egyptians believe they are unemployed due to their lack of vocational skills.

Forms of Formal Labor

Although it is rarely a major source of household income, some are engaged in agriculture.

Agriculture and Property Rights

Most households in rural areas barely survive on subsistence agriculture. However, the land parcels they were allocated, like those of all Albanians, were very small, generally only one hectare. Agriculture is usually subsistence because of lack of infrastructure and irrigation, as well as high maintenance costs. Agricultural production is also discouraged by the competition from imported, lower-priced agricultural produce from neighboring countries. A Roma *kryeplak* from Levan said: "Personally, I want a long-term loan, with exact specification on when I have to pay it back. I will put myself to work, and make a greenhouse for tomatoes."

Trade in Used Clothes

The used clothes business has been a major income source for many Roma and some Egyptian families. It provided a key income source for many Roma families in the cities of Korça, Elbasan, Tirana, Fushë Kruja, Fier, and Berat. Retail markets for used clothes exist in most Albanian cities and are mainly dominated by Roma families. Used clothes are also traded in the informal sector. Many Karbuxhinj and Cergar families, who had engaged in small-scale business and were able to accumulate savings during the socialist period, began selling used clothes in 1991. Some purchased clothes in bulk in Macedonia, Bulgaria, Romania, and Turkey and sold them in Albania.

Arben, a well-to-do Roma businessman from Elbasan, explained the development of the used clothes business in Albania: "Small textile business is a part of our tradition. Even during the socialist period, Roma women who were not begging or fortune-telling engaged in small textile business. When the transition period began, we started going to Macedonia to buy used clothes there and sell them here. After a couple of months, we were able to go to Turkey by bus, through Bulgaria and Greece. We went everywhere. . . ."

In recent years, however, the used clothes market has been in decline. Subsequently, many went bankrupt or lost their savings because of less demand, poverty, and competition. More specifically, as the breadth and depth of poverty have increased during transition, fewer people can afford to buy even used clothes. Increased competition from other poor Roma, some Egyptians, but also, increasingly, Albanians, means that the used clothes trade is now less profitable, as respective incomes decrease. As a result, some Roma are forced out of the market, and pushed further into poverty.

The used clothes business increased from 1991 until the mid-1990s because of high demand and low prices for these goods. A Roma *kryeplak* from a village near Fier said: "At the beginning of transition, we earned a lot of money. Although goods were difficult to find, it was only us who were dealing with it, so we made huge profits. Our houses were constructed during 1992–1996, when we were making a good living. Starting from 1997 onwards, the white hand, who knows nothing of this trade, has entered the market. Other people also entered the market that own land and are wealthy. This led to the decline of our income, and caused us to be in a bad economic situation."

Today, most Roma families are still involved in the used clothes trade. They purchase clothes in bulk from non-Roma wholesalers, who transport used clothes from Italy or Greece when returning from international migration.

To cope with the declining market in used clothes, some Roma businesses survive by borrowing from wholesale providers. Debts further contribute to the economic dependence and future economic uncertainty of Roma families.

A small number of Roma families that were successful in trading used clothes during the early transition years moved on to sell new clothes or other goods. They purchase goods from wholesalers and sell them in stores. Luljeta, a Roma woman from Tirana who sold used clothes in open markets during the early transition period, now sells handbags in a shop. Some Roma families from Gjirokastra sell used household appliances and construction materials that they purchase in Greece.

Forms of Informal Labor

While informal work helps families make a living and survive in the short-term, it further contributes to erratic livelihoods and economic uncertainty in the long-term. This causes many people to migrate within Albania or to neighboring countries in search of employment. A large labor force outside the formal market has negative effects on government tax revenues, economic productivity, and the establishment of a stable market economy.

Casual Work and "Omonia" Places

In Albania, unemployed people gather to be hired for casual or temporary work at public places within cities and most large villages called "Omonia."[64] Every morning, employers and

---

64. De Soto, and others (2002). The name "Omonia" refers to a public square in Athens, where many Albanian international migrants assemble and look for work.

workers, including job seekers from smaller surrounding villages, meet at a local Omonia in Albanian cities and large villages.

Those who are hired at an Omonia supply cheap labor for basic construction and public works projects, agriculture, or work as porters or dockers. Daily wages depend on local supply and demand. They range between L500 and L1,000. In the Liria quarter in Shkodra, young Egyptians wait for trucks along a major road, hoping for work in portage. Agron, a Roma from the city of Korça, waits with his friends outside the city's warehouse three times a week in hope of casual work.

Internal Migration

When economic conditions are poor, unemployed people commute or migrate to other Albanian cities that have a growing construction sector and thus higher labor demand.

In the cities to which unemployed workers commute or migrate, competition in the local labor markets increases, and daily wages decrease. In some cases, tensions emerge between the commuting migrants and local unemployed workers. A Roma in Vlora complained: "To have order in the city and to avoid turmoil like in 1997, it is necessary to create new job opportunities. It's fine that people have come here from other cities, but it would be better if they looked for jobs in their own cities. . . ." (De Soto and others 2002).

Still, there are seasonal opportunities for informal work in agriculture when other sources dry up. In Pojan, both groups work as agricultural day laborers in the village of Kreshpan, especially during periods of bean picking. Roma from Llakatund hire out during olive picking. Roma from Akërni are hired as day laborers in agriculture in Tre Vëllazër, Panaja, and Cergovina, while those from Novosela are hired as low-skilled construction workers there or in nearby villages.

Musical Performance

Another form of informal work for both is musical performance. Organized bands exist in almost every city and village where both groups live, and they usually perform at weddings and other festive ceremonies. Bands include several different musical instruments, such as clarinets, accordions, violins, and cellos.

The demand for musical performance is especially high during summer and autumn, when most weddings occur. Arian, a young Egyptian from Gjirokastra, explained: "During the summer, we perform every week at weddings. . . . Income from each wedding varies from L20,000 to L30,000 per person. . . . With this money we can support ourselves for two or three months. We give the money to our parents, who use it for daily household needs."

Bandleaders, who are usually clarinet players, receive a 10 percent higher wage because they also serve as band managers who sign contracts and receive payments on behalf of the band.

Well-known bands are often hired by families from surrounding districts. Some Roma bands from Durrës villages are hired for weddings in Tirana or Kruja. Bands in Fier are hired to perform in Vlora and Lushnja. One band from Delvina is hired to perform in Greece for Christmas festivities or weddings held by Albanian migrants. Skënder, a Roma from Delvina, said: "I started playing in bands at weddings when I was 13 or 14. I've played the accordion and the violin. We Roma play music by ear, not by notes . . . People hire us and give us an advance of L15,000 to L20,000, depending on the number of people invited to the wedding. . . . The music we play depends on the region where the wedding is held. In the villages where the Greek minority lives, we mostly play Greek music, but we also play authentic Albanian music. In Konispol, they ask us to play *Çam* music."[65]

Handicrafts and Traditional Occupations

In certain areas, families engage in unique forms of casual work, such as basket weaving, metalwork, or horse dealing. In Pojan, some deal in horses and mules, which they purchase in city markets and sell in villages. Some Roma from Gjirokastra make and sell baskets in the city and in surrounding villages. In Levan, and Delvina, Cergar and Bamill, families make and sell pans and containers that are used to produce *raki*.[66] In Delvina, some families collect and sell medicinal herbs during certain seasons.

Egyptian families in Pojan cut and sell firewood. In Fushë Kruja, others produce and sell processed limestone for construction. In Delvina, they make and sell charcoal, while in Korça, some Roma girls work for months at a time in snail processing.

Begging, Fortune-Telling, and Other Occupations

Another form of casual work for both is begging in cities and villages (De Soto and Gedeshi 2002). Most beggars are women, or children up to the age of 12. They beg for money, used clothes, and food. Most activity takes place at major city intersections and streets, and in cafes, restaurants, and other businesses. Many can earn as much as casual laborers—from L400 to L1,000 daily—but beggars with physical disabilities earn more. Women and children who earn money begging give it to the head of the household.

Beggars commute to cities where incomes are higher or where they believe that local residents are more inclined to hand out money. For example, many Roma families from Durrës, Fushë Kruja, and Tirana regularly commute to Shkodra. Roma in Fushë Kruja travel as far as Shkodra, Durrës, and Tirana to beg, while many Egyptian children in Bradashesh travel to Tirana. Roma children from Levan commute to the cities of Fier, Vlora, and Durrës, while women and children from the village of Çuka travel to Saranda to solicit during the day. Kujtim, a Roma originally from Durrës, stated: "We come to Shkodra because there are more opportunities for begging here. The citizens of Shkodra are the most generous ones."

In addition to begging, some Roma women tell fortunes to pedestrians in cities. Nadire, a Roma woman from Fushë Kruja, said: "When someone wants to have their cup of coffee read, we tell their fortune and make around L100, but we mostly beg."

Many Roma and Egyptian women and children also collect and sell tin cans and metal scraps. Roma in Levan travel as far as Vlora and the city of Fier to collect metal to sell. "At 3 p.m., you can come and see women and children hauling the tin cans they collect in Vlora and Fier to sell them here. They also gather copper scraps and wires, which they sell either here or in Durrës for L200 to L300 per kilogram." Egyptians in Bradashesh gather metal

65. *Çam:* an ethnic group that originated in Greece. They moved to Albania after World War II and now live mainly in southern Albania.
66. *Raki:* the local Albanian hard liquor.

scraps near the former metallurgy plant, while Roma women from Morava travel to the city of Berat to collect tin cans from garbage bins. In Zinxhiraj, collecting and selling metal is a major source of household incomes.

In some cities, women from large families sell blood to local hospitals. Mimoza, a teacher in Bradashesh, explained: "Conditions for Egyptian families are very poor, partly because they have 10 or 11 children. In order to raise their children, mothers have to sell their blood." Arben, a Roma university graduate, recalled that his mother used to sell blood to pay for his expenses.

Perception on Improving the Labor Situation

The majority of assessment participants envision increased overall employment opportunities in Albania as key to expanding their work opportunities. Ninety-two percent of Roma and 90 percent of Egyptians mentioned that there are not enough jobs in Albania, but consider it a responsibility of the Albanian government to remedy their employment situation. Few think of the private sector as an alternative.

However, others think that better education is the main issue to be addressed to improve the current employment situation. A member of a Roma association in Elbasan points out that education of Roma children is a necessary precondition for their attendance at vocational training. He stresses that without basic reading and writing skills, Roma children will face major difficulties in the labor market.

A full 76.7 percent of Roma consider vocational training an aid to improving their current employment situations. They say that they would prefer to take these courses in specific cultural centers. A Roma from Elbasan suggested instituting training courses such as tailoring, construction, plumbing, and transportation, in which prospects for future employment are high.

Roma and Egyptians who work in the agricultural sector believe that access to agricultural credits would enable them to make the necessary agricultural investments. This would also improve their production, profits, and overall economic situation.

Conclusion

The transition period has several negative implications for the labor market, such as agriculture, which has been reduced to mere subsistence farming for many Roma and Egyptians. In addition, the demand for handicrafts has decreased. Furthermore, income from trade in used clothes has also diminished as a result of both lower demand and increase in competition. This has contributed to an increase in poverty, in terms of both breadth and depth.

Without a significant increase in educational enrichment programs that minimally cover basic reading and writing skills, both groups will remain disadvantaged in Albanian society. Their employment opportunities will continue to be restricted to low-skill jobs with high uncertainty and low wages. As a result, they are likely to remain caught in the poverty trap.

CHAPTER 8

Migration and Remittances

International migration is a coping mechanism for poverty and social exclusion among poor population groups in Albania. For many Roma and Egyptian communities:

- International migration is the determining factor in a family's economic situation because it distinguishes the very poor from the poor.[67] As a result of extremely high unemployment rates, remittances from Roma and Egyptians employed in neighboring countries are the only major source of income for many villages and urban areas.
- International migration, extremely common among these groups, poses lasting social, economic, cultural, and institutional effects on the entire population.

Many Roma and Egyptian migrants acknowledge the negative effects of international migration—such as family break-ups, stress, and poor health—but the necessity of that migration is overwhelming. Unemployed and confronting discrimination, they have few alternatives. So, despite the drawbacks, they continue to migrate to cope with the poverty and social exclusion that characterize their lives in Albania.

Most international migrants go to Greece and Italy; some also go to the United Kingdom, Germany, and Switzerland. Given the geographical proximity, many people who live in southern Albania migrate to neighboring Greece.

Albanians migrate abroad out of necessity. Albanian international migration was widespread during the last decade, with 22 percent of the country's population migrating between 1991 and 2001 (INSTAT 2001). The consequences of international migration for the Albanian economy have been significant. Remittances play a crucial role in the sub-

---

67. The categories of "very poor," and "poor" have been identified in De Soto, and others (2002).

sistence of many poor communities, but the brain-drain phenomenon affects many private sector industries and government agencies across Albania.

Origins of International Migration

The Roma began migrating internationally immediately after Albania opened its borders in 1991. What began as a short-term, sporadic phenomenon involving men and boys has evolved into an annual, often organized process that encompasses entire families and communities. The mayor of Delvina said that 60 percent of his town's Roma migrate to Greece for a portion of the year. The head of one Roma association in Levan remarked that about half of Levan's Roma have migrated to neighboring countries. In Risili, one migrant stated that 30 percent of local Egyptians work abroad.

International migration experiences differ between and among Roma, Egyptians, and Albanians. Among Roma, 49 percent of migrants work in agriculture and 21 percent beg, while others work in construction or collect used clothes. Egyptians work mostly in construction, but also in agriculture. Roma migrate most often to agricultural regions in Greece that are close to the Greek-Albanian border. Egyptians migrate to Greek cities, such as Thessaloniki and Athens, but also to Italian urban areas, like Florence.

Why Migrate?

Frequent international migration is a direct result of the high rates of unemployment and underemployment among these groups in Albania. Employment abroad is the only consistent work available for them, and therefore the only means of generating substantial income.

In the southern Albanian towns such as Berat and Gjirokastra, international migration is high. Because of their proximity to Greece, these communities are prosperous compared to those in the northern towns of Fushë Kruja and Shkodra, where the long trip to Greece or other distant destinations deters international migration.

Economic levels of individual communities and families are largely determined by whether there are family members able to migrate abroad. In Novosela, one commented: "The poorest are those that don't have sons who migrate internationally." Small pockets of relatively prosperous families or communities that are surrounded by poorer ones often have higher rates of international migration than those in surrounding areas. In the village of Baltëz—the most prosperous Roma community in Fier—residents attribute their relative economic success to migration. And in Rrapishta it is said that: "If we didn't migrate abroad, we would be finished." However, if international migration wards off extreme poverty, it is rarely a means to escape poverty altogether.

The Role of Remittances

Remittances are important to the livelihood of both groups' households because families spend them on basic family consumption items. In Risili, one Egyptian stated: "We have many who work [abroad], but it's only for feeding ourselves. There are very few who can save."

In a majority of cases, many explained that income earned abroad simply allowed families to survive and to avoid extreme poverty. A woman in Gjirokastra reported: "With international migration, you only live. It isn't something that improves your economic situation." And, more succinctly, one Roma migrant added: "Families who have migrants abroad are in a better economic situation, but it doesn't solve everything."

A few families that migrate abroad, especially those who migrate frequently, use remittances to purchase small luxury items and to repair or construct their homes. One migrant stated that as a result of international migration, he can purchase "expensive food items" and home furnishings One Roma migrant from Korça, who regularly travels to Greece, stated that he has been able to purchase a bed, a tape recorder, and a television, to which he referred as "new and good things."

However, income earned abroad is rarely applied to commercial or public investment, since little is left over after the basic needs have been purchased. Then, too, there is an overall lack of investment opportunities and stable investment climate, and in some communities also a lack of basic infrastructure. One person mentioned that his family does not invest in agriculture because there is "no guarantee that the produce will sell." When asked if he invested his money earned abroad, one Morava man retorted: "Invest in what?"

Who Migrates?

Most international migrants are young men, but families, including children, also migrate abroad frequently. While important economic benefits are associated with international migration, only those who have sufficient funds and social capital are able to go. Compared to Albanians, Roma and Egyptians are at a disadvantage because they earn substantially lower incomes. Some compensate for low incomes with social networks in Albania and Greece that they use to find employment.

Families and Young Men. Depending on the districts, the makeup of international migrants varies. Forty-seven percent of Roma indicated that international migrants in their neighborhood were young men, while 36 percent were entire families.[68] For Egyptians, 56 percent were young men, and 27 percent, whole families. Distinctions also exist between Roma fise, since more Cergars and Bamill families migrate abroad than Meçkars and Karbuxhinj. In Gjirokastra and Delvina, international family migration is very common.

Families with Disposable Income. Initial migration costs are high, so only families with disposable income can afford to have family members migrate abroad. Migrants who enter the destination countries must pay legal visa and passport costs. Visas cost between US$30 and US$50. However, many international migrants purchase visas on the black market at the current cost of L100,000 for a three-month visa, and L200,000 for a six-month one.

The actual travel costs to host countries, which may involve a combination of foot and automobile travel, can also be very high. An automobile ride to Salonika from Rrapishta can cost L40,000. A trip to Greece from Llakatund can cost a family L20,000 and upon arrival, another 40 euros (US$52). From Shkodra, international migrants need about L3,000 to travel to the border, and 50 euros (US$65) for train or taxi fares upon arrival. Collecting sufficient provisions for such a trip may make it prohibitive. International migrants must also

---

68. The make-up of Roma international migrants stands in contrast to the make-up of international migrant Albanians, which is overwhelmingly young male (De Soto, and others).

be able to gather enough food to sustain them through 12 days of foot travel. One Egyptian migrant from Shkodra carried a backpack filled with salami, cheese, olives, coffee, sugar, and water. An Egyptian man from Shkodra explained: "So we Egyptians stay here because we don't have this money. . . ." This is reaffirmed by a Roma man from Fushë Kruja, who says that: "[We] don't go because we don't have money to go with." It is unlikely that families with extremely low food allowances can afford to make this expensive and difficult trip. Table 8.1 depicts the length and cost of a first international migration.

Table 8.1. Length and Cost for Initial Travel

Initial Migration Travel and Costs	
Length of Foot Travel: Elbasan to Salonika: 7–8 days/nights. Albanian border to Kardhica: 7 days.	Black Market Greek Visa 3-month visa: L100,000 (US$697) 6-month visa: L200,000 (US$1,394)
Legal Greek Visa/Albanian Passport 3-month visa: US$30 6-month visa: US$50	Black Market Albanian Passport L500,000 (US$3,500) Legal Albanian Passport US$30

Source: "From social exclusion to social inclusion—a Needs Assessment for Roma and Egyptian communities," 2003.

While migrants require disposable income to travel abroad, having social capital is critical. As one Egyptian from Shkodra commented, "To go to Greece, you need money, people to go with, and contacts to find you work and a place to live."

Families with Social Capital. Social capital[69] has a significant impact on the feasibility of migrating abroad. Having it makes the difference in how much migrants can earn and how frequently they can migrate. Solidarity and trust are important forms of social capital among all three groups and those who migrate in international migration circles. Trust is also important between international migrants and their hometown shops that allow families to put their food purchases on the list. In fact, social capital is important throughout all stages of international migration, from the point of departure to the point of sending remittances home and returning home.

First, international migrants rely on social capital in their hometowns. Roma and Egyptians commonly identified an extended family as a necessity for international migration, since the assistance of family members remaining at home makes it possible. One Fushë Kruja couple left their children in the care of an older relative while they worked in Greece for two weeks. A Rrapishta couple left their children with grandparents. Roma have the advantage of a particularly large segmentary[70] *fis* organization. Although this has

---

69. For a full description of the types and uses of social capital, see Chapter 10.

70. Segmentary *fis:* a kinship descent system, defining descent categories with reference to more and more remote apical ancestors so that the descent categories form a treelike structure (including successively wider ranges of descendants) (American Anthropological Association).

weakened during the transition period, the *fis* still provides aid to local extended family members.

In turn, family members who remain at home often rely on the trust of local businesses to allow them to purchase their goods with a shop list, while the breadwinning family members are abroad. Relations between the migrants and local businesses are equally crucial, since many rely on these local shop lists that businesses provide to sustain their family members at home. While many Roma (80 percent) and Egyptians (77 percent) depend on such lists for survival regardless of international migration, families with migrants abroad are particularly dependent on lists because migrant family members can be away for several months at a time. Some families have lists that have not been paid for seven to nine months. Debts incurred by family members who remain home are paid when the internationally migrating family members return home. Those who are unable to borrow from local businesses are less likely to migrate.

Second, illegal migrants rely on a unique form of social capital—international migration circles—to travel to Greece. International migration circles, which consist of 30–300 migrants, form in home districts in central or southern Albania and travel to Greece en masse. These circles offer safety for illegal migrants. Migrants also use the circles to find work in Greece.

Solidarity with Albanians is also necessary for successful international migration, especially during travel to recipient countries. Migrants reported how networks with Albanians made international migration possible. One migrant from Shkodra explained: "The time that I went there, it was nine of us. I was the only Egyptian, whereas the others were white. They did me a big favor by taking me, as they were my friends." In fact, in Shkodra, where migration is rare, all Egyptians who had migrated previously had done so with Albanians. Communities with more Albanian networks tend to have higher rates of migration. Some Roma communities in Fier, Berat, and Vlora have strong relations with Albanians and, in some cases, travel together to host countries.

Third, international migrants rely on social capital within these countries. Many Roma who migrate internationally benefit from solidarity with Roma living in Greece to find work and housing while there. In some cases, Greek-Roma lent money to Albania-Roma until the latter found employment.

Table 8.2 shows how financial and social capital are essential to the different stages of international migration.

Roma and Egyptians from Southern Districts and Meçkars. In general, Roma and Egyptians from southern districts are more likely to migrate internationally than those from northern districts:

Albanians who live in the south have an advantage in international migration for several reasons. Their proximity to Greece lowers transportation costs. Moreover, Greek visas are more easily acquired in southern districts, particularly Gjirokastra, thus making travel there much easier and safer. In addition, many Roma from southern regions began migrating in the early 1990s and have developed important Greek social connections to secure employment. Repeated trips strengthen these networks and even enable some migrants to learn Greek, making subsequent trips more successful.

Meçkars migrate abroad for longer periods and generally benefit more from migration than those from other *fise*. Meçkars mainly work in agriculture, which often provides consistently high wages compared to other forms of migrant labor.

Table 8.2. The Role of Financial and Social Capital in the Different Stages of International Migration	
1: Home	a) International migrants need money to purchase passports/visas.
	b) International migrants unable to purchase legal passports/visas purchase black market passports/visas.
	c) International migrants unable to purchase illegal passports/visas travel to recipient countries clandestinely.
	d) Extended family cares for family members left behind.
	e) In some cases, primary *fis* members also watch out for family members left behind.
	f) Trust of local businesses allows family members left behind to purchase goods on list.
2: Travel	a) International migrants require food stocks for long travel to recipient countries.
	b) International migration circles enable illegal international migrants to travel safely to Greece. Some international migrants also use the international migration circle to find employment in agriculture.
3: In Host Country	c) Roma international migrants in Greece use solidarity with Greek Roma to find employment and/or housing.
	d) International migrants use family members/friends/acquaintances to send remittances home.

Source: Socioeconomic household questionnaires with Roma and Egyptians for the Needs Assessment (2002/03).

Historical reasons also explain the advantages that Meçkars enjoy when it comes to international migration. These Roma receive preference for hiring because they worked in agriculture during the socialist period. Various Roma *fise* are traditionally connected to distinct skill sets. Skills honed during the socialist period were factors that would influence postsocialist era migration rates.

Roma from other *fise,* particularly Karbuxhinj and Cergars, were low-skill workers in state enterprises. However, these two groups also engaged in small, private business. With the border's opening in 1991, many Karbuxhinj traveled to Turkey and Romania, purchased market products in bulk, and sold them in Albania. By working in business during the socialist era, the Karbuxhinj and Cergars had considerable savings compared to other Roma and Egyptians at the beginning of the transition period. Thus, at socialism's end, these Roma had distinct advantages over Meçkars.

With little savings, Meçkars were at a disadvantage. In contrast, Meçkars lost their jobs when socialist collective farms were closed and, without any savings or employment opportunities in Albania, were thus forced to migrate abroad soon after the Albanian border's opening. So while Karbuxhinj engaged in small business, Meçkars established migration networks in their districts and in Greece.

After 1994, the Karbuxhinj and Cergars' initial advantage over Meçkars declined because of competition with Albanians, and business became unprofitable. During the same period, Meçkars gained an advantage in migration because, by 1995, the only reliable source for steady income for Roma and Egyptians was migration.

The migration networks developed by Meçkars over the years have helped them reduce the risks and costs of international migration. In some cases, when Meçkars migrate abroad, they phone landowners in Greece to inquire about available employment, and travel to Greece only when they are told by landowners that employment is available. One Meçkar from Orizaj explained: "When I want to go to Greece, I call up the Greek [landowner], and I tell him that I'm going to go, and when he has work he tells me to come."

Host Countries and Regions

Roma migrants (89 percent) overwhelmingly choose Greece as their destination. Even in Vlora and Fier, districts with direct sea access to Italy, 94 percent preferred Greece. Only Roma in Durrës preferred Italy, although international migration was much less frequent in Durrës than in central or southern districts. Most Egyptian migrants also selected Greece as their recipient country, but do not migrate there as frequently as Romas. The Egyptian preference parallels that of Albanian international migrants, of whom 60 percent choose Greece as a host country.[71]

Figure 8.1 illustrates the countries to which Roma and Egyptians migrate.

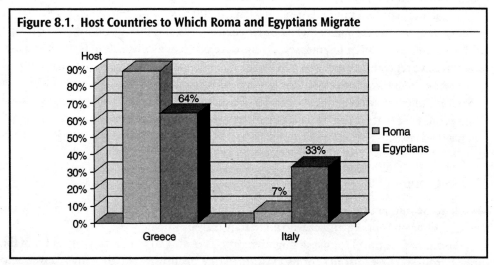

Figure 8.1. Host Countries to Which Roma and Egyptians Migrate

Source: Socioeconomic household questionnaires with Roma and Egyptians for the Needs Assessment (2002/03).

Favored host regions in Greece are agricultural areas near the Albanian-Greek border. Some Roma return *en masse* to specific Greek villages and towns. Korça residents head for Prespa and Larisa. Delvina Roma work in Patra and in the nearby town of Arta. Gjirokastra's Roma families can be found in Larisa and Patra. Some Baltëz families from the Fier district work in Kardica and Kavala, while Llakatund and Levan families work in Patra,

---

71. Of all Albanian international migrants: 60percent migrate abroad to Greece, 40percent to Western Europe/North America. De Soto, and others.

Volos, and Lamias. For those migrants in nonagricultural professions, Thessaloniki and Athens are preferred cities.

Roma migration outside the southern districts is less organized, and recipient areas are determined by each small international migration circle. Most agricultural workers generally migrate to the same areas as residents of southern districts. Most Egyptians migrate to major cities or towns, but Egyptian farm workers migrate to the same agricultural areas as the Roma.

Forms of International Migration

How Roma and Egyptians migrate abroad predicts how successful they will be in the host country. Forms of international migration vary in legality, modes of travel, and frequency.

Legal and Illegal International Migration

Because of the visa and passport costs and the difficulty of getting a visa, most migrate abroad illegally, though illegal migrants face many risks. Many are caught by Greek authorities and immediately returned to Albania. Collected goods are often confiscated by authorities.

Legal international migrants generally have better migration experiences. They travel to their destinations through official border checkpoints and thus avoid the risks of clandestine travel. They often migrate seasonally, develop strong networks in Greece, and as a result receive regular income. Many Baltëz Roma, for example, migrate abroad legally and have higher living standards than Roma from other towns. However, because of high visa costs, only migrants with frequent or seasonal employment benefit from legal international migration. Frequent or seasonal employment is required to cover "overhead expenses," such as visa costs.

Travel Groups

While some migrants travel by car for a portion of the trip to Greece, most clandestine travel is done on foot. Egyptians who go to Italy travel by boat.

Forms of foot travel for illegal migrants vary according to the size and make-up of the travel groups. Three distinct forms exist: (a) large group travel, (b) family travel, and (c) small group travel. Large group travel, commonly organized by Roma migrants from Berat and Vlora, usually involves groups of 30–300 men, women, and some children. These groups elect as leader the individual with the best knowledge of the route and terrain, who decides on such details as departure and rest times. Agricultural workers will often seek work jointly by selecting the more articulate group members to approach landowners. Otherwise, the group separates and individual families search for work independently. Family travel, commonly practiced by Roma migrants from Delvina, Elbasan, and Gjirokastra, is similar to large group travel, but includes entire families. Parents often carry small children on their backs during travel periods. Small group travel involves groups of 10–30 individuals. These are sometimes interethnic. Members are either experienced migrants who know the terrain very well, short-term migrants living near the Greek border, or less experienced migrants.

These last have fewer contacts in Greece and usually have greater difficulties in securing employment.

Small group travel: A Roma from Baltëz

"We went by car up until the border. Afterwards we traveled by foot for seven days and went to the village of Kardhica. We went out to the village and asked around for food at first. We didn't know anybody there, and we were dirty, exhausted. When a villager saw us, that we were hungry, tired, and thirsty, he gave us food to eat, and he kept us there to work. Afterwards, others came and took us, and we were organized into work groups. I stayed there one month the first time, working in cotton, harvesting, and stables. At that time they paid you 2,500 drachmas. We slept outside or in a shed. We hardly left the place, even to eat, and we brought back home very little. I brought back 60,000 drachmas the first time. We would go there and the police would bring us back. This continued until 1997. But now we have our documents. I go when I have work there and stay as long as there are crops. I make 20 euros (US$16) a day. We aren't very happy with this wage because we pay for six-month visas, and whenever we renew them, we pay 400 euros (US$520)."[72]

Return trips from Greece to Albania require relatively less organization, since Greek police are reportedly more "lenient" on departing international migrants.

Frequency of International Migration

Frequency of travel abroad and length of stay also vary. Many migrants, particularly in agriculture, practice established annual patterns. Their stay may last weeks, seasonal months, or years.

Some agricultural workers stay abroad for sowing and harvesting periods and return home when employment is unavailable in July and during the winter months. International migrants to the Greek villages near Prespa and to Larisa work from April until June and again from September through October, harvesting beans and tomatoes. In Patra, where most Delvina residents work, watermelons are picked in the first weeks of June, tomatoes and grapes in July and August, and oranges and olives from the end of October through the end of June. Employment can be frequent if migrants possess proper visas or are willing to work illegally. In fact, one Delvina farm worker asserted that he can be employed in Patra for 250 days out of the year. Still, most limit their stays. Migrants from Pojan with six-month visas work from May to October, for example.

International migrants who do not work in agriculture or are unable to attain Greek visas stay for shorter periods of time. Most Pojan residents migrate annually for less then one month at a time. One Durrës Roma works in Greece from late February through late

---

72. For rates of exchange at the time of this study, refer to the Glossary of Terms.

May. Others' length of stay varies from sporadic two-week trips to long-term international migration.

Informal Labor and International Migration

The most common form of migrant labor for Roma is agriculture (49 percent), followed by begging (21 percent). Other, less frequent forms of migrant labor include construction and collecting used clothes. For Egyptians, the most common form of migrant labor is construction (41 percent), followed by agriculture (24 percent). Strong distinctions exist between Roma *fise*, since more Meçkars work in agriculture than those of any other *fis*.[73] Figure 8.2 shows a breakdown by Roma and Egyptians of the various informal labor sectors for migrants.

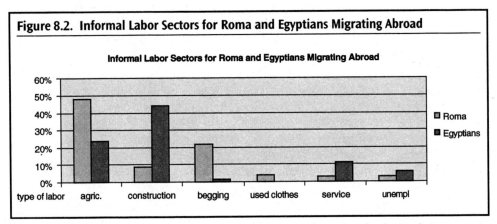

Figure 8.2. Informal Labor Sectors for Roma and Egyptians Migrating Abroad

Source: Socioeconomic household questionnaires with Roma and Egyptians for the Needs Assessment (2002/03).

Wages and Remittances

In agriculture, pay is standard and currently stands at 15–20 euros daily (US$19–26) for a 12-hour day. In nonagricultural forms of migrant labor, income varies. A woman from Salonika claimed she earned L100,000 a month begging with her children. An Azotiku woman who collected clothes in Salonika earned L200,000 in two months. Others stated that a child can earn 10 euros (US$15) a day by begging. One Roma from Elbasan claims that in three months, his family brought home L100,000 from begging and collecting scrap metal.

While 80 percent of international migrants send money or goods back home, it is difficult to determine how much money they actually bring home. Most migrants mention that they save 70–75 percent of total wages earned and that average monthly remittances total approximately 120–150 euros (US$156–195). One Rrapishta man in Greece claimed that he brings home about L100,000 after three months of work. One Llakatund man who works in agriculture in Patra said that after two or three months, he returned home with 270–300 euros (US$351–348).

---

73. When asked about forms of informal migrant labor in destination countries, many Bamill Roma responded "other," without further elaboration. Thus, data for this Roma *fis* are incomplete.

Delivering Remittances: "The delivery man"

Almost all remittances from 97 percent of Roma and 94 percent of Egyptians are sent home by the migrants themselves or friends acquaintances. Many migrants send remittances home through "delivery men," relying on trusted people from their own neighborhood or village to deliver money home to their families.

Delivering remittances is stressful and dangerous. International migrants who carry remittances on their persons can make tempting robbery targets. One Roma who was delivering 1,000,000 drachmas from Greece told how he was robbed in the district of Librazhd by a group of individuals dressed as police. Another account described theft by Greek police while migrants were returning to Albania from abroad.

"The Delivery Man": A Roma Athlete from Llakatund

"It was my last day there. The other guys would come later. Dealing with the money issue was difficult, but I told them that if they heard about me getting beat by the police not to ask for their money. When I got to Kakavia, I was very scared because there are many difficulties there. I had a lot of money; one man had [given me] 150,000 lekë (US$1,100) and others a little less. Right after I got there, I knew everyone and there weren't any problems. Afterwards I went directly to the families, and only then did I go to my own family. I had letters for everyone packed up. They were for Roma acquaintances of mine, as well as non-Roma friends."

Working and Living Conditions

When entire families or couples migrate together, different forms of labor are sometimes assigned to different family members. Agricultural migrant families will often work together in the fields. In nonagricultural forms of migrant labor, men often work in construction or collect metal scraps, while women collect used clothes or beg.

Work and living conditions are difficult and often hazardous. International migrants in agriculture work 10- to 12-hour days, even during summer temperatures that reach the low 40s (centigrade).[74] One migrant said: "They collect tomatoes and throw them into crates. They do this for up to 80 drachmas per crate, and go without lunch. I myself wasn't able to do more than 70 crates because I didn't have the strength, but the others stayed even until 7:00 in the evening. The pesticides on the tomatoes and the mosquitoes were unbearable. When the tomatoes were finished, they went on to onions or grapes." They sleep outside or in makeshift shelters. Food consumption can be very little, as landowners will pay workers higher wages if lunch is not provided.[75]

Children sometimes beg in the streets with their mothers or alone. They beg by drifting in and out of local businesses by day, and on sidewalks at night. Accounts from children describe workdays that last until midnight to 2:00 a.m.

---

74. This translates into the 100s °F.

75. Only two accounts described amounts and kinds of food eaten during international migration. One told of two meals eaten per day; the other, of salted tomatoes and bread.

Effects of International Migration

International migration is often a traumatic experience involving entire communities. While it is difficult to distinguish the effects of migration on these communities from the effects of other social phenomena, some trends that have emerged during the transition period can be attributed at least in part to the frequency of migration. International migration's direct consequences appear substantial, affecting(a) individuals and families, (b) cultural institutions, (c) child literacy and education, (d) future economic security, and (e) health.

Impact on Families and Individuals

Many describe migration's direct negative effects on individuals and families. As one Roma from Korça stated, "International migration breaks families up." Families separate for long periods of time, resulting in significant emotional stress and marital separation. Single-entry visas can force extended stays, because migrants cannot afford to pay for multiple visas. A Roma from Baltëz described his community's experiences with international migration: "Here most marriages end because there are those who go abroad and stay for months and even years without coming back. . . . About 20 families here have this problem." The elderly and children in particular experience psychological stress when children or parents are away for long periods. Explained another Egyptian woman from Risli: "There are women here who have lived separated from their husbands for up to 10 years. Their children miss their fathers." Some family members who live better abroad choose to stay. Added one Roma woman from Tirana: ". . . there are cases when they stay there, because here it's poverty, but there it's different. Over there, it's a different world. You have food to eat and things to wear. There are youth who have . . . stayed there because they can't bear it here anymore."

Culture and Cultural Institutions

Cultural institutions are also affected by the Roma and Egyptian community's high migration rate. One Roma familiar with Roma social issues stated that musical traditions are being lost among Albanian-Roma migrant families, because families of musicians work entire days in agriculture and cannot pass down musical traditions to children.

One troubling practice among Roma and Egyptian migrants applying for Greek visas is name changing. These migrants claim that Greek consulates act more favorably toward visa applicants with Greek-Christian names. Roma and Egyptians, who commonly have Muslim names, change them to Greek-Christian names to improve their chances of getting papers. Names like Ramadan, Lutfi, Islam, and Selamet become Marko, Kristo, Thimjo, Vasil. One Roma from Delvina said: "To get a visa, I changed my name to Kristo. . . . I am a Muslim. When I changed my name, I received a three-month visa." This practice is also common among Muslim Albanians. Although the effect of name changing on Roma identity is unknown, its practice is worth noting.

Child Literacy and Education

Another drawback of Roma and Egyptian international migration is that it prevents children from attending school. Another result of international migration on communities is increased child illiteracy. Few children attend school while abroad, because any education they receive at home is interrupted for a significant part of the year. Thus, as one migrant complained, "A portion of [Roma] children born after 1990 are illiterate."

This assertion is supported by quantitative data. The international migration of families by Roma *fise* is highest among Bamill, which means that greater proportions of Bamill children migrate abroad than children of other Roma *fise*.

Future Economic Security

International migrants are not enrolled in state pension programs that contribute to long-term economic security. Noted one Roma: "It has been 10 years; all the boys who went at first were 20, and now they're 30 and uninsured . . . A large part of them are not on pension. Youth pass through poverty, but old age will also be like this for them." Thus, as Roma age, poverty will continue.

Health Effects

International migrants seldom associate health problems with migration, which is possibly less a reflection of reality than low levels of health awareness.[76] Nevertheless, migrants describe difficult and hazardous working conditions, including heavy exposure to pesticides and long working days with little food. However, no medical assessment of Roma and Egyptian migrants has recently been undertaken, so any association with international migration and specific health effects would require further study.

Conclusion

Because of the Roma and Egyptian communities' high rates of unemployment and under-employment, international migration is a crucial source for meeting families' basic needs and expenses. As one Roma from Elbasan remarked, "If you don't go to Greece, you're dead here."

Although many families have been migrating annually since 1992, few long-term commercial or public investments have been made. It appears that no long-term benefits can result from migration. On the contrary, international migration is reinforcing long-term poverty and social exclusion.

While Roma and Egyptians use international migration to cope with poverty and social exclusion, migration only enables them to survive in the short term and surely leads to further poverty and social exclusion.

- The costs associated with international migration, such as travel and visa and passport costs, are high.

---

76. A report on Roma in Central and Eastern Europe made this conclusion about Roma parents and their assessment of their own children's health. The report noted that many Roma parents claim that their children are in good health, even though morbidity and infant mortality rates were high. (UNDP, 2002).

- International migrants who work in low-skilled positions often receive low wages.
- Children who migrate abroad do not attend school, and international migrants are not enrolled in pension programs.
- International migration breaks up families, which leads to further negative economic consequences.
- Most international migrants spend remittances on basics or on paying lists taken out from local shop owners, rather than savings or investment.

CHAPTER 9

Prostitution and Trafficking

Although many quantitative studies on Roma in East and Central Europe address issues such as unemployment, education, and poverty, other important challenges that affect these communities go unrecognized, such as prostitution and the trafficking in children and drugs—among the most often used coping mechanisms against poverty and social exclusion.

A minority of Roma families and women use prostitution and trafficking of children and drugs as coping mechanisms of last resort, as a means to survive only when alternatives such as informal labor or international migration are no longer available to them, or are insufficient to meet their basic survival needs.

Prostitution and trafficking are more common among Roma than Albanians. In reality, prostitution and trafficking offer little possibility of lifting families out of poverty. Although many hope that they are exit strategies out of poverty, prostitution and trafficking simply exacerbate financial distress.

Poverty is the biggest cause of prostitution and trafficking of children and drugs. In some cases, Roma parents have been found to be involved in these arrangements; a more common practice, however is that parents organize early and arranged marriages.

Prostitution

Many Roma girls and women are sent into prostitution by families hoping to deflect poverty, but in most cases their families receive little or no remittance. The social costs of prostitution are high. They affect both family cohesion and child welfare, including decreased school attendance for young girls and marriage at an early age. As virginity is highly valued, families marry off their girls very young to avoid prostitution. However, early marriage can put women at greater risk of poverty and might eventually steer them into prostitution to cope with lack of income. Thus, while often regarded as an escape from poverty, prostitution actually increases the poverty of both the women working as prostitutes and their families, and contributes to further socioeconomic problems.

Entry Points into Prostitution

Roma and Egyptian women enter into prostitution in one of four ways: (a) they are coerced; (b) they receive deceptive marriage proposals from Albanians; (c) they are sold or rented by their very poor family members; or (d) they are kidnapped by organized trafficking groups. In many cases, women were taken to Italy by "white" Albanian traffickers.

Coercion. The most common form of induction into prostitution involves women who migrate to Italy in search of employment opportunities not available in Albania. Most women who become prostitutes do so out of desperation or family obligation. Marriage problems, such as abuse or abandonment by husbands, lack of education, or low vocational skills are also factors that force them to enter into prostitution. In these cases, young women are often obliged to care for their children. Edlira, a Roma woman from Durrës, remembered: "She left for Italy by speed boat . . . She came back here and I told her not to go again, but she said that she was going to go back because she had nothing here to live on." And in Levan, a Roma explained: "Those that returned home went back there (abroad) again— I say because of economic conditions. They stay here one week or one month, are unemployed, and then they leave again. They come from poor families."

Deceptive Marriage Proposals. Many young girls are lured into prostitution by Albanian men who make deceptive marriage promises. Most are vulnerable women under the age of 20, often single mothers who are facing separation or divorce. Out of desperation, they accept a proposal from a man about whom they know little, and learn only later that they are being taken into prostitution in Italy.

The "Italian husband" myth is often used by Roma families to explain that their daughters who are living abroad are married to foreign, generally Italian, men. These stories may also be used by daughters and parents to ease tension within the family caused by the shame associated with that occupation. In some cases, it is Albanians who approach a girl's parents and offer to marry her and take her to Italy. Frequently, those parents learn later that their daughter has been turned into a prostitute, but they did not object to the arrangement when money was sent home.

Families Sell or Rent Girls and Young Women. Some girls and young women in extremely poor families are sold or rented by family members. As Albin, a Roma from Fushë Kruja, explained: "The parents who live in shacks deliver the girls themselves." Typically, Albanians approach Roma families and offer to take a daughter to Italy in exchange for payment. Family members decide on whether to offer the female family member for financial gain, with or without her consent. A woman who was a small business owner in Korça described a transaction handled by her sister-in-law, a mother who sold her daughter into prostitution: "An Albanian showed up and he told her: 'I will give you L200,000 and you give me your daughter as a wife.' He took the girl to Italy, and he now sends my sister-in-law L300,000–400,000 every three to four months."

Kidnapping. Kidnapping, the fourth entry point into prostitution, is believed by the Roma and Egyptians to be common. Despite kidnapping's low frequency, this belief is disproportionately influential in the Roma communities. Eighty-three percent of Roma and Egyptians believe that women and girls are aware of the threat of trafficking, but many still think that prostitution stems mainly from kidnapping. One Egyptian girl from Pojan commented: "My parents teach us always, they tell me to stay indoors and to do my work, and not to associate with bad friends, not to go out of the village because there are bad boys around . . . Our cousins also teach us this." While girls are constantly warned of the imminent threat of kidnapping, they are not warned of the prostitution that may result from leaving school, marrying too young, or having children at an early age. Instead, kidnapping is promoted as the greatest threat to girls and women.

While kidnapping was commonly mentioned as leading to prostitution, very few concrete examples were provided. Nevertheless, this disproportionate fear probably stems from the dramatic events relayed after an incident. Drita, a Roma woman from Delvina, narrated the kidnapping of her 19-year-old cousin: "He was in a car with two other guys, then while he was making conversation with her . . . the two guys grabbed her. They kidnapped her while holding a pistol to her head. . . . She didn't scream because she was scared. They took her to a brothel in Rome. . . ." In this example, Drita did not actually witness the kidnapping, but nonetheless the story instilled an unwarranted fear of kidnapping in its retelling. Blerta, an Egyptian woman from Pojan, added: "We've heard about [cases of prostitution] on television, so I tell my daughter to keep her eyes open."

However, once the girl is lured away, pimps control her income. Few, if any, remittances are sent home. Meanwhile, the families of prostitutes with children fall deeper into poverty because they have more family members to support.

Causes of Prostitution

Most agree that poverty and social exclusion are the main causes of prostitution. In many cases, women who enter into prostitution through deception, being sold or rented by their families, or out of coercion are extremely poor. However, the majority of poor girls and women, as well as their families, try to avoid using prostitution as a poverty-coping method as long as other survival strategies are available.

Specific poverty-related factors, such as marriage practices common among Roma couples, help explain why poor women and poor families opt for prostitution as a solution. Some norms and values held by certain Roma families hold prostitution as an acceptable poverty-coping method. Frequent interaction between Roma and Albanians also has an impact in this regard. The data shows that Albanians tend to recruit poor Roma girls and women for prostitution, however, in some case, prostitution also occurs among less-poor Roma girls and women.

Early and Arranged Marriages

The downward poverty spiral begins when poverty is combined with common Roma marriage customs. In combination with poverty and social exclusion, some aspects of Roma marriages contribute to high prostitution rates among Roma. These include early and arranged marriages, childbearing at a young age, alcoholism, and domestic abuse that leads to high divorce rates among Roma. Women in abusive marriages who wish to separate from their husbands regard prostitution as one of the few exit strategies available to them in terms of life choices and economic survival.

When couples with children separate, mothers are left to care for the children. If single mothers cannot earn income at home, they may enter prostitution to support their children. "They feel bad for their children and are required to do this for them," explained one Roma from Elbasan.

So when women and their families become vulnerable to the enticements of an Albanian trafficker, who provides them with an opportunity to earn income, the women enter prostitution, leaving children at home with grandparents or other family members.

Family and Community Norms/Values

In some Roma families, cultural norms and values make prostitution an acceptable poverty-coping method. In these families, prostitution is not an affront to family bonds as long as it is undertaken to cope with poverty.

Accordingly, prostitution is more often tolerated than rejected in Roma communities because of its necessity among poor families. Prostitution is so widespread in some Roma localities that attaching a universal stigma to it would be destructive to many families. The common acceptance of prostitution was explained in part by a Roma woman from Pojan: "[Village residents] talk, but they don't want to know, since the girls bring food which allows the others here to eat."

Eighty-two percent of Roma claimed that prostitutes were accepted by their families, and only 16 percent claimed that they were rejected by both family and community. In Fushë Kruja, where poverty rates among Roma are very high, 94 percent indicated that trafficked people tend to return home. In extremely poor communities, such as Bregu i Lumit, some returning prostitutes have remarried.

Roma attached a strong, universal stigma to prostitution, but complaints about prostitution were centered only on the dangers posed to very young girls. This suggests the importance of female virginity in Roma culture, rather than outright opposition to prostitution.

Relations with Albanians

Most studies on Roma analyze the positive aspects of increased Roma interaction with majority populations. However, prostitution represents a possible downside to increased interaction with majority populations because in Albania, prostitution is strongly associated with that interaction.

Surprisingly, even in many relatively prosperous Roma localities, such as Morava and Baltëz, prostitution rates are also high. These Roma are relatively well-off and enjoy high international migration rates, high levels of education, basic infrastructure, and good relations with Albanians. These characteristics would lead many to believe that a phenomenon such as prostitution, which is usually associated with extreme poverty, would be uncommon.

However, among Roma, such localities are ripe for prostitution, because in these localities Albanian traffickers benefit from relatively easy access to vulnerable families and women. The traffickers succeed in bringing girls and women into prostitution by gaining their trust or the trust of their families in everyday interaction, through false marriage proposals, or in the case of selling or renting of girls and women, through business arrangements with family members. Ben, a Roma from Korça, explained: "Albanians, by talking to the girl and her parents, by them getting to know each other, are able to convince the parents to allow him to take the girl. Whites don't go into poor communities, only to wealthier ones." Such transactions are more difficult to make in segregated Roma neighborhoods and villages, because Albanians who enter isolated Roma areas are immediately viewed with suspicion. Thus, an Albanian trafficker can only operate in extremely poor communities, where Roma are most desperate, and in relatively prosperous communities, where interaction between Albanian and Roma is frequent.

The Effects of Prostitution: Remittances and Social and Economic Costs

Prostitutes send very few remittances home. In some cases, particularly when girls and women are rented by family members, families receive remittances, but in most cases these are inconsistent and few. Most often, families benefit very little from prostitution.

Remittances

Very few prostitutes' families receive any substantial income from their daughter's prostitution because pimps control their earnings. Fushë Kruja was the only district in which many local Roma indicated that they knew of someone in their community profiting from trafficking (94 percent) and, of these cases, that profiting was a very widespread phenomenon (47 percent). Compared to Fushë Kruja, those in Fier (66 percent), Elbasan (31 percent), and Vlora (40 percent), large districts considered important trafficking centers, were less likely to know of someone in their community who profited from this activity. In other districts, such as Tirana (34 percent), Korça (30 percent), and Durrës (29 percent), percentages were even lower.

Respondents from different communities, as mentioned above, explained that the amount of remittances received by families of prostitutes varies widely. Those in Bregu i Lumit stated that remittances can be up to L100,000 annually. One Bregu i Lumit woman claimed that her mother was able to build a house with the L500,000 she received from a prostitute family member. One Roma woman from Baltëz explained that her sister-law's remittances from Italy allowed the family to build the two-story house in which they currently lived.

Families are more likely to receive income from prostitution if parents rent their daughter and make arrangements for regular payments with the trafficker. Extremely poor families, such as those in Fushë Kruja, appear to benefit from prostitution more than relatively prosperous families, because remittances constitute a greater proportion of income for extremely poor families. Yet, overall, few or no remittances are sent home, because remittance levels depend entirely on the pimps. Gjergj, a Roma from Bregu i Lumit, stated: "[Pimps] can keep for themselves L500,000 and give the girl L200,000–300,000 for two years." Bukura, another Roma woman from Bregu i Lumit, added that her sister does not send money home when she is with "a bad person."

Edlira, a Former Prostitute from Korça

"I was married at 12, and I left him when I was 14. When I married and moved in with him I regretted it because I saw that we didn't get along well, but also that [his family] didn't run things as they should have. They didn't have a bedroom, just a sofa to sleep on. . . . My husband beat me because he was jealous, and he told me to not go out, don't even look out the window. When I finally asked him what was going on he told me that he had a girlfriend and that he didn't love me anymore. I left and went to my mother's. I was pregnant and I later had an abortion through a doctor. I was 14 and a half when I had the abortion."

Social and Economic Costs

The social costs of prostitution are high and they outweigh the financial gains for girls and young women working as prostitutes and their families. These costs are: decreased education for young girls and early marriage for young women. For families, the social costs of prostitution are increased poverty when prostitutes rejoin the family household and high tensions within the family.

Prostitution is directly related to low education levels for girls. Parents end their daughters' education early, fearing that they will be kidnapped on the way to school. Elida, a Roma woman in Driza, explained: "They are scared because times now are bad. Even I will only allow my daughter to attend school for two more years until she turns 12. Then I will pull her out. I'm scared that they will take her from me." Some girls even leave school of their own accord. One Roma mother explained: "A 12-year-old girl from our *fis* was kidnapped and taken to Italy. My girls were told that [this girl] didn't come to school because she was kidnapped by people in a car, and out of fear, they stopped going to school."

In Roma minds, early marriage is an antidote to prostitution. Eni, a Roma woman from Fushë Kruja, stated: "We Roma marry young. For us it's a good thing, because times now are bad; you raise them and somebody takes them from you. Nowadays they are kidnapping 12- or 13-year-old girls and taking them to Italy." In fact, it is more likely that early marriage itself is a contributing factor to subsequent prostitution.

Attitudes Toward Prostitution

"When they come back, there's a sort of disdain for them. They aren't liked in the same way as all other women from the neighborhood. Their families accept them. In general, they don't help their families financially, but in some cases, they do send money once in awhile. The families who have daughters in prostitution are the very poor ones. One [prostitute] was unmarried, so was another girl. Some girls had children . . . one left a nine-month-old baby with her parents because she had separated from her husband. . . ."

Many Roma described family and community tensions created by prostitution. However, attitudes toward returning prostitute daughters are not monolithic. They vary from one household to another, from neighborhood to neighborhood, and from one village to another. In some instances, only certain family members accepted a trafficked family member back into their household. Some prostitutes, rejected by parents, moved in with a sibling, for example. Moreover, the social and economic costs of children left home by their mothers forced into prostitution should also be considered. Because most prostitutes do not send remittances home, parents of prostitutes are often left without the financial support to care for their grandchildren, which increases the family's poverty.

Prostitution also affects the emotional and physical health of prostitutes. There are many instances in which prostitutes have been beaten and tortured by their traffickers or pimps.

The shame associated with prostitution compels many to remain abroad. When they return to Albania, their family's economic condition has worsened. Lacking education and job skills, and unable to generate income at home, the prostitutes who return to Albania leave once again for Italy and re-enter prostitution.

In sum, prostitutes and their families lose out from prostitution. Prostitution constitutes a downward spiral into poverty for Roma communities.

Trafficking of Children

Among, Roma, the trafficking of children is more common than among Albanians, since Roma suffer from higher rates of poverty and unemployment. Higher levels of trust among Roma are also contributing factors to child trafficking. However, the costs of child trafficking on Roma children include increased child illiteracy and undereducation, while the effects on the Roma communities include tensions and stress.

Table 9.1 shows the daily income of trafficked children in three situations.

Table 9.1. Daily Income of Trafficked Children
Begging in Tirana: L300 (US$2.31)
Begging in Greece: 10 euros (US$13)
Working in Agriculture in Greece: 15–20 euros (US$19–26)

Source: Interviews and focus groups with Roma and Egyptians for the Needs Assessment, 2002/03.

Definitions

When discussing the effects of child trafficking with Roma, it was difficult to explain its definition. The term is ambiguous and culturally contingent, and could include all children who are used by families for financial gain, or only children who are rented to other families. There were problems in interpreting data, and so this study relies more on anecdotal evidence than on quantitative data.

Certainly, most Roma distinguished children who work alongside their families from children who are rented or sold to other families, and only the latter fell under the category of child trafficking. Nonetheless, most categorized all cases as "prostitutes," regardless of age.

Therefore, child trafficking in this study includes all cases in which children are lent or sold to other families for profit; as well as other cases not involving prostitution in which children leave their locality, alone or with family members, for their family's financial gain or that of another family.[77]

Forms of Trafficking Children

Three basic forms of child trafficking are practiced by some Roma families:

- Children are rented to other families for financial gain.
- Children are sent by families to nearby cities and towns to work.
- Children migrate abroad with families and work as informal migrant laborers.

Children who are Rented or Sold by their Families. In cases in which children are rented to other families, parents place their child in the care of another family for a specified period, and that family supervises the child's informal work, usually begging. The child's family receives a percentage of the child's earned income or a fixed sum. In most cases, children are rented to families migrating to Greece or Italy. Children who beg abroad can earn 10 euros a day, and their families receive approximately L10,000 per month, which is approximately one-fourth to one-fifth of the child's earned income. Supervising families, meanwhile, use the remainder of the child's income to pay for living and transportation expenses. In some cases, supervising families arrange for false passport and visa documents. Otherwise, children are transported illegally.

Hana, a Rented Roma Girl from Korça

"I went to Greece one time. I was 11 years old then . . . We didn't have any food and so I went with a friend of my father's. I worked all day. I got up in the morning, ate breakfast, and from 3:30 [pm] went out begging, and I would go back home at night. I begged and sold flowers . . . I would come back home up to 12 at night. I didn't count the money [I received], but I got a lot, and I gave all of it to my father's friend. He gave my father L10,000 a month. He had a wife . . . and they would stay near me while I begged. I stayed a long time, around two months. I came back because the police caught me, but [the couple I was with] had documents, so they stayed."

Children Are Sent to Work to Nearby Cities and Towns. In cases where children are sent by families to nearby cities and towns to work, they are usually sent to beg on the streets. Sajmirë, a Roma boy in Bradashesh, explained: "There are seven people in my family. I am 14 years old and I go to beg in Tirana and Elbasan . . . My parents are at home and un-

---

77. Prostitution is not included in this section because of the difficulty in distinguishing cases that involved females under the age of 18 from cases that involved females over 18. All prostitution cases are used for analysis in the "Prostitution" section of this chapter.

employed. I go to Tirana by minibus and [the driver] takes me there for free. I beg in front of the Pyramid. My father's friends help me. I sit down on the street or beg in the stores . . . They feel sorry for me so they give me money. I end up with L200, L300, up to L500."

Many Roma explained that trafficked children are more commonly sent to work by their own families than rented to other families.

Children Migrate Internationally with Families. The third form of child trafficking involves children who migrate abroad with their families and work in various forms of informal migrant labor. Most cases involve children who migrate to Greece, which is very common among families in Gjirokastra, Elbasan, and Delvina. Some children work in agriculture, and usually earn wages equal to other family members—15–20 euros daily or US$0.28 per crate of picked tomatoes. Others beg beside their mothers in cities and towns, earning as much as 10 euros a day.

The frequency of children migrating with their families and working abroad is considerable. As noted in the chapter on migration, when survey respondents were asked who from their neighborhood or village migrates, one third indicated entire families, including children.

Eni, a trafficked Roma girl from Morava

"When I went to Greece in 1999, I went with my mother and father. Over there, I begged in front of the cemeteries, sometimes by myself and sometimes with my mother. We were in Asir. I went out to beg when I had free time. I would do work around the house, then afterwards I would go out to beg. I made L400, sometimes L500. I would stay out from 8 until 12 in the evening. Some people gave us money, but some didn't want us around at all. In the beginning, I was ashamed of begging, but little by little, I stopped feeling ashamed."

Who Gets Trafficked?

When Roma and Egyptians were asked if children were obliged to beg for their family, it was important to know that they did not differentiate between child begging in home localities and child begging *outside* home localities. Therefore, data cannot provide information strictly on child trafficking as defined in this chapter. However, if survey data are combined with qualitative data, they paint a general picture of child trafficking among Roma and Egyptians by gender, *fis*, and district.

Gender. When asked about family responsibilities assigned to boys and girls, 44 percent of Roma and 27 percent of Egyptians responded that boys were required to beg, while only 36 percent of Roma and 20 percent of Egyptians believed that girls also ought to beg. The differential can be explained in part by their beliefs that more girls are expected to undertake household chores, and by the fear that, by begging alone in public, girls might be kidnapped and thrust into prostitution. More boys than girls are obliged to beg for their families.

Cergar and Karbuxhinj Roma. Child trafficking is more common among Cergar and Karbuxhinj Roma than among Meçkar Roma. The head of the Rrapishta branch of Amaro Drom stated: "There are cases of children being taken to beg in Greece, but in comparison with other districts, Roma from Elbasan are particularly known for this. If you are a poor family, the head of the household goes with his wife and children to Greece. They stay there for months." Many claimed that Cergars from Fier and Karbuxhinj from Pogradec were "experts" in child trafficking. A likely explanation for lower child-trafficking rates among Meçkars is that they are more likely to have alternative poverty-coping methods at their disposal, such as subsistence agriculture and migrant agricultural work. For many Karbuxhinjinj and Cergars, child trafficking is one of only a few sources of consistent income.

Observers describe high frequencies of child begging in Fier, Elbasan, Fushë Kruja, Durrës, and Tirana, but lower rates in Korça and Berat. In Shkodra, although child begging is common, child trafficking is less likely, since Roma families in Shkodra are Karbuxhinj migrated to Shkodra from Tirana and Fushë Kruja because there were better opportunities for begging. Notably, Egyptian child-begging frequencies are much lower than Roma frequencies, even in extremely poor districts such as Shkodra.

An Egyptian Father and Child Begging

"There are six people in our family, myself, my wife, and four children. My oldest son is 20, but we haven't heard from him in five years. A man took him to Italy to beg, but when they got there, the guy drugged him and forced him into distributing drugs. My son was scared and refused. The guy beat him. . . . He was 14 when I sent him to Italy to beg with a man of the white hand from Berat. The man promised that he would send us L500,000 per month, but he didn't send us anything. I made a six-month agreement with him, and afterwards my son was supposed to return to Albania with this man. I sent the boy because I was very poor and I felt that through begging, he would send us some money for us to live on . . . He used to go out to beg here or wash car windows, and sometimes he would bring us L300, L400, or L600 a day, and we lived on that. My son had been sick since he was a small boy . . . he was crippled. I talked it over with my wife and explained to the boy the reasons why he should go. He himself also wanted to go. One time before he tried to take off with another man from the white hand without telling me a thing. . . . I sent him to this second person instead."

Causes, Social and Economic Costs, and Financial Benefits

Like prostitution, child trafficking is caused by poverty and social exclusion. Families resort to child trafficking when other poverty-coping methods fail to provide families with basic needs. Again, Roma exhibit great trust when renting their children to other families within their localities. Trust allows these children to be placed in the care of another family for up to several months. Most Roma who rent their children to other Roma families receive regular income. Few cases involve Roma who rent out their children to Albanian families.

Unlike prostitution, child trafficking provides families with small but consistent income. Children who are rented to other families to beg in Greece can provide their families with as much as US$75 for each month they spend abroad. Even children who travel to nearby urban areas to beg can bring families L1,000 a week.

Like prostitution, the social costs associated with child trafficking far outweigh the benefits to families. Child trafficking results in poor education for children. Karbuxhinj and Cergar Roma children have extremely high illiteracy rates compared to Meçkar or Egyptian children, who are less commonly trafficked than Karbuxhinj and Cergar children. The average number of school years completed by Karbuxhinj and Cergar children is also low compared to that of Meçkar and Egyptian children.[78]

Although data on health are insufficient to make any definite correlations between child trafficking and health problems, the health effects of trafficking on children must also be considered.

Trafficking of Drugs

In the districts of Tirana, Elbasan, Korça, Berat, Fier, and Vlora, Roma are widely engaged in drug trafficking.[79]

Who Traffics Drugs?

Drug trafficking is conducted primarily by young Roma men, usually heads of households of poor or very poor families. They enter into arrangements with organized groups of traffickers for cash benefits. The reason organized groups approach Roma to traffick drugs is there are high risks involved and relatively low financial returns. Moreover, for many Roma, this activity is not considered a shameful occupation.

Reason for Drug Trafficking

The main reason for drug trafficking is poverty and social exclusion. Those individuals who engage in trafficking of drugs come from poor families and see this as a poverty-coping mechanism because they are able to provide their families with temporary cash income.

Economic and Social Costs, and Financial Benefits

However, the economic and social costs can be very high. As with prostitution, the consequences of drug trafficking can be severe for the individuals who sell illegal drugs, as well as for their families.

Some of the drug traffickers were detained by the police in the neighboring country and sentenced to several years in prison. Skenderi, a Roma from Berat, said: "I have been in prison, in Greece. I was sentenced to six years for drugs transportation. Albanians gave

---

78. For statistical data, see Appendix D, and Chapter 9, Prostitution and Trafficking.

79. In this study, drug trafficking refers only to the transportation of drugs from one location to another or within a given locality, as well as the distribution of drugs in these locations.

me a bag of drugs to take it someplace and for this, I got 426 euros (US$550). While I was in prison, my family stayed in Albania. My youngest son was six months old when I left and, when I was back, I found him six years old."

As with female prostitution and child trafficking, drug trafficking also has serious negative consequences for families. Kujtime, a Roma woman from Tirana, lives together with her children in a shack by the Lana River. She explained: "I have two children. I sold the house for L1,500,000 (USD$11,000) and I put the money in the pyramid schemes. But we lost all of it and we were left out on the streets. Because of poverty, my husband migrated to Greece, but in the year 1998, he was detained and sentenced to prison for drug distribution. The children don't go to school and I can barely raise them in this shack. I can't even get the *ndihme ekonomike*[80] because they do not give it if the husband is not here."

In many cases, the woman leaves the home, abandoning even the children. Nimete, an old woman from Berat said she lives with her three nephews: "My son is in prison in Greece, whereas his wife went as a prostitute abroad and left the children with me. I benefit from the *ndihme ekonomike,* I sell some used clothes in the villages, or simply beg."

There are links among prostitution, child trafficking, and drug trafficking. In some cases, children can be rented for drug trafficking. Such is the case of Estref, an Egyptian from Berat. "I sent my son to Italy because I was very poor and I thought that through begging, we would have some money to live on. I made a deal with the person who took my son . . . He was supposed to give me L500,000 Albania (US$240) per month for a six-month period. But he was giving drugs to my son and was forcing him to sell drugs"

In other cases, criminal networks exploit women for prostitution with the pretext that "we need money from you to release your imprisoned husband." Nimet, a Roma leader from Tirana, said: "There are men connected to the mafia who are involved in the drug-trafficking business. They give the drugs to Roma, who carry it in bags and hand it to the Greeks. They walk for 40 km. They get L20,000 for each bag. Anyone who gets caught by the police ends up in prison. In such cases, the trafficking leaders tell the wife she should go to Greece to take her husband out of prison, and they even get her a visa. They take the woman with her two or three children and they take her directly to a hotel where they exploit her for prostitution. If she refuses, they threaten to kill her children."

Conclusion

Prostitution and trafficking of children and drugs are employed by Roma families as poverty-coping mechanisms when other income-generating opportunities are unavailable or fail to meet the families' basic needs. For instance, trafficking of children and drugs is a more frequent phenomenon in neighborhoods or villages where income from informal employment is extremely low. Notably, there are cases in which both prostitution and child trafficking are employed by the same family.

While qualitative data link poverty to prostitution, trafficking of children, and drug trafficking, other important determinants also help to explain the high frequencies of these phenomena in Roma communities. These are particular to their situation.

---

80. See Chapter 5, Income and Living Standards for a more detailed description of *ndihme ekonomike.*

One aspect of life in all Roma communities—the deeply ingrained custom of early marriage for Roma girls—is strongly linked to prostitution. Indeed, unique forms of social capital that are common in that community are also linked to prostitution and child trafficking. For instance, Roma who have good relations with Albanians, including relatively prosperous ones, have unexpectedly high prostitution rates. Moreover, the high trust that Roma exhibit allow some families to rent their children to other families. Policies that aim to reduce prostitution and child trafficking require careful attention to these unique Roma characteristics. Drug trafficking, however, is not unique to Roma, since it is also pursued by Egyptians and Albanians. Despite the inherent risks of being caught by police and imprisoned, many poor Roma traffick drugs because it serves as a means to survive and is thus a coping mechanism against poverty and social exclusion.

CHAPTER 10

Social Capital

D uring the socialist period, the state and Roma *fis* system forged a mutually beneficial relationship. The state system provided jobs and housing, for example, while the *fis* handled such day-to-day matters as marriage and informal private business. However, with the weakening of the state during the transition period, Roma no longer enjoy the economic and political benefits and living standards in employment, education, housing, and health care that they had under the socialist state.

At the same time, the established "social capital" within the Roma *fis* has been sufficient to meet the socioeconomic and institutional challenges and new demands of the transition. Poverty and internal and international migration, as well as other transition phenomena, have weakened the *fis* system, and Roma have developed new forms of social capital to survive. Today, rather than rely on the state and kinship system, Roma rely on forms of social capital that are based in local, regional, and even trans-national relationships. Ervin, a Roma from Korça, referring to his own *fis*, stated: "Poverty has broken us up."

On one hand, both Roma and Egyptians benefit from a wealth of cognitive social capital[81] that enables them to migrate abroad and to purchase food with lists, for example. On the other hand, they are poor in the structural social capital that is particularly crucial to allow their participation in decisionmaking processes at local, regional, and national policy levels.[82] They certainly lack effective political representation. Their existing associations are fragmented and unable to advocate effectively their interests and solutions to challenges. Therefore, both groups will remain ill-equipped to face poverty and social exclusion until their structural social capital grows stronger.

---

81. Cognitive social capital refers to very intangible values, norms, and attitudes that govern behavior.

82. Structural social capital refers to formal or informal associations or networks that facilitate collective action.

Definitions

Social capital refers to the "institutions, relationships, attitudes, and values that govern inter-actions among people and contribute to economic and social development" (Grootaert and van Bastelae 2002). Most social scientists categorize social capital as "horizontal" or "structural" social capital, and "vertical" or "cognitive" social capital.

Many economists grapple with social capital. The fact that social capital is frequently intangible poses difficulties for respective measurement and monitoring. Until now, intangi-ble concepts like "trust" and "norms" were never associated with "capital" which can be obtained, held, and used. These concepts were left to anthropologists, who often disagreed with the perspectives of economists while exploring kinship, betrothals, or religious rituals in their village case studies. Anthropologists and sociologists also use certain notions of social capital in their work on social organization, illustrating individual behaviors through societal structures and institutions at the policy level. These qualitative concepts, however, were fre-quently not acceptable to traditional economists, who tended to dismiss them as intangible and subjective experiences, statistically immeasurable notions, and unempirical anecdotes.

Recently, interdisciplinary research in sociological, anthropological, and economics dis-ciplines has attempted to describe and measure human and policy determinants of collec-tive action and productivity. The notion of "human capital" emerged, referring to the skills and talents of individuals and their roles in facilitating productive activity. This meant that an individual's education and training, for example, became measurable. Social scientists and economists could link social processes with economic productivity. This advanced the research agenda, which moved from the individual level of behaviors to the level of groups and their collective action, and ultimately to societal interaction with the notion of dynamic processes at the policy level. As a result, the concepts of norms and values, as well as social organization and networks, were acknowledged and their linkages recognized.

Structural social capital refers to "social structures, such as networks, associations, and institutions, and the rules and procedures they embody" (Grootaert and van Bastelae 2002). For example, structural social capital can be an association of construction firms that lobbies a local government to expedite construction permit procedures.

Cognitive social capital refers to intangible values, norms, and attitudes that govern behavior. For example, cognitive social capital can be the trust that allows informal bor-rowing or lending between clients and businesspersons.

Trust is one common indicator of cognitive social capital. According to the economist James Coleman, a "group whose members manifest trustworthiness and place extensive trust in one another will be able to accomplish much more than a comparable group lack-ing that trustworthiness and trust" (cited in Dasgupta 2000). The role of solidarity in the welfare of communities has also been analyzed within the framework of social capital. Respective analyses investigate whether community members would assist an individual in crisis and to what extent family welfare is affected (Grootaert and van Bastelae 2002).

In order to cope with poverty and social exclusion, both Roma and Egyptians employ cognitive and, to a much lesser extent, structural forms of social capital. Higher levels of social capital among some make them better equipped to face poverty and social exclusion than those with lower levels.

In fact, varying levels of social capital could possibly help identify why some are extremely poor and completely segregated from Albanian society, and others are poor but relatively well-off compared to extremely poor. Thus, social capital may help explain why the impact of poverty and social exclusion on the different Roma communities varies greatly.

After socialism, many Roma are unemployed, marry early, and have low education qualification. And while levels of savings and income fluctuated immediately after 1990, by now most Roma are simply poor, and financial capital is not great enough to explain differences in the way some Roma live. What makes Meçkars Roma in Morava say that their lives are "a little better" compared to "the time of the Hoxha," while Karbuxhinjinj Roma in Shkodra reminisce about the socialist era? Why are only a few Roma and Egyptians from Shkodra capable to find ways to migrate abroad, while most of their neighbors are unable and stay home As one economist (Coleman 2000) has argued, "Like other forms of capital, social capital is productive, making possible the achievement of certain ends that, in its absence, would not be possible." It seems to appear that some Roma groups enjoy better connections, trust relationships and networks, i.e. social capital which they build upon and utilize for migration.

An analysis of social capital can also identify areas of interest for policymaking and lead resources and investments to the invisible strong points in Roma and Egyptian localities that otherwise would have gone unnoticed. An in-depth analysis of social capital among both groups in Albania requires anthropological, extended-case-study methods, which this study does not claim to have carried out. An analysis would require "on-the-ground investigation of community organization" (Krishna and Shrader 2002), because their norms, values, associations, and networks are little known, and thus analyses of social capital are heavily exposed to misinterpretation by a short-term observer.

However, qualitative and quantitative data do allow for a sketch of the forms of social capital present in some of their communities, and of basic assumptions about how they matter to the general welfare of Roma and Egyptians.

Cognitive Social Capital: Trust and Solidarity

During the socialist period, both groups exhibited trust and solidarity, either as members of a working class or, for Roma, as members of a *fis*. With the weakening of the state and the *fis* organization during the transition period, they have been forced to extend levels of trust and solidarity to new groups in order to survive. Today, trust and solidarity among the two groups exist at the local, regional, national, and trans-national levels, and trust and solidarity between all groups are more fruitful for Roma and Egyptians than trust and solidarity that are confined to a single ethnic group.

Trust

Trust plays an important role in facilitating economic activity and both groups maintain a high level of trust with their neighbors. In fact, 48 percent of Roma and Egyptians assert that they have full trust in their neighbors. Trust is important for survival, and it allows them to do such things as borrow small amounts of money from neighbors. And, 58 percent of Roma and Egyptians indicated that they knew unrelated people who would lend money. Meçkars (65 percent) knew more unrelated people on whom they could rely for small loans than did Karbuxhinj (53 percent), Cergars (50 percent), or Bamills (33 percent).

Figure 10.1 illustrates the depths of trust of Roma and Egyptians have in their neighbors.

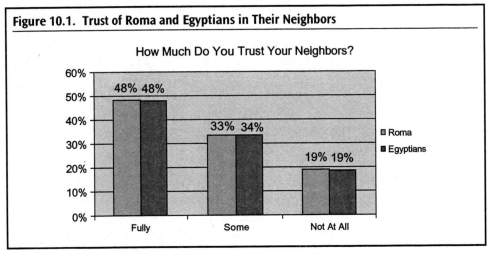

Figure 10.1. Trust of Roma and Egyptians in Their Neighbors

Source: Socioeconomic household questionnaires with Roma and Egyptians, 2002.

In the absence of a fully functioning state institution and *fis* organizations, high levels of trust help Roma and Egyptians to face poverty and social exclusion. Trust has become so important in the transition period that, in some cases, common trust-based transactions have evolved into informal institutions. Two strong examples of the importance of trust are the "delivery man," who delivers remittances to hometowns, and the shop owner, who allows them to purchase goods with lists. These examples are noteworthy because delivery man and shop owner transactions often take place in the absence of some external arbiter, such as a *kryeplak* who can enforce agreements between two parties. Moreover, in the case of the shop owner, almost all transactions take place among the three groups, constituting perhaps the country's single most important daily interethnic transaction.

Trust as Cognitive Social Capital: The Shop Owner

Many Albanian shop owners in Roma and Egyptian localities permit the two groups to purchase goods, mainly food, on lists. Use of lists is widespread and crucial for the well-being of Roma and poor Egyptians. When asked "What do you do when you don't have money to buy food?" 65 percent of Roma and 52 percent of Egyptians responded that they bought food with lists. Those who are unable to purchase with lists from local shops are left without a vital poverty-coping method. Since Egyptians are more likely to borrow money from relatives, friends, or employers, they are less likely to buy with lists. To Roma, lists appear more valuable than small loans provided by others, because Roma, though lacking cash, can get food and avoid starvation by resorting to lists.

Many lists range from US$25 to US$300 for one family, and can run for a few weeks to several months. Lists are paid when income is received from temporary employment, international migration, or state assistance. Sami, a Roma in Delvina, stated: "There are four of us, and you can take a look at the list of how much I've borrowed. When the flowers bloom we'll go out and collect them and then pay back the list." In Pojan, customers can take as long as five months to pay lists. When lists are paid, the list process begins again. In Tirana, some families take out lists from different shops: "We've taken out loans from four shops. Here I've borrowed L600; here, L2,500; and another L1,000 somewhere else."

Most lists are used entirely for food purchases. Gjergj, a Delvina store owner, stated: "[My] total list amount has gone from L120,000 up to L130,000. The ones with loans are mostly Roma. They pay them back when there's a wedding[83] or when they come from Greece and bring money. They mainly buy food, pasta, rice, sugar, vegetables, etc. A loan for one person is as high as L10,000, but I don't give any more than that because I'm in my own situation and I would have problems afterwards. They bring the money and afterwards start another list."

In Tirana, some customers had been on lists for three months because pension checks are arriving late. Ladi, a shop owner, explained: "About 10 Roma families come here and purchase by list. It's now two to three months since they have received any economic assistance. One family has a loan of around L40,000–50,000, they pay them back when they get their pensions. . . . The loans were smaller before, but now they're taking out more."

Poor Albanians also employ lists. Shop owners, however, report that Egyptians and Roma take longer to pay back loans, borrow larger amounts, and borrow in increasing amounts. Therefore, higher levels of trust are needed for transactions with Roma and poor Egyptians than for transactions with Albanians. Kristo, a Durrës shop owner, stated: "I keep lists with Egyptians, but the white hand buys with list for one or two days and then pays it back, whereas Egyptians have a lot . . . All of them buy with list."

What makes the list so dependent on trust is that shop owners have little means of acting on unpaid loans. There are no legal ramifications for unpaid loans. Often, lists are simply written on a slip of paper. In fact, in some neighborhoods, customers can delay repaying loans because there are other nearby shops available for list purchases. This is particularly true in Tirana, where customers have more than one neighborhood shop from which to purchase goods, and so do not need any single shop. While shop owners could be motivated to lend to customers because these customers constitute a percentage of business, many, when asked for their motivations, expressed sympathy-based motivations other than profit-based ones. "They use it to buy food," said one shop owner simply. In some cases, they explained that they too had borrowed from local businesses and thus were more inclined to lend to their own customers.

Because lists are based on trust, shop owners confirmed that, in most cases, lists are repaid. However, problems exist for shop owners when, for example, most customers are on lists and "welfare" assistance or pension checks arrive late. Marrenglen, a shop owner in Elbasan, claimed to have over US$2,000 out on list and was thus near "bank-

---

83. Families of Roma and Egyptian brides and grooms receive money as wedding gifts, which helps to cover wedding expenses.

ruptcy." Most owners who lent in smaller amounts experienced fewer problems with the list.

Without trust as a form of social capital, Roma and Egyptians would not be able to depend on shop lists. They would also be less likely to migrate abroad, and extreme poverty in the form of hunger would be even more common.

Trust as Cognitive Social Capital: The Delivery Man

As described in the chapter on migration and remittances, delivery men are international migrants who return home and deliver the remittances to the families of migrants who remain abroad. Approximately 15 percent of remittances are brought home to Albania by friends and relatives acting as delivery men. While relatives who make deliveries are motivated by family norms, deliveries made by friends and acquaintances are based on high levels of trust. To a great extent, trust facilitates the delivery of remittances with demonstrated results.

Earnings are collected in Greece and transported by foot across the Greek-Albanian border. In border areas, delivery men who can transport amounts up to L150,000 are especially vulnerable to robbery or police harassment. The delivery process can be dangerous, and as noted before, robberies occur. Thus, not only must friends and acquaintances trust the integrity of delivery persons, but they must also trust in their ability to elude robbery.

In the delivery man example, trust also has tangible results. The next most popular option for remittance delivery is Western Union, which charges up to 13 percent of the money amounts transferred out of Greece.[84] International migrants either pay these fees or wait until they can return home to make deliveries themselves. Trust in the delivery man reduces remittance losses.

In some cases, Albanians delivered remittances on behalf of Roma. Most frequently, this occurred in Baltëz, where good relations existed between Roma and Albanians. In the same village, some Roma claimed that they could also borrow money from Albanians if necessary. Nonetheless, in most cases, the delivery men that carry the earnings of Roma international migrants are Roma themselves.

Solidarity

Solidarity-based social capital facilitates coordination and cooperation during crises that affect a collective group, such as a neighborhood or village, a segmentary *fis*,[85] a primary *fis*, or Roma and Egyptians. Among Roma, solidarity that facilitates collective action exists on the neighborhood or village, segmentary *fis*, primary *fis*, and transnational levels. For Egyptians, solidarity exists at the neighborhood or village level and to a lesser extent at the kinship level.

---

84. Western Union's fee for amounts between US$150–220 is US$19.75; US$23.50 for US$220–300, and US$27.00 for US$300–365.

85. Segmentary *fis*: a kinship descent system, defining descent categories with reference to more and more remote apical ancestors so that the descent categories form a tree-like structure (including successively wider ranges of descendants) (American Anthropological Association).

The Kryeplak: An Indicator of Solidarity at the Neighborhood and Village Level

The waning strength of the *fis* system for both Roma and Egyptians has meant that roles traditionally associated with the *fis* are now being played by non-*fis* individuals. Among these important roles is conflict resolution. In the absence of the traditional *fis* leader, a new figure in local neighborhoods and villages—the elected *kryeplak*—often plays the role of conflict mediator. His status in the community enables him to facilitate cooperation and productive behavior. His presence indicates solidarity at the neighborhood and village level.

The *kryeplak* is an elected village leader who adjudicates disputes between two or more families and is consulted for or makes decisions affecting the entire local community. He is involved in resolving conflicts between families and, when necessary, facilitating assistance to certain families in need. Explained Ferit, a Roma *kryeplak* in Tirana: "When two cars crash, and it's the other guy's fault, we don't start a conflict, we pay them the money in order to put an end to the dispute. When they ask for, be it millions, we don't leave them to kill one another, but we get together the money and give it to them. And when one family or neighbor doesn't have anything, and I do, I give them money because we can't leave the children without food." In Pojan, one *kryeplak* described his role in resolving conflicts: "When one family has a disagreement with another I reconcile them. I tell them that they should resolve the disagreement together. . . ."

Neighborhood and Village Solidarity as Cognitive Social Capital

Both display high levels of solidarity when members of their neighborhood or village are in need. Forty-six percent of Roma and 47 percent of Egyptians have neighbors that would help one another in the event of a crisis.

When asked if neighbors assist community members who are sick, Genc, a Roma in Delvina, simply stated: "We watch out for each other a lot." While Egyptians are less likely to respond to crises that affect their community, they often respond to crises that affect their local neighborhood or village.

Although less common, villages in certain districts benefit from solidarity between Roma and Albanians in times of crisis. In these cases, Roma not only benefit from solidarity that is based on one's segmentary or primary *fis*, but on solidarity with the majority population. Solidarity between Roma and Albanians is more common in rural areas. Hamit, a Roma from Novosela, explained: "One man was hospitalized . . . in Tirana. We will get everyone together and chip in L500 or however much we have and will make L5,000 and give it to him. . . . He is our fellow villager so we will help him. The whites also help us." And in Llakatund, one Albanian teacher stated: "We have a tradition here that when a person gets into a bad economic situation, we help him; when there's an illness, we collect whatever money we can." Neighborhoods or villages that display solidarity between Albanians and Roma generally have higher living standards than those that display only ethnic solidarity.

Egyptians benefit from higher levels of solidarity with Albanians. Egyptians, who more frequently than Roma live in neighborhoods or villages that are integrated with Albanians, cope with economic uncertainty by associating themselves with Albanians and thus reap the benefits of solidarity with the majority population.

Kinship Solidarity as Cognitive Social Capital

Many traditional aspects of the *fis* system that governed collective action during socialism have waned during the transition period. However, elements of the *fis* system, such as solidarity, still thrive today. Although no longer governed solely by kinship rules and rituals, kinship-based solidarity still plays an important role among both Roma and Egyptians and constitutes an important form of social capital.

Kinship-based solidarity is directly associated with international migration. Many families with members who migrate abroad are assisted by extended family members, such as grandparents, or uncles and aunts, who take care of children or wives who stay home.

Solidarity among Roma often extends to the primary *fis* level. When asked if solidarity existed among members of Roma *fise*, Ladi, a Roma in Xhafzotaj, responded: "Yes, naturally, with our *fis* there's no question; we find out where there are deaths or people sick. I've gone all the way to Baltëz in Fier and I didn't know them." Some international migrants also credit primary *fis* members for watching out for other family members who stay home. When facing poverty and social exclusion, many Roma benefit from solidarity based on both their segmentary and primary *fis*.

Roma or Egyptian Solidarity at the National Level

Roma in Albania rarely display solidarity with Albanian society at the national level. While solidarity is common within a primary Roma *fis*, it is uncommon between two different primary *fise*. These low levels of inter-*fise* solidarity are shared by Egyptians, who prefer to interact with Albanians rather than Roma because they benefit from solidarity between the two.

The lack of Roma solidarity at the national level has strong implications for members of a primary *fis* that live among Roma belonging to another primary *fis*. These are less likely to migrate abroad, for example. Isolated families of one primary *fis* are less likely to benefit from the coordinated activities associated with primary *fis* solidarity. Moreover, the lack of solidarity between and among Albanian Roma impedes coordinated political activity. Their lack of solidarity prevents benefits stemming from neighborhood- or village-based bonding from becoming countrywide.

The Egyptian community in Shkodra is a strong example of the low level of solidarity between Egyptians and Roma. In this town, they live on two sides of a river, and there is little interaction between the two groups. Compared to Roma, Egyptians lack this important form of social capital. Although many Egyptians claim unique origins and traditional occupations, very little social capital results from this affiliation. Again, at the national level, Egyptians instead associate themselves with Albanians.

Solidarity at the Transnational Level

While displaying little solidarity at the national level, Roma often display solidarity at the transnational level. Albanian-Roma and Roma in neighboring countries often act together in solidarity as Roma, while the latter assist the former in securing employment and in facilitating business transactions with non-Roma in foreign countries. Edi, a Roma businessman from Tirana, described solidarity with Romanian-Roma: "Back then, people were saying that goods [in Romania] were much cheaper than in Albania, where there was a food and clothing crisis . . . I didn't know anyone in Romania, but this isn't a problem for us, because wherever we go we meet other Roma who help us find and purchase goods for reasonable prices." Solidarity is common between Albanian and Greek-Roma, especially in agricultural areas. According to international migrants' accounts, Greek-Roma refer international migrants to landowners seeking workers. They also assist in times of crisis. According to Arben, a Roma from Elbasan: "When we lose a child, we ask around with Greek-Roma and they tell us where he is."

Structural Social Capital

Roma and some Egyptians are rich in cognitive social capital that is manifested in informal organizations. They display levels of trust and solidarity that generally exceed the levels of trust and solidarity displayed by Albanians. However, their cognitive social capital is almost nonexistent on the national level, where solidarity and trust are crucial for political representation. To fill this gap in cognitive social capital, new and alternative forms of structural social capital have emerged between them.

Structural social capital refers to formal or informal associations or networks that facilitate collective action. During the socialist period, kinship and government institutions were some of the few forms of structural social capital in Albania. Weakened by increasing poverty and social exclusion during transition, the traditional kinship structures are no longer able to meet the changing needs of their communities. Transition also affected previously available government institutions and social policies, thus forming new networks and associations. Yet, compared to cognitive social capital, structural social capital is extremely weak among Roma and Egyptians. Therefore, both groups are limited in their ability to facilitate collective action.

Roma and Egyptian Associations as Structural Social Capital

Roma and Egyptian associations represent one of the rare forms of structural social capital operating within these communities. Associations are the only form of social capital among these groups that many economists would call "formal." While their associations have the potential for facilitating organized interest representation, they cooperate very little with each other. Reportedly, they have only occasional contact with Roma and Egyptians, and thus receive low levels of trust from these communities. Figure 10.2 depicts those levels of trust.

Two Egyptian and seven Roma associations direct cultural, educational, and awareness programs in various country districts.[86] However, 64 percent of Egyptians and 51 per-

---

86. Roma and Egyptian associations include Amaro Drom, Amaro Dives, Rromani Baxt, Disutni Albani, Romanies for Integration, Alba Rom, Kabaja, Nefreta, and Vellazerimi.

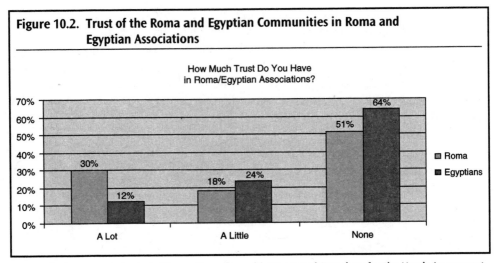

Figure 10.2. Trust of the Roma and Egyptian Communities in Roma and Egyptian Associations

How Much Trust Do You Have
in Roma/Egyptian Associations?

Source: Socioeconomic household questionnaires with Roma and Egyptians for the Needs Assessment, (2002/03).

cent of Roma do not trust their associations. Lower trust levels among Egyptians can be explained by their identification more as Albanians than as Egyptians.

The weak rapport of Roma associations with Roma communities is also linked with the lack of solidarity that exists between the different Roma primary *fise*. Two Cergar Roma in Kthesa e Ariut helped explain this relationship. While Roma in the district of Durrës number 1,100, most are Meçkars. Cergars are represented by only 20 families. So when asked about the local Roma association, two Cergars responded: "Those from the association have lied to the people and have taken money or aid from the government and they haven't given anything to the people. They are never interested in us. They have opened up shops and clothing stores for themselves . . . Those that founded the association in Shkozët are Meçkars . . ." Further: "Aid has come, but they haven't given us anything. It would be good if we Cergars would have our own president." Roma and Egyptian associations, while having strong potential, do not facilitate significant collective action.

The International Migration Circle as Structural Social Capital

International migration circles formed spontaneously when both began migrating 10 years ago. An international migration circle, an *ad hoc* network of international migrants that forms to confront the dangers of travel abroad, facilitates important collective action among these international migrants.

A large international migration circle of 30–300 illegal migrants that band together to travel abroad represents the most productive example of structural social capital employed by Roma and Egyptians. These circles form in home districts, and travel to the Albanian border on foot. Some, such as those that form in Elbasan, receive members from far-off districts such as Shkodra, where international migration is less frequent.

Members of international migration circles elect one leader who plans the route and rest periods. Leaders are elected for a combination of experience and integrity. One elected circle leader explained: "The people of my neighborhood elected me because I have experience and I'm honest. We don't abandon anyone on the road, and when someone gets sick, we stay and help them. I don't receive any compensation as the leader." International migrants reported no discipline problems or challenges to the authority of an elected leader of an international migration circle.

By leading a large group of international migrants and making life and death decisions for the group, the leader has more authority for the duration of the trip—often up to a dozen days—than any other Roma and Egyptian has in any leadership position. In some ways, the leader of the international migration circle temporarily plays the role of the traditional *fis* leader.

Notably, these migration circles have other uses as well. The circle is also employed for the exchange of information and knowledge on employment sources in the destination country. Today, they represent a lasting form of social capital.

Political Representation and Social Capital

As mentioned previously, the political representation of Roma and Egyptians is very weak. Some feel politically represented at the national level by the United Party for Human Rights, which is considered by other sources to be controlled largely by Albania's Greek minority (Koinova 2002). Others, however, see their interests represented by the National Socialist Party or the National Democratic Party. In general, most are not politically represented at the local, communal, or national levels. Only a few Roma have been elected to office at the district and communal level, such as the Roma representative on the district council of Bilisht, the commune council of Otllak, and the commune council of Lushnja (Taho 2002). Overall, though, Roma have not been able to translate social capital into the structures of political organizations, and Egyptians have fared no better. According to Beni, a Roma in Korça: "I don't see any good in belonging to any party, because we've been used by both the Socialist Party and the Democratic Party. They make promises but don't do anything." A Roma in Korça explained that: "There is discrimination, for example . . . when we go to their offices, they don't support us."

Implications of Social Capital

Roma and Egyptians' wealth of cognitive social capital represents the cultural elasticity of these ethnic groups and their diverse and desperate attempts to deal with what is growing worse and still stronger—poverty and social exclusion. The illustrations above are describe social capital in their communities. The examples represent different forms of capital because of their role in facilitating activities, such as migration, "list-buying," support by the *fis,* etc., that possibly would not have occurred without networks, trust, and connections Before the transition period, much of these activities, facilitated by social capital, were either unnecessary or handled by the state or *fis* system. But today, social capital has become a necessary coping mechanism and often spontaneous effect of economic uncertainty and desperation.

Notably, social capital can explain distinctions in the living standards of some Roma and Egyptians, for social capital that forms between Roma and Egyptians and Albanians is more productive than social capital that is confined to one's own ethnic group. Albanians are connected to resources that make social capital more productive. Not only do relations with Albanians assist in meeting immediate needs, but in most cases they also break down discrimination and stereotypes. Examples of the impact of relations with Albanians are the few Shkodra international migrants who, against heavy odds, managed to migrate to Greece through help from Albanian acquaintances. In the districts of Berat, Vlora, and Fier, many Roma and Albanians benefit from good inter-ethnic relations and at times even migrate abroad in mixed groups.

In many localities in which Roma and Egyptians were relatively prosperous compared to those in other localities, good relations existed among Albanians, Roma, and Egyptians. In the city of Korça, Roma described frequent interactions with Albanians. Albin, a Roma boy in the sixth grade, explained: "I sit at a desk with a white friend. I have friendships with them and I go to their houses. The teacher is good to us." The relatively well-off Roma in Xhafzotaj were the only ones in the district of Durrës to consistently describe good relations with Albanians. Roma families living in the city of Delvina among Albanians are better off than Roma living in their own mono-ethnic neighborhoods. Egyptians living in mixed quarters are better off than Egyptians living in segregated quarters, such as those in Shkodra. Family welfare is associated with frequent interaction with Albanians and with trust and solidarity that cross ethnic boundaries.

In general, Meçkar Roma are better off than Roma belonging to other *fise* because of relatively strong relations with Albanians. When asked if he had seen discrimination committed against Roma in his hometown, Beni, a Meçkar Roma from Lapardha, responded: "No, no, they respect us and even invite us to their weddings." More Meçkars described solidarity and trust with Albanians than Roma from other *fise*. This trust and solidarity has its benefits. Edi, another Meçkar Roma from Lapardha, said: "I also borrow money from the white hand; we have very good relations with them . . . They have given us respect at all times." Possible explanations for relatively high levels of solidarity between Meçkars and Albanians include Meçkars' traditional profession—agriculture—which brought Meçkars and Albanians together on collective farms and agricultural cooperatives during the socialist era. Stated one Meçkar from Morava: "We were together in the agricultural cooperatives and there were no distinctions in any way; we ate together; we Roma were mixed together with the whites. We got along without *fis* or color distinctions. For the good and the bad, we were united." Solidarity with Albanians has helped Meçkars survive the transition period.

To be sure, there is a direct association between good relations with Albanians and prostitution in Roma and Egyptian communities. This association explains why prostitution was so widespread in some relatively prosperous Meçkar communities. Traffickers, who are almost always Albanian, enter Roma and Egyptian communities more easily if relations among Roma, Egyptians, and Albanians are good. Traffickers also use trust among Albanians, Roma, and Egyptians in these neighborhoods to take advantage of particularly vulnerable Roma and Egyptian females and their families.

While relations with everyday Albanians are known to benefit Roma and Egyptians, interethnic relations less frequently extend to Albanian public administration workers. Ervin, a Roma businessman from Elbasan, suggested the importance of having relations with these Albanians: ". . . a white person has a friend that works in a ministry, in parliament or somewhere else and in this way he gets by easily." Lacking valuable relations with Albanian public administration workers, Roma and Egyptians lose out. Even in areas where everyday Albanians displayed knowledge of Roma and Egyptians, Albanian government workers often expressed gross generalizations regarding Roma and Egyptians. While social capital exists in the form of solidarity between some communities of Roma and Egyptians and everyday Albanians, these relations, especially for Roma, do not extend to the more immediately powerful and influential Albanians.

There is a ring of desperation to social capital. Among the two groups, financial resources and structural social capital are too weak to transfer high levels of cognitive social capital into comparably high living standards. Had Roma in Driza collected all their scraps of money earned in international migration, collective action would not likely result in higher living standards. Genc, a Roma from Llakatund, stated: "Yes, [we work together], but you must know that our standard of living is very low. . . . The labor power of our village is not absorbed by another place." When asked if his neighbors would help a neighborhood family in need, one Roma from Korça responded: "Yes, whoever is able to help. Most people here go to sleep on empty stomachs." Even relations with everyday Albanians have limited benefits, for many Albanians themselves are poor.

Conclusion

Numerous forms of cognitive and structural social capital among Roma and Egyptians have emerged during the transition period to confront poverty and social exclusion. In general, Roma and Egyptians are rich in cognitive social capital, but poor in structural social capital.

CHAPTER 11

Social Exclusion

According to a European Commission definition, social exclusion is "evidenced by several types of deprivation and barriers, which alone or together, prevent the full participation in areas such as employment, education, health, environment, housing, culture, access to rights or family support, as well as training and job opportunities."[87]

Social exclusion is a multidimensional and dynamic concept. It is based on the combination and interrelation of socioeconomic, institutional, political, and historical processes, at the levels of both the individual and society. Social exclusion is the consequence of constraints of historical, socioeconomic, political, and formal and informal cultural institutions and organizations (Beddies 2000). Furthermore, social exclusion creates "insiders" and "outsiders." Insiders are individual actors or groups of actors that can participate in and govern the processes that affect their individual livelihoods, solidarity towards other members of society, and social cohesion within society. On one hand, "outsiders" cannot participate in or govern these processes because of their exclusion from them. On the other hand, social inclusion refers to opportunities for change for these institutions and organizations by creating the right incentives and removing barriers to development opportunities.

Social exclusion is brazenly discriminating and aims to deny access to public and private goods and services, markets, and development opportunities, such as social safety nets, market capacity, training and job opportunities, and education.[88]

---

87. COM (2000). 79 final: "Communication from the Commission: Building an Inclusive Europe," 1 March.

88. COM (2000). 79 final: "Communication from the Commission: Building an Inclusive Europe," 1 March.

This study assessed the socioeconomic, historical, and institutional situation of Roma and Egyptian communities in Albania. It was found that they face social exclusion in many aspects of their lives. From the analyses, a pattern of linkages and dynamics emerges between economic restructuring, unemployment, poverty, weak government capacity, discrimination, and social exclusion. These factors and their linkages increasingly trap these families into poverty and make the majority of Roma and Egyptians the "outsiders" of Albanian society. Thus, in contrast to mainstream society, these population groups are denied participation in, and governance of, numerous aspects that affect their lives.

Albanian Roma Within a Regional Perspective

This study focused on two of the most marginalized groups in Albanian society: the Roma and Egyptians. Albanian Roma need to cope with similar socioeconomic problems as the Roma population in other Southeast Europe (SEE) and Central Eastern European (CEE) countries. A 2003 World Bank draft report has reported the Roma population estimates in several of these countries, as shown in Table 11.1.

Table 11.1. Distribution of Roma Population 1991–94
(thousands)

Country	Roma Population	Total Population	% of Roma
Albania	95	3,421	2.0
Bosnia & Herzegovina	45	4,383	1.0
Bulgaria	750	8,459	8.9
Croatia	35	4,788	0.7
Czech Republic	275	10,323	2.7
Hungary	575	10,280	5.6
FYR Macedonia	240	2,191	10.9
Poland	45	38,446	0.1
Romania	2,150	22,761	9.4
Slovak Republic	480	5,345	9.4
Slovenia	10	1,993	0.4
Yugoslavia	425	10,675	4.0

Notes: Roma population estimates are midpoints of ranges.
Source: The World Bank (2003). "Draft: Social Development in Europe and Central Asia Region: Issues and Directions." Washington, DC: Environmentally and Socially Sustainable Development, Social Development Team, Europe and Central Asia. March, pp. ix, x.

The same report states: "Although the CEE countries have indeed avoided violent conflict, ethnic relations between Roma and majority populations has reportedly deteriorated to a significant extent in the last decade. Unlike other minorities, who benefit from psychological, and sometimes material and political assistance from their "homelands," the estimated seven to nine million Roma who live dispersed throughout Europe and the former Soviet Union, with the largest concentrations in Macedonia, Bulgaria, Slovakia, and Romania, lack this support" (World Bank 2003).

Throughout the region, Roma suffer the same difficulties in procuring and keeping employment. In fact, their unemployment in CEE is estimated to be between 50 to 90 percent. Moreover, like the Roma in Albania who worked on collective farms during the socialist period, those in both CEE and SEE countries also lost their agricultural jobs when, during their transition, the state returned the land to their original owners. In one instance, in Bulgaria, where Roma constitute only 6.5 percent of the population, the percentage of households that live under the poverty line is 84 percent. Similarly, in Romania, where Roma are only 2.3 percent of the total population, more than 78 percent live in dire poverty (Ringold 2003).

Throughout these countries, the Roma retreat to neighborhoods on the periphery that are unconnected to sewage systems and lack utilities and transportation alternatives. Living in such unsanitary conditions, with little health care and health basic information, they generally live 10–15 years less than non-Roma.

Few Roma children move beyond elementary school education because of poverty, low cultural valuation on education, and often severe discrimination at school (World Bank 2003). Roma school children in these countries also suffer discrimination and difficulty because they do not speak the majority language. As a result, they are described as "mentally disabled."

Rural Roma in these countries who move to towns do not qualify for unemployment or social assistance because they are not registered as residents of that town, and these exclusionary rules are replicated at the various levels of public sector governance. For instance, Roma in the Czech Republic must produce documents proving permanent residence or the absence of a criminal record for five years.

In contrast to Roma in other CEE and SEE countries, Albanian Roma have a unique form of social organization, the *fis*.[89] The key functions of the Roma *fis* are the support of individuals and communities in sustaining their livelihoods though social cohesion, trust, and solidarity.

As a social organization, however, the *fis* is subject to socioeconomic and structural change in both structure and function. This affects individual Roma as well as the community as a whole. Extensive *fis* networks played a special role during the socialist period. Social capital[90] held the *fis* together and provided its members with essential connections for finding markets and trade goods in the informal sector.

The significance of the *fis*, however, has weakened during the transition period. Dramatic socioeconomic downward trends that have occurred with Roma families have weakened the *fis*'s social organization and have worked against the close solidarity that existed between the families under socialism.

While market liberalism sparked economic uncertainty, political liberalism during the 1990s allowed Roma and Egyptian communities to achieve some gains in national and international recognition. Throughout Eastern Europe, in fact, Roma and Egyptian communities established political parties, NGOs, and newspapers, with such aims as cultural

---

89. ???
90. Social capital is discussed fully in Chapter 10.

awareness, economic development, and political representation. Shortly after the end of communist rule, several NGOs were established in Albania, including Amaro Dives, Rromani Baxt, Amaro Drom, Rromani Braxt, Disutni Albania, Alb Rrom, Roma for Integration, Rromani Kham, the Jevg Association, Nefreta, Kabaja, and Vëllazërimi.

Recently, Roma communities received a powerful boost from the European Union, because candidate countries are rushing to improve their human rights record (World Bank 2003). This offers the Albanian NGOs an opportunity to encourage the government to devise and implement measures to solve some of these problems. In doing so, the NGOs will rightfully gain the trust of their peoples.

Yet the structural capital of Roma has continued to be weak. It is significant that Albanian Roma have scarcely any representation in the government. Few are employed at the local, regional, or national administrative level, nor do they have any elected officials on any level. Without such representation, they have only limited voice to address their concerns.

Summary of Findings

Linkages and dynamics associated with social exclusion emerged from analyses presented in the areas of focus described below.

Culture

Roma and Egyptian cultures are distinct both from each other and from the majority Albanian culture.[91] Roma identified distinguishing cultural markers such as language, music, community celebrations, family ceremonies, and wickerwork. Egyptians describe their culture in terms of metalwork and music. Both Roma and Egyptians emphasized the importance of preserving these cultural markers.

However, poverty has strongly affected the ability of Roma and Egyptians to preserve these cultural markers. Poverty has contributed to strong declines in the transmission of folktales, handicraft making, and Roma and Egyptian music. Many families are too poor to hold traditional wedding ceremonies. Moreover, Roma *fis* structures and functions, which are traditional forms of social capital, are fading away.

Income and Living Conditions

Extremely poor living conditions—including lack of sanitation and other basic infrastructure—and health distinguish many "outsider" Roma and Egyptian communities from the "insider" majority population.[92] Though 7 percent of Roma and 17 percent of Egyptians have a telephone in their home, only 13 percent of Roma and 20 percent of Egyptian families have a shower or bath. Indeed, more than 40 percent of Roma and 30 percent of Egyptian families do not even have potable water in their homes. Approximately half of

---

91. For a more detailed discussion of Roma and Egyptian culture, see Chapter 3, Culture.

92. For more detailed discussions of Roma and Egyptian income and living standards, see Chapter 5, Income and Living Standards; Chapter 7, The Labor Market; and Chapter 8, Migration and Remittances.

them cannot afford to pay their electricity bills. Based on self-assessments, both groups are suffering from declining health, partly because of their inability to afford health care, and only 25 percent of Roma and 29 percent of Egyptians say that they have enough money to buy medicines. Moreover, because health care services have decreased in rural areas, many Roma there are increasingly vulnerable to declining health care.

Marriage and Family Planning

Early age at marriage and in childbearing has been the norm during the transition period, and is deemed by both groups as directly causative of increased poverty.[93] In addition, the effects of early marriage and childbearing on women include high illiteracy rates, low educational qualifications, lack of vocational skills, and separation and divorce, which all contribute to future and increased financial uncertainty and, ultimately, to social exclusion.

The majority of Roma and Egyptians do not receive formal marriage and family-planning education. Contraceptive usage is low, either because they have little knowledge of contraceptives, or husbands refuse to use male contraceptives. One consequence is that average family sizes are larger for them; the national average for Albania is 4.2 but it is 6.4 for Roma and 5.2 for Egyptians.

Education

Reportedly, 64 percent of Roma and 24 percent of Egyptians ages 7–20 have never attended school; as a result, 62 percent of Roma and 24 percent of Egyptians are illiterate. Of the majority population, with whom they must compete on the labor market, only 2 percent are illiterate.[94]

The biggest barriers to their education are related to poverty and social exclusion. Families cannot afford to pay for school books, supplies, or fees, nor to feed and clothe children sufficiently for them to attend school. Moreover, many Roma children who speak Romani exclusively at home face difficulties when they begin school. An Albanian teacher in a Roma kindergarten in Shkozet, for example, asserted that Roma children under the age of 6 cannot speak Albanian. The result is that some Roma children who struggle in classes during the first years of primary grades eventually drop out of school.

Other barriers include limited access to education facilities. In some areas, the long distance of schools from homes prevents children from attending school.

The Labor Market

Both groups bring poor health, low educational levels, and low vocational skills to the shrinking formal labor market—and largely fail.[95] While the overall national unemployment rate was around 16 percent at the end of 2002, the unemployment rate for Roma was 71 percent,

---

93. For a more detailed discussion of marriage and family planning, see Chapter 4, Marriage and Family Planning.

94. For a more detailed discussion of Roma and Egyptian education, see Chapter 6, Education.

95. For a more detailed discussion of labor issues, see Chapter 7, The Labor Market.

and for Egyptians, 67 percent.[96] Many became unemployed when state enterprises were restructured beginning in 1991.

Many face discrimination and social exclusion in the formal labor market. In fact, 30 percent of Roma, and 32 percent of Egyptians consider ethnicity as the main reason for their unemployment. Indeed there is evidence that some private sector enterprises do not hire Roma and Egyptians, or prefer to hire Albanians instead.

Facing poverty and exclusion from the formal labor market, they both turn to the informal labor market, mainly in casual work, musical performance, can and metal collection, and begging. These forms of labor provide only limited incomes to their families, and lower the odds against achievement of future economic security. While enabling many to afford some daily needs, the informal labor market nonetheless contributes to the existence of two separate groups: (a) those with steady employment, and low or medium wages and (b) those with uncertain employment prospects and extremely low wages.

Migration

When income sources from formal or informal work are insufficient to meet daily needs, both groups attempt to migrate abroad for short-term periods.[97] International migration is a poverty-coping method that allows many of their families to subsist in the short term, but it eventually leads to increased poverty and social exclusion.

Most international migrants travel illegally because they are unable to procure legal visas to host countries. The costs associated with illegal migration—such as travel to these countries and black-market visas—are high. So, international migrants can often work only in low-skilled positions that pay low wages.

Most international migrants spend remittances on basic consumption items or on paying lists[98] taken out from local shop owners. So, after international migration costs and basic consumption expenses, many international migrants end up with less money than when they started. Children who migrate abroad do not attend school, and international migrants are not enrolled in pension programs. Meanwhile, lists are increasing among them, and unemployment in Albania remains high, which forces many to continue migrating. Consequently, poverty and social exclusion continue.

Prostitution and Trafficking

Prostitution and trafficking emerge from and perpetuate social exclusion.[99] Many Roma girls and women enter prostitution to cope with poverty. For example, women in abusive marriages who wish to separate from their husbands regard prostitution as one of the few

---

96. The national unemployment figure is derived from INSTAT, 2002. Roma and Egyptian unemployment data results from the socioeconomic household questionnaires with Roma and Egyptian for the Needs Assessment (2002/03).

97. For a detailed discussion of Roma and Egyptian migration, see Chapter 8, Migration and Remittances.

98. A "list" refers to informal credit granted by a shop owner to a customer that permits a customer to take goods now and pay later. For a sample of a "list," see Appendix J.

99. For a detailed discussion of Roma and Egyptian prostitution, see Chapter 9, Prostitution and Trafficking. See also Appendix 5, for "More Voices from Albania."

exit strategies available to them, in terms of both life choices and economic survival. The effects of prostitution include decreased school attendance for young girls and young marriage ages for women—both connected to poverty. Thus, while often regarded as an escape from poverty, prostitution actually increases the poverty level of the women and their families, and contributes to further socioeconomic problems.

Among Roma, the trafficking of children is more common than among Albanians, since Roma suffer from higher rates of poverty and unemployment. However, child trafficking contributes to low education levels for children.

Social Capital

Both groups employ social capital to cope with poverty and social exclusion. It is social capital that enables them to migrate abroad and to purchase food with lists, for example.[100]

They both benefit from a wealth of cognitive social capital[101] but are weak in structural forms of social capital. However, because they are poor in structural social capital, it is particularly crucial to foster their participation in decisionmaking processes at local, regional, and national policy levels.[102] They lack effective political representation. Their existing associations are fragmented and unable to advocate their interests and needs effectively. Moreover, these associations lack the trust and rapport from the majority. Both groups will remain ill-equipped to face poverty and social exclusion if their structural social capital remains weak.

Causes of Social Exclusion Identified by Roma and Egyptians

A clear pattern of social exclusion has made Roma and Egyptians outsiders, with limited access to aspects of life available to the insider majority population: employment, education, and infrastructure, for example. The ability to express their cultural markers, another important factor in social exclusion, is limited. Most attribute these forms of social exclusion to poverty and discrimination.

Poverty

Most forms of social exclusion, according to both groups, stem from poverty. They, like Albanians (De Soto and others 2002), have a multidimensional understanding of poverty. For them, poverty is understood in terms of the inability to afford food, clothing, and shelter; emotional stress; and the feeling of being excluded from social and economic life. They also understood poverty as feelings of vulnerability and insecurity and the inability to continue family traditions.

---

100. For detailed discussions of social capital and its forms among the Roma and Egyptians, see Chapters 8 (Migration and Remittances) and 10 (Social Capital).

101. Cognitive social capital refers to intangible values, norms, and attitudes that govern behavior.

102. Structural social capital refers to formal or informal associations or networks that facilitate collective action.

Definitions of Relative Poverty

Both groups agreed that the ability to afford food, clothing, and shelter, in terms of both quantity and quality, was a main indicator of social exclusion. Moreover, levels of social exclusion varied in part according to a family's ability to afford material needs.

To compare and contrast, these families were categorized into four socioeconomic levels, according to their ability to afford material needs: very poor, poor, non-poor, and relatively prosperous.

Families that "cannot afford to buy food" or that "cannot afford daily necessities" were categorized as very poor, while families that "can afford food, but cannot afford clothing" were categorized as poor. Then, on one hand, families that "can afford daily necessities" were categorized as non-poor. On the other, families that "have enough money to save" were categorized as relatively prosperous. Table 11.2 shows the breakdown of those categories, and Figure 11.1 shows the distribution of those categories among Roma, Egyptians, and Albanians.

Table 11.2. Self-Assessment of Family's Socioeconomic Conditions			
Assessment of Socioeconomic Conditions	% that selected this assessment		Socioeconomic Category
	Roma	Egyptians	
Cannot afford food	40	41	Very Poor
Cannot afford daily necessities	35	29	Very Poor
Can afford food, but not clothing	7	9	Poor
Can afford daily necessities	14	16	Non-Poor
Have enough money to save	4	5	Relatively Prosperous
Total	100	100	

Source: Socioeconomic household questionnaires with Roma and Egyptians for the Needs Assessment, 2002/03

Compared to the majority population (29 percent; De Soto and others 2002), the percentage of Roma (75 percent) and Egyptian (70 percent) families categorized as very poor is high. According to self-assessments, their families fall into two extremes: very poor and poor families, which together represent 80 percent of all families, and relatively prosperous or well-off families, which represent 5 percent of all families. Very poor and poor families face higher levels of social exclusion, because they are less capable of affording daily needs, but also because they are less likely to participate in and govern processes that affect their individual livelihoods, such as employment and education.

Characteristics of Very Poor Families

The average family size of very poor Roma and Egyptians (Roma, 6.4; Egyptians, 5.3) is higher than the average family size for both groups.[103] However, most of their families belong to this group. Their main difficulties are a shortage of food; poor housing conditions; and lack of a

---

103. The average family size is 6.4 for Roma and 5.2 for Egyptians.

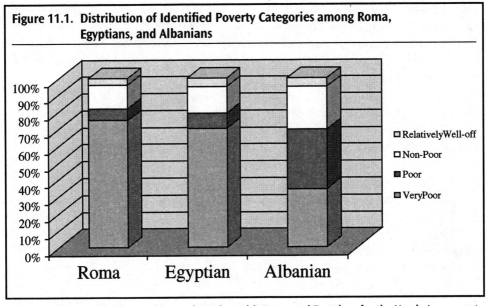

Figure 11.1. **Distribution of Identified Poverty Categories among Roma, Egyptians, and Albanians**

Source: Socioeconomic household questionnaires with Roma and Egyptians for the Needs Assessment, 2002/03.

sewage system, potable water, and electricity. These families indicated that these problems have worsened since 1990, and more than 90 percent stated that the main cause of this deterioration is unemployment. Approximately one-half expressed that their main problems have worsened since 1990 because of a lack of interest from the state, while one-third stated that it was their ethnicity. Main income sources are casual work, self-employment, pension benefits, *ndihmë ekonomike,* begging, and, for Egyptians, wages. Very few migrate abroad.

Most report that their health has worsened since 1990, and malnourishment is identified as the major factor in their declining health. Food consumption is low, and diets are composed mainly of bread, pasta, and rice. They consume meat, milk, butter, and fruit once every two weeks, and eggs and cheese only once a week. Some families in rural areas do consume home-grown vegetables regularly, but both city and rural Roma and Egyptians may also go without any food at all for several days a month.

Very poor families purchase with list in one or more shops. Most of the children of these families do not attend school because they cannot afford books and school supplies, or because they are forced to contribute to family income through work.

Living conditions for most families have deteriorated during transition, partly as a result of an increase in family sizes and increased poverty, and because many have sold apartments which they had owned during the socialist period. Most of these families live in shacks or dilapidated houses with small surface areas (Roma, 45m²; Egyptians, 41m²). Most families own a television (Roma, 64 percent, Egyptians, 77 percent), while few families own a separate bed for each family member.

Characteristics of Poor Families

The main difficulties identified by poor Roma and Egyptian families are similar to those identified by very poor families: lack of food, potable water, and electricity, and poor health, housing, and road conditions. Most of these families indicated that their difficulties have worsened because of unemployment and neglect by the state. Most income for poor families comes from casual work and self-employment for Roma and wages for Egyptians. Unlike very poor families, another important income source for poor Roma families is income from migration abroad.

The average family size of poor families (Roma, 6.9; Egyptian, 5) is higher than the average family size for all Roma, but lower than for all Egyptians.

Like the very poor, their diets consist mostly of bread, vegetables, pasta, and rice. Eggs and cheese are consumed two to three times per week, while meat is consumed once per week. One-quarter of poor families may have nothing to eat for several days during the month. Poor families associate malnutrition and stress with their declining health.

Average home surface area is 48m^2 for Roma and 58m^2 for Egyptian families. Most families belonging to this group own a television (Roma, 86 percent; Egyptians, 93 percent) stove, refrigerator (Roma, 55 percent; Egyptians, 70 percent) tape recorder (Roma, 64 percent; Egyptians, 57 percent), and in more than 50 percent of all households, there is a separate bed for each family member.

Characteristics of Non-Poor Families

Those from non-poor families indicated that the main difficulties they face are a lack of electricity, and access to potable water, lack of sewage network connection, and poor road conditions. Non-poor families explain that the causes of their difficulties are unemployment, low education levels, and, like their very poor neighbors, disinterest from the state. Main income sources for these families come from self-employment,[104] casual work, international migration income, and, for Egyptians, wages.

Although 54 percent of non-poor Roma families also identified lack of food as a major problem, they indicated that their situation has improved since 1990. Their diets are more balanced than the diets of poor and very poor families. Non-poor families consume meat, milk, cheese, butter, rice, pasta, and fruits two or three times a week, vegetables almost daily, and sweets or desserts twice a week. However, these families still purchase food with list (Roma, 52 percent, Egyptians, 38 percent).

The number of families whose health status has worsened is smaller for non-poor families than for very poor and poor families. Non-poor families associate poor health with old age, stress, and an inability to pay for medical treatments.

The pon-poor average family size (Roma, 6; Egyptians, 5.1) is lower than average family size for both.

Living conditions are better for non-poor than for very poor and poor families. Average home surface area is 81m^2 for Roma and 70m^2 for Egyptian families. Many or a large majority of families own a television (Roma, 94 percent; 100 percent, Egyptians), a refrigerator (Roma, 72 percent; Egyptians, 94 percent), and a washing machine (Roma, 40 percent; Egyptians, 75 percent). Some non-poor families (Roma, 19 percent; Egyptians, 16 percent) own an automobile. However, not all families own a bed for each family member.

---

104. Self-employment includes trade in used clothes and can and metal collection.

Characteristics of Relatively Prosperous Families

Relatively prosperous families represent only 4–5 percent of families. This group can afford to meet all essential daily needs and to save money. Relatively prosperous families consider that their main difficulties are a lack of connection to a sewage or water network or an electricity grid, and poor road conditions. However, many of them own villas or apartments with large surface areas ($162m^2$ for Roma and $96m^2$ for Egyptians). They own cars, refrigerators, electric stoves, televisions, washing machines, stereos, and cellular phones.

These families indicated that they associate their major difficulties with state indifference. Main income sources for relatively prosperous Roma are formal business, particularly the wholesale trade of new and used clothes, and self-employment, while for Egyptians, self-employment and wages.

In spite of their relative comfort, relatively prosperous Roma and Egyptian families experience financial uncertainty and stress about the future, which they link to their ethnicity. In addition, these families do not live among other Roma and Egyptians, but in mixed neighborhoods.

These families consume bread, vegetables, eggs, dairy products, meat, fruits, and sweets several times per week. Most in this category aver that they have good or average health and that health care service has somewhat improved since 1990. In contrast to poor and very poor families, the main cause of illness for this category is old age.

Their average family size (Roma, 6, Egyptians, 4.7) of the relatively prosperous group is lower than the average family size for both, but still higher than the average family size at the national level (4.2).

Factors Contributing to Uncertainty and Vulnerability

In addition to food, clothes, and shelter, Roma and Egyptians also linked poverty to a feeling of insecurity, vulnerability, and the inability to continue cultural traditions for a number of reasons.

The inability to sustain traditions such as weddings, births, or funeral ceremonies deepens their feeling of isolation and exclusion. Most blame low incomes for the weakening of their cultural traditions. Arjan, an Egyptian in Korça, illustrated: "I don't have any friends. I hang out with my brothers and in-laws . . . because to hang out with friends, you need to sit at a café and drink coffee. But I don't have any money." Xhemal, an unemployed Roma from Maliq (Korça), explained that he was unable to organize a wedding for his son: "I really wanted to have a wedding, because that day is remembered for the rest of your life. During the 1980s, when my oldest son was born, I invited 10 friends over for a celebration. They came and congratulated me and brought gifts. But weddings now depend on your economic conditions. So, being unable to have a wedding, my son 'kidnapped' his fiancée and brought her to our home."

Social Exclusion at the Institutional Level

With limited resources and poverty among the majority population, many Roma and Egyptians are excluded from equal access to public institutions, including state assistance offices and municipal and communal governments, the legal system, and schools.

Local and Communal Government. Like many Albanians, Roma and Egyptians expressed the inability to voice their needs to their local and communal-level governments. For, in contrast to Albanians, few are represented in government, and fewer still in government administration. According to the head of a Roma association in Korça, "You won't find any one of us in local administration."

Consequently, many complained about social exclusion by state assistance employees that resulted in the late distribution of state assistance. While the distribution of state assistance is also a problem for many Albanians, the Roma and Egyptians discussed how they feel that they receive lower-quality service in general from state assistance employees. A Roma in Elbasan explained that his local commune "gets a lot of assistance, but they don't give it to us." The local *kryeplak* added: "I go to the commune as their *kryeplak* to deal with the issue, and they tell me to 'get out of here, you're a Gypsy.' "

Some local officials did appear to be unresponsive to the needs of local Roma and Egyptians. When asked to explain high poverty levels among local Roma, one mayor of a town in Fier stated: "Well, maybe that's all they want out of life." Moreover, "There's no reason for them to be poorer than us because we are equal citizens by law and by land, but it all depends on the way they manage their lives."

In the cases in which public officials appeared to be responsive to their Roma and Egyptian constituencies, both groups felt more included in public life. The mayor of the city of Delvina, who in an interview appeared to be very familiar with issues affecting them, is a perfect example of what a public official taking a personal initiative can accomplish. Most Roma in the city of Delvina explained that the mayor had constructed roads, provided running water and electricity, and was even someone who "cared" about Roma. In giving Roma their due, rather than neglect, Roma felt acknowledged and included in public life.

The Legal System

Both groups have described a sense of exclusion from the legal system in Albania, in terms of discrimination during court proceedings, but also because they didn't understand the legal processes. Exclusion from the judicial system has especially affected land ownership and property rights.

Many in several districts told of irregularities in land distribution procedures that were implemented during the transition period. Erjon, an Egyptian in Kruja, explained that: "When the reform was enacted, they gave me eight dynym of land, but then the owner showed up and threatened me, and told me to not work or harvest the land."

Exclusion from the Albanian Legal System: 15 Families in Pogradec

"The legal system does not treat Roma as it should. If a Roma is involved in a trial, he doesn't know where to turn for information concerning his rights, since there is no public information office. To find out his rights, he would need to spend a lot of money. There are cases in which Roma involved in court trials are threatened with long sentences. When a Roma is involved in a property dispute, he never wins. The most recent case took place two weeks ago in Pogradec, when a group of 15 Roma families submitted a complaint that a former owner of the land they have been living on since 1998 is threatening to evict them from their apartments. The families have documentation from the national homeowners agency that their land used to be state-owned, and was given to them by the state. After the complaint was submitted, the owner purchased all 15 apartments at a price of L2 million, or US$1,500. The Roma families refused to leave their apartments and sued the former owner. The former owner won the first trial, and the appeal was held in the absence of the Roma families, which the owner also won. Prior to a second appeal, I sent a statement out to the Helsinki Committee, OSCE, and Gazeta Shqiptare, and I hired a lawyer to issue a formal complaint to the District Attorney and the second appeals court, because the Enforcement Office had decided to execute the first court's verdict to evict the families from their apartments."

Of course, many Albanians have also experienced problems with the government's land distribution procedures. Legal ambiguities have resulted in court battles between individuals claiming to own property titles dating back to the interwar period, and individuals who received the same properties directly from the state following 1991. In such cases, legal processes are lengthy and complicated and require a general knowledge of the Albanian legal system and access to a lawyer. Roma and Egyptians involved in these disputes often give up their land without attempting to settle claims in court, because they are unfamiliar with legal procedures, cannot afford legal costs, or feel that Albanian courts are biased against them. Finally, they believe that trying to settle a dispute in court has no chance for success.

Law Enforcement

In some areas, Roma described mistreatment or neglect by law enforcement authorities. This was especially the case in Fushë Kruja, where 89 percent of Roma evaluated police work as "poor." According to Ervehe, a Roma in Fushë Kruja, "The police behave very badly in this neighborhood. When they catch you, they beat you, even on the streets. Even when you're not guilty of anything, they beat you." Mistreatment results in lower-quality law enforcement service for some Roma families. According to a leader of a Roma association in Tirana, "Compared to Albanian families, there are . . . more cases of mistreatment by police towards Roma when it comes to handling or solving the same problem. The way I see it, this happens because the police consider Roma a group of people that can be mistreated more easily, or a group from which, with less pressure, they can get bribes."

Schools

The two groups give mixed reviews of the treatment of Roma and Egyptian school children. As mentioned in the chapter on education, parents and children described different forms of frequent mistreatment by teachers in some localities, such as Korça and Tirana. Anecdotal evidence reinforces the notion that many are made to sit at the back of classrooms. One report (Taho 2002) on Roma in Albania noted that Roma parents complain that their children are "being beaten by non-Roma children and that they are being discriminated against, even by the teachers." However, most admit that discrimination by teachers is not widespread, and the treatment of school children is dependent on the attitudes of individual teachers.

A general problem in Albanian education is its lack of multicultural content. Social science textbooks that are used in public schools primarily reflect the experiences of Albanians, and Roma and Egyptians are absent from these textbooks.[105] A report on Roma in Albania concurred: "[Roma] suffer from the official refusal of the majority to recognize their culture and traditions. . . ." (Taho 2002). Albanian, Roma, and Egyptian students are denied the opportunity to learn about non-Albanian cultures within their country, and Roma and Egyptians feel more excluded from the Albanian education curriculum. According to the principal of a kindergarten in Gjirokastra, "It would be good to teach the history of Roma, their characteristics, and other things. I, for example, am an older person and I didn't know anything about the history of Roma, and I felt bad about the discrimination committed against this part of society. If the state were to support them, there wouldn't be a [bad] reaction from the general population."

Social Exclusion and Discrimination

About 25 percent of Roma and Egyptians believe that discrimination is another factor in social exclusion and that their ethnicity was a cause of it.

Some studies of Roma in Eastern and Central Europe,[106] while describing high levels of anti-Roma discrimination, also point to many positive examples of coexistence. These examples commonly occur where there is a high level of interaction between Roma and the majority populations. A UNDP report claimed that " 'neighborhood' relations and contacts intermediated by children seem to dominate interactions" between Roma and majority populations.[107] Moreover: "Inter-community interactions were reported to be higher than expected, reflecting inter-group contacts and support determined by survival needs. Interactions between the poor Roma and non-Roma are, however, more frequent, which suggests the existence or emergence of class (rather than ethnic) solidarity."[108]

A study of Roma in Slovakia (World Bank 2002a) reiterated the efficacy of geographic integration: "In integrated communities, the level of contacts and interactions between Roma and non-Roma was naturally higher and relationships were reportedly smoother." The study also suggested that negative attitudes toward Roma were based on stereotypes, rather than direct experience.

Interaction between members of all groups in most districts is frequent, except in poor urban areas. Only some localities, such as Fushë Kruja, Shkodra, and some Tirana neighborhoods, are completely segregated from Albanians. As the studies above concluded, relations between Albanians and these groups tend to improve with increased interaction.

---

105. The teaching of "minority issues" on the subject of interethnic relations is generally limited to two or three hours of class time per school year.

106. See UNDP (2002); "Poverty and Welfare of Roma in the Slovak Republic," World Bank (2002); World Bank.

107. UNDP (2002), p. 4.

108. UNDP (2002), pp. 4, 5.

However, the benefits of frequent interaction are limited. Even though, in many rural areas where interaction among all groups[109] is frequent, Roma and Egyptians felt that they commonly face discrimination.

Perceptions of Roma and Egyptians about Discrimination

More than half of Roma and Egyptians said that they have experienced discrimination because of their ethnicity. In fact, 34 percent of Roma and 30 percent of Egyptians experience discrimination often, as shown in figure 11.2, below. Levels of perceived discrimination vary by district:

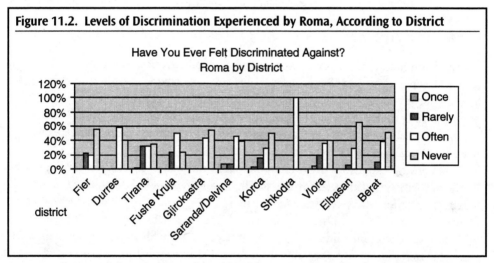

Figure 11.2. **Levels of Discrimination Experienced by Roma, According to District**

Source: Socioeconomic household questionnaires with Roma and Egyptians for the Needs Assessment (2002/03).

In general, Roma in poor, segregated neighborhoods such as those of Shkodra and Fushë Kruja experience higher levels of discrimination at the hands of the majority population. In contrast, more Roma in central and southern districts, except Delvina, claimed "never" to have experienced discrimination than Roma in northern districts. This is to the result of the higher proportion of rural populations in central and southern districts, which are less segregated than urban and rural populations. However, even in Durrës, where most Roma live in rural areas, levels of perceived discrimination are high. Levels of perceived discrimination among Egyptians also varied by district. Figure 11.3 illustrates levels of discrimination against Egyptians, by district.

Like the Roma, Egyptians in Shkodra claimed that they had often experienced discrimination. "Here, as soon as you go out, they curse you and offend you," stated an Egyptian

---

109. Some Egyptians are physically indistinguishable from Albanians. Anti-Egyptian discrimination during casual interaction involves dark-skinned Egyptians only.

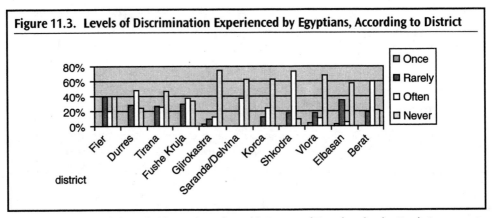

Figure 11.3. Levels of Discrimination Experienced by Egyptians, According to District

Source: Socioeconomic household questionnaires with Roma and Egyptians for the Needs Assessment (2002/03).

woman from Shkodra. However, more than half of all Egyptians surveyed in Gjirokastra, Korça, Delvina, Vlora, and Elbasan claimed never to have experienced discrimination. Lower levels of perceived discrimination among Egyptians compared to Roma can be explained in part by the fact that some Egyptians are indistinguishable in appearance from Albanians. In addition, in districts such as Gjirokastra and Vlora, Egyptians are more integrated with the majority population than those in other districts.

Both groups experience discrimination mainly through a sense of inferiority projected by the majority population. According to Elmaz, an Egyptian in Korça, "We feel discriminated against; they tell me condescendingly that I am Egyptian. They treat us very differently from the others . . . Nor do they give us work." Both associate this form of discrimination with their socioeconomic situation. Arjan, an Egyptian from Shkodra, explained that: "It is a fact that this community is separate from the majority population, discriminated against. Egyptians are seen as inferior. Being looked upon by society as inferior, this community has remained underdeveloped."

Most discrimination comes in the form of rude behavior and verbal offense (79 percent for Roma; 89 percent for Egyptians). However, more Roma (12 percent) than Egyptians (5 percent) claimed to have been refused service. Also, more Roma (10 percent) than Egyptians (5 percent) claimed to have experienced physical abuse or violence because of ethnicity.

Perceptions of Albanians about Roma and Egyptians

Albanians who live or work near these minorities have mixed attitudes about them. Among their reactions, 49 percent perceived them to be "hard-working," while only 20 percent perceived them to be "lazy." And while 27 percent of families described their neighbors and coworkers as honorable, only 8 percent described them as untrustworthy. The most common negative perceptions held by Albanians were that Roma and Egyptians were "drunks" (45 percent), "noisy" (35 percent), and "uncultured" (28 percent). Table 11.3 depicts Albanian perceptions of Roma and Egyptians.

Table 11.3. Albanian Perceptions of Roma/Egyptians	
Hard-working	49%
Drunk	45%
Noisy	35%
Uncultured	28%
Honorable	27%
Clever	21%
Lazy	20%
Dirty	16%
Family-oriented	15%
Untrustworthy	8%
Intelligent	8%
Clean	5%
Wealthy	3%
Unemployed	3%

Source: Socioeconomic household questionnaires with Albanians for the Needs Assessment (2002/03). *Note:* 459 Albanian families were surveyed. Survey respondents were allowed to select up to three options. Results are percentages of total Albanian families surveyed having a given perception about Roma and Egyptians.

Albanians who live or work near Roma and Egyptians confirm levels of discrimination described by both. Forty-four percent of Albanian families agreed that they would not accept their children's Roma friends, while 40 percent would not allow their children to have Egyptian friends. In addition, 47 percent of Albanians would not live next to Roma, and 40 percent, next to Egyptians. To bolster that assertion, 39 percent of Albanians surveyed would not accept working with Roma, and 26 percent, with Egyptians.

A clear line exists between acceptable and unacceptable forms of interaction. Albanians who frequently encounter Roma and Egyptians limit their levels of contact to casual and "passing acquaintanceship." Taho made the distinction between "quite friendly" relations between Roma and Albanians in "rural, traditional, and 'nonprofit' life," and less amicable relations between the two groups in "urban, modern, and profit-making society" (Taho 2002).

The consequences of limited interaction can lead to increasing social exclusion. For example, at a kindergarten in Gjirokastra that holds classes for 75 Roma and Albanian children, teachers were forced to add Albanian-only classes after some Albanian parents complained about integrated classrooms.

Ways of Addressing Social Exclusion According to Roma and Egyptians

Both groups were asked to identify ways to address social exclusion in Albania. The most common suggestions were:

▨ Create more jobs (Roma, 96 percent; Egyptians, 90 percent).
▨ Provide ways to attend universities (Roma, 91 percent; Egyptians, 94 percent).
▨ Hire them to work in state administration offices (Roma 90 percent; Egyptians, 86 percent).
▨ Hire them to work in local administration offices (Roma 88 percent; Egyptians, 85 percent).

Responses reflected some of the difficulties both groups described as the barriers to escaping poverty and social exclusion, such as unemployment and low education levels, but also the expressed desire to be represented in government agencies. According to them, their employment in local and state government offices would make these agencies appear more accessible to them, which would enhance their sense of social inclusion.

They also expressed a need to have their own political representatives at the local, communal, and state levels. According to an Egyptian leader in Vlora, "The main threat that we face is a lack of participation in [public] institutions. This barrier results from racial discrimination and intolerance. We represent a large community in Vlora. But who's going to convey our problems to the municipal council? Only through our own government representatives would it be possible to solve even a few of our problems. Having government representatives would change something." An informal leader in Fushë Kruja added: "We need to have a representative in Parliament, because one or two members would do a lot of things; they would raise their voices in the defense of our rights."

More Roma (81 percent) than Egyptians (56 percent) expressed their belief that supporting cultural identity was one way of eliminating social exclusion. Arben, a community activist in Korça, explained: "Our aim is for the education and integration of the Roma people. With integration, I mean cooperation with the other part of society . . . We don't want to lose our Roma identity, but to preserve its best qualities. We are going to advance in society with the name Roma, without ever losing our name." More Roma than Egyptians responded that the support of cultural identity was important, possibly because more Egyptians associated themselves with Albanian culture.

CHAPTER 12

Social Inclusion

Recommendations and Policy Implications

The Roma and the Egyptians have been identified as the poorest and most marginalized population groups in Albania. They are frequently denied access to education, employment, information, participation, voice, and justice. The result is that they suffer from low educational qualifications and vocational skills, high unemployment and underemployment, and limited access to public goods and services. Then, they are excluded because Albanian public and private institutions are not transparent and their organizations are not accountable to them. According to several studies, including this assessment, Roma and Egyptians have been affected particularly negatively by the social change during transition because they are excluded from access to governance and decisionmaking processes in key aspects that affect their livelihoods. For the majority today, social exclusion has become a part of their daily lives, and multiple institutional barriers obstruct their development opportunities in Albania.[110]

Social inclusion is defined as "the removal of institutional barriers and the enhancement of incentives to increase the access of diverse individuals and groups to public good and services, and development opportunities."[111] The challenge now is to address their social exclusion and to develop policies and programs that foster their social inclusion.

Therefore, within the framework of the Albanian National Strategy for Socio-Economic Development (NSSED), the government of Albania has requested a Needs Assessment to

---

110. UNDP (2000). "Albanian Human Development Report"; Dudwick, N, Shahriari, H. 2000. "Education in Albania: Changing Attitudes and Expectations," The World Bank; De Soto, H, Gordon, P, Gedeshi, I, Sinoimeri, Z, (2002). "Poverty in Albania. A Qualitative Assessment," Washington DC: The World Bank; UNDP (2002). "Avoiding the Dependency Trap." Bratislava: The World Bank.

111. World Bank (2002), "Social Development Department. Social Analysis Sourcebook: Incorporating Social Dimension into Bank-supported Projects." Washington DC. The World Bank.

gather information on Roma and Egyptian needs for and challenges to sustainable liveli-hoods. The government has further asked for advice on how better to consider these needs and challenges in the national efforts for poverty reduction and social inclusion, and for meeting some of the EU recommendations on ethnic minorities.

In this effort, tailoring policies for different local problems is key. The following rec-ommendations provide a wide spectrum of possible public choices. These could be taken individually, in combination, or in sequence. Implementation is possible at the local, dis-trict, or national level, exclusively, combined, or incrementally. Realization of recommen-dations could further draw on the support and partnership of a variety of actors that include different government organizations, NGOs, Roma and Egyptian community orga-nizations, the private sector, and international partners.

According to the collected empirical data, the causes of poverty and social exclusion for Roma and Egyptians in Albania are lack of education, employment, and basic infrastructure. The symptoms of poverty and social exclusion are seen in their informal sector activities, migration, aid dependence, and prostitution, which they employ as coping strategies in their daily lives. Their overall approach is to use cognitive social capital, evident in different kinds of trust relationships. However, while these coping strategies help to sustain their livelihoods at the edges of mainstream society, these equally constitute further constraints and barriers to their inclusion as de facto traps into poverty and social exclusion. Within this context, effective policy recommendations must address the core of the problem, that is, the multiple causes of poverty and social exclusion, not simply the symptoms. The comprehensive iden-tification of their multidimensional poverty and social exclusion, meaning the various con-straints to their inclusion, serves as an opportunity for policymakers to engage in a dialogue to devise policies and actions that will truly overcome the barriers to their socioeconomic, cultural, institutional, and political inclusion into Albanian society.

The analytical framework that guided the study, can be found in Appendix L.

Access to Public Goods and Services

Both groups frequently lack access to public goods and services, primarily the public edu-cation system, water and sanitation networks, adequate housing, and health care.

Education

In the eyes of many Albanian, Roma, and Egyptian parents, the long-term benefits of edu-cation are uncertain compared to the immediate benefits of removing their children from school to fulfill family duties and contribute to the household income in the informal sec-tor. Improving education levels for Roma and Egyptians in the long term requires solutions that address Albania's education system as a whole.

The lack of educational qualifications and limited access to educational facilities are primary consequences of, and reasons for, poverty and social exclusion. As a direct result, there are major implications for individuals, communities, and the economic, social, and institutional development of the country as a whole.

Unlike the Egyptians, whose own language has been lost and who therefore speak Albanian, the majority of Roma children suffer from lack of access to education because they face difficulties with the Albanian language in first grade. Although Roma children learn the Romani language from their parents at home, it is not formal language training, which is necessary to overcome illiteracy. However, being able to master the Albanian language is a prerequisite for Roma children to follow the curriculum in public schools, and is an important long-term method for creating possibilities for Roma students to attain educational qualifications, and vocational skills.

Policy choices could include preschools, where Roma learn Albanian in tailored language courses that are taught by Roma teachers. In areas with large concentrations of Roma, public schools should provide two to three hours of class instruction in Romani by a qualified Roma teacher.

Furthermore, the lack of school facilities for physically and mentally challenged children was identified. In contrast to current practice, policies are needed that provide for facilities and equipment in public schools for physically challenged children, and special-needs schools and facilities for mentally challenged children. More and improved schools and facilities are required, and their geographical dispersion across Albania is needed.

Parents and children both described the impediments to class participation. Among them is reported frequent mistreatment by teachers in some localities, such as Korça and Tirana. In these areas, more Roma and Egyptian students are made to sit at the back of classrooms, and receive punishment from their teachers more frequently than white students. Policies to create inclusive and participatory teaching by qualified teachers should be developed and implemented. To effect this, one option would be to train teachers not only to provide technical knowledge, but also to meet the needs of all pupils equally. Training in their cultural values and more would raise teachers' awareness of the different needs of their pupils, and provide them with the qualifications to address these needs. This should also be true for both public and special-needs schools for physically and mentally challenged children.

Classes open to all could include the history and culture of the Roma and Egyptian peoples. This could increase a respect for diversity at public schools, and also raise awareness among Roma, Egyptian, and Albanian children about their respective backgrounds and ways of life.

Weak government capacity impedes the realization of the eight-year-minimum compulsory education. Policies that support the government in implementing the education law could be designed so that parents who receive education grants or scholarships for their children but who do not send them to school would be ineligible for future support. International partners can support the government in strengthening existing and building further capacity at the central and local levels.

Lack of access to education based on income-poverty could be addressed with free access to school services, facilities, and amenities. This would support Roma and those Egyptian households that cannot afford to send their children to school because of limited financial means to pay for school books, clothes, or other school charges such as meals, or the use of education facilities. Humanitarian aid in the form of food, clothes, and basic amenities could also be provided to their very poorest families, conditional upon their children's regular school attendance.

Making secondary and higher or university education accessible could be addressed through specific scholarships, conditional upon central and local government capacity to establish, administer, and monitor the scholarship and grants schemes.

Frequently, lack of vocational skills leads to social exclusion. Public schools could provide vocational training courses that are tailored to the geographical or sectoral demands of the labor market. Businesses could offer business fairs, open houses, in-house visits, or short- or long-term internships for Roma and Egyptian trainees to help them choose a suitable future employment sector and business, as well as ease their transition into later working life.

One of these solutions would be to promote and provide vocational training, where qualifications are tailored to the demands of the respective geographical or sectoral labor market to open greater formal employment opportunities for all Albanians. A concerted effort among the government, NGOs, and the private sector is needed to accomplish this goal.

A mentoring program could help these disadvantaged pupils and their parents to recognize the long-term benefits of educational qualifications and vocational skills. Mentors such as students at secondary schools and universities, teachers, trainees, or public and private sector specialists and professionals from all walks of life would act as examples for pupils, sharing their personal educational development experiences and future aspirations.

Water, Sanitation, and Housing

The majority of Roma and Egyptians live in extremely poor living conditions with limited access to or lack of potable and household-use water supply, sanitary facilities, health care, electricity, heating, and adequate housing. Lack of infrastructure was cited as a pervasive problem. Limited access to or exclusion from the public water and sanitation network has major implications for health, and poor health was identified as one of the main reasons for absence of children at school or employees at work, chronic severe illnesses, and high morbidity rates. Very poor Roma and, to a lesser extent, Egyptians, live in housing conditions that do not meet the internationally accepted standards for health and hygiene. Policy changes could provide the necessary access to public water supply, sanitation and electricity networks by ensuring, that where infrastructure exists, these services are actually provided. For families who live outside of the formal water supply, sanitation systems, and electricity grid and are not yet connected to these systems, the government could better promote the expansion of these respective networks and service providers with the support of the private sector and international partners. Concerted efforts among the Government, the private sector, and international partners can address these issues.

More poor Roma and Egyptians also live in very crowded, dilapidated, inadequate housing lacking even the basic amenities. Public policy changes could include the provision of building materials and resources for home construction for these homeless at low or no cost. Basic humanitarian aid, such as beds—a frequently identified need—could be provided to very poor and large families.

Health

Many in these groups have limited access to public health services because they lack the necessary financial means to pay for in- and outpatient treatment. Policy choices could include the free provision of basic medical treatment, such as vaccinations, medical checkups, and treatment for illnesses.

Frequently, however, Roma and, to some degree, Egyptians referred to lack of access to health care based on discrimination against them by medical personnel. They cited the need to pay for extra charges for treatment or consultations. The government must develop policies that identify, monitor, and act upon the misuse of public service provision. Illegal surcharges for medical treatment must be eliminated, and the offending personnel made accountable. The government could draw on the assistance of international partners with experience in countering this offensive practice.

Lack of access to health services is also tied to geographical distance. A large number of Roma and some Egyptian communities are located in remote geographical areas far from the nearest health facility. Possible policies could focus on outreach activities with provision of basic medical services and treatment and personnel in remote areas free of charge.

Since many in these two groups do not use health facilities because they are unaware that their medical conditions require treatment, policies could focus on teaching an understanding of basic health conditions that do require professional attention. Respective education and raising awareness could be provided in health centers and schools, or by medical personnel that travel to the different communities.

State Assistance

The government provides state assistance in the form of economic assistance (*ndihmë ekonomike*), retirement benefits (pensions), unemployment benefits, and disability payments. Currently, too many are excluded from receiving different types of state assistance or from receiving this assistance as long as is necessary. Policy options could include welfare reforms for state assistance covering general eligibility, actual provision, and its duration and reliability. These changes will have a great impact on the very poor, their families, and, in fact, entire communities. For instance, currently, eligibility for assistance is conditional on the actual presence of the male head of household at local social security offices to collect monthly benefits. In numerous cases, however, long-term unemployment in Albania forces many poor Roma to migrate abroad for work. As a result of the high financial and physical risks, most international migrants must remain abroad for extensive periods of time. One policy option that would solve this problem would be to allow economic assistance to be collected by another designated family member, regardless of his or her status as the head of the household.

The majority of these who are unemployed long term identified the lack of access to unemployment benefits as a symptom of social exclusion. At present, only those unemployed less than one year are able to receive benefits. However, because long-term unemployment is a frequent condition in these communities, the benefits run out before families can gain any kind of stable employment. Reforms extending the duration of eligibility for unemployment benefits are crucial. Policy changes could include a time-scaled benefit system, in which benefits would be scaled down over an extended time period and cut only after this extended time.

Market Opportunities and Employment

For the majority, the lack of market opportunities and employment is linked to social exclusion. Changing demands of the labor market during the transition forces them into unemployment, migration, or prostitution to cope with poverty and social exclusion.

Labor Market

The labor market has been identified as one of the primary consequences of, and reasons for, poverty and social exclusion. For both groups, limited employment opportunities, frequent or long-term unemployment, and underemployment have characterized their employment during transition.

Both Roma and Egyptians have particular skill in producing handicrafts. As a result of the restructuring of former state-owned enterprises in handicrafts, and the general decline in demand for these products, policy options could be to develop existing and create new local, national, and international markets for handicrafts. In collaboration with the private sector and international partners, the government could organize trade fairs and exhibitions to promote handicrafts. Furthermore, since both are very skilled in musical performances, policy could further advance the already existing market at the local, national, and international levels.

A number of Roma and some Egyptians referred to their skills mismatch to the labor market as another reason for social exclusion. The value of their educational qualification and vocational skills has decreased during transition. As a result, their educational and vocational skills do not meet the demands of the present labor market. Thus, they are forced into the informal sector, where they find low wages, job insecurity, and high vulnerability to social exclusion. Policies should focus on vocational training of skills and qualifications that are needed in the labor market, and for jobs and locations where employment opportunities exist. This requires the joint efforts of the government and the private sector. International partners could equally provide assistance. For instance, in extremely poor localities, the government could encourage the private sector to hire local Roma and Egyptians with tax incentives or copayments to social security benefits for these employees.

Lack of access to the formal market pushes the majority of Roma into the informal sector. Their income comes mainly from informal work, casual work, or self-employment. The government, private sector, and international partners could elaborate policies to improve the formal business environment to attract investment and thus improve formal employment opportunities. Specific policies could promote the creation, viability, and sustainability of small and medium-size enterprises.

The lack of market and employment opportunities for many Roma and, to a lesser extent, Egyptians compels them to retreat into internal and international migration as a strategy for survival. In the short term, in-cash, or in-kind income and remittances from migration support their families as well as the migrant. In the long term, however, migration remains a poverty-coping mechanism. It does not allow the migrant or migrant families to break out of the poverty cycle, because income and remittances are not invested in Albania. At present, there is little investment opportunity, but policy changes could improve Albania's investment climate by creating a business environment that attracts the national or international private sector. Policies should be tailored to specific growth sectors and geographical locations with prospective industries. The active role of the private sector is crucial, and partnership with national authorities and international donors would be particularly useful. Increased demand for a steady workforce and supply of necessary employment opportunities would lessen the need for these groups to turn to migration.

Furthermore, migration and remittances are often tied to seasonal work that, in the case of international migration, involves high risks. Without the financial means to purchase official visas, many international migrants are forced to obtain visas at lower rates on the informal market or travel without one. This makes international migrants vulnerable during the illegal, long, and dangerous trip, but also in the host country, where lack of a visa limits their work to the informal sector with its low wages and unsafe working conditions. In addition, internal and international migrants working in the informal sector are not enrolled in social security schemes. If migrants cannot travel because of illness or old age, they do not earn income, are not eligible for state assistance, and face increased poverty as soon as this survival strategy is no longer available to them. Public choices would have to address the issues of visas and work permits through international agreements. State assistance could be provided to migrants if their status were changed from informal seekers of work to formal migrant workers through work permits and visa.

Prostitution has been identified as a poverty-coping mechanism of last resort that women are forced into because of their lack of access to formal market and employment opportunities. It is a survival strategy that not only traps people in poverty, but also, through its implications for individuals, families, and communities, causes their fall into even deeper poverty. Prostitution and trafficking have been identified as a downward spiral into poverty. As a result of higher poverty rates and lower levels of educational and vocational qualifications, divorced women are more vulnerable to prostitution. Policy options could include government assistance programs, where divorced women become eligible for state economic assistance. Their associations and community members could also assist by encouraging divorced women to attend vocational training courses. Both groups identified cultural centers as a preferred location for vocational training courses.

Access to the Justice System

Both groups described the lack of transparency and accountability of the judiciary as another manifestation of social exclusion. For most, judicial procedures are unclear, access to lawyers is limited, laws and regulations are not always applied equally, and sentences are thus seen as not always entirely objective. New policies could foster judicial transparency and accountability by dissemination of information on judicial processes and procedures, objective enforcement of laws and regulations, and legal advice and counseling. Others mentioned the problems with property rights following the government's 1992 land distribution. Policies need to include clear land titling, ownership rights, dispute resolution, and compensation for loss of land in unresolved disputes.

Most consider themselves excluded from the legal system, especially in the case of divorce of an unregistered marriage. Since the majority of Roma and some Egyptian couples marry below the legal age, their marriages cannot be formally unregistered. Divorced women, who traditionally take care of the couple's children after divorce, particularly suffer. Without formally recognized rights and responsibilities, women do not have legal levers to demand and enforce alimony and child support payments from their children's father. Even in the case of registered marriages, divorced husbands stop paying alimony when they marry again. The government could develop policies that make former common-law wives eligible for alimony and enforced payment. In parallel, Roma and Egyptian associations could organize a public awareness campaign in which the negative effects of early marriages, unregistered marriages, and legal accountability of common-law husbands for spousal and child support are outlined. Cultural centers could provide space for information dissemination.

Lack of formal marriage registration also has negative effects on birth certification of most children. Without official papers, these children are denied citizenship and their essential human, civil, and political rights. As a result, they are destined to a life in poverty and social exclusion from formal work, mainstream society, and legal access to public good and services. The government must develop policies that address unregistered marriages and unregistered childbirths by allowing citizen status.

Access to Information

The majority feel that they cannot fully participate in society and are excluded because they lack information on government policies, decisionmaking processes, the rule of law, and rights and responsibilities. For Roma, information is particularly difficult to obtain. One reason is location, since they tend to live in rural and remote areas. The main reasons, however, are language difficulties and illiteracy. Possible policy remedies could be translation of key documents and information material into the Romani language, while broadcasting them over local radio stations as public service announcements. Key information could further be disseminated through community meetings and village councilors, and information centers where Roma would receive help in obtaining and handling documents such as service contracts, property rights documents, application forms, and notifications. Furthermore, these minorities would be trained for various occupations to work in the local and national media to help support this communication and information effort. They could serve as advocates to voice their communities' needs and interests, foster their understanding of governance processes, and promote their participation in decisionmaking processes of different aspects of Albanian society. The government, NGOs, community representatives, Roma associations, and international partners could join forces in this communication and dissemination effort.

Safety and Security of Livelihoods

In some areas in Albania, parents' concern for the security of their children on their way to and from school is another barrier to school attendance, literacy, and inclusion. The main reason cited was lack of safety measures provided by local governments for the long walk to the nearest school. Policies should involve central and local government in devising and implementing anticrime measures, protecting citizens, and assisting crime victims. Increased security measures for protection of property must also be installed.

For the poor, and particularly very poor, Roma and Egyptians, the lack of security in their livelihoods is directly causative of their social exclusion. They spend the majority of their incomes on meeting their basic needs: food, health care, and list repayment. Policy choices that address these financial uncertainties could be in the form of humanitarian aid for food, clothes, and basic amenities given on a conditional basis. For instance, the eligibility for this aid could be linked to their children's school attendance and completion of compulsory education, or to trainees' attendance and completion of vocational training courses.

Social Capital, Voice, and Participation

Social capital has been identified as a mechanism to cope with poverty and social exclusion. Roma and Egyptians, for instance, use cognitive social capital to migrate abroad, since they share values, norms, and attitudes that govern their behavior. However, they are weak in structural forms of social capital, such as formal or informal associations or networks that facilitate collective action. This form of social capital is particularly crucial for helping them to voice their needs and interests, and for encouraging their participation in the local, regional, and national policy decisionmaking processes. They will remain ill-equipped to escape poverty and social exclusion as long as their structural social capital remains weak and they have no voice or participation in those aspects that affect their livelihoods.

Therefore, Roma associations are important, especially in view of the declining role of the Roma *fis* during transition. Both the structure and function of the *fis* have weakened because of socioeconomic changes during this period, and the close solidarity that existed between Roma families under socialism has been affected. As a result, the social organization of the Roma *fis* has changed, in both breadth and depth. The knowledge of local Roma communities is valuable for the implementation of policies that foster their social inclusion in Albanian society. However, cooperation between the different existing Roma associations is weak at the moment; they lack a strong support base within each community, suffer from low membership rates, and have very limited funding.

Furthermore, both groups expressed little trust in their associations and whether they were representing their issues effectively or adequately. As a result, many consider that these associations are unable to produce benefits for local communities. In the short term, the government could help build trust between the communities and the associations by including both in the planning and implementation of programs for the community as a whole. By attaching associations to programs that would benefit both, trust and rapport between the local Roma and Egyptians and their associations would grow.

Furthermore, trust between these associations, communities, and central or local government in the decisionmaking process is important to gain effective political representation, solidarity, and social cohesion. Policy options would include greater transparency of institutional mechanisms and decisionmaking at the local and central government levels. With more information and understanding of these processes, government would become accountable to both groups—a prerequisite for good governance, solidarity, and cohesion.

International NGOs should strengthen and encourage coordination between Roma and Egyptian associations by making funding conditional on cooperation between them, as well as between associations and the communities.

In the long term, international NGOs and the Albanian government should help increase the national and international links between these associations in Albania with related associations in other European countries. These international links would familiarize association leaders with projects for these groups that are being implemented outside Albania, which would assist these leaders in replicating workable local projects.

Roma Cultural Centers as a Means for Social Inclusion

Albania's Roma and Egyptians are acutely aware of their desperate need for financial aid, services, and education to improve their living conditions during this period of socioeconomic change. Like the Roma in the Gold Coin folk-tale, they lament that the dire strat-agems, especially migration, to which they must resort if they hope to make even a basic living have had the effect of further eroding the family structure and the knowledge and practice of their cultural heritage that nourishes their identity. As a result, both have strongly expressed a desire for cultural centers where they could gain pride by restoring and enriching their venerable cultures and engender social inclusion by disseminating this information to all Albanians.

Cultural centers are seen as a first step to bringing the far-flung Albanian Roma together, supporting expressions of their cultural practices, and helping to strengthen their social capital. These centers would provide formal instruction in the Romani language, tra-ditional crafts and customs, music, dance, and history. They would also give participants sites at which to display their family's historical handicrafts such as wedding clothing and delicate iron and basketwork.

They would also provide other training and services that address needs identified by the Roma and Egyptians themselves. First and foremost would be adult vocational train-ing aimed at the realities of the local job market, not only in trade skills but also, for the more literate adults, training in basic grant proposal writing and accounting. To remedy high illiteracy, both suggested that reading centers housed there would be helpful.

Women have expressed a need for information on basic health and hygiene, repro-ductive health and family planning, and parenting. A large number have also requested legal advice, marriage counseling, and counseling for abused women. The formation of informal women's groups to help support women in making decisions that affect their lives, such as on early marriage, would be encouraged. Those in rural areas without access to medical facilities would find basic medical services life-saving.

After-school classes that most Roma parents identified as crucial to improving their children's education levels could be held there, where both preschool and older children who receive humanitarian aid for daily school attendance would have lunch, take Alban-ian language classes, and, if appropriate, receive homework help from bilingual Roma teachers. These services could also be provided for local Albanian and Egyptian pupils, who would not only work toward improving their low school performance, but also learn about each other's culture. This interaction would begin the process of fostering cultural, social, and institutional inclusion.

Cultural centers could also help promote community-based development, in which Roma and Egyptians themselves rebuild their communities with the assistance of local, national, and international partners. With Albanian cooperation, Roma and Egyptians voic-ing their needs and interests would be encouraged by being heard. Through bottom-up social inclusion, Roma, Egyptians, and Albanians together would contribute to social cohesion.

A detailed policy matrix that summarizes the possibilities to ameliorate the causes of social exclusion can be found in Appendix K. The following is a summary of the short-term and most urgent policy recommendations.

Summary of Short-Term and Most Urgent Policy Recommendations

The illustrated policy recommendations include short-, medium-, and long-term mea-sures for inclusion. In order to address the insecure livelihoods of Roma and Egyptian communities within the short term, policy recommendations in the four policy areas of education, infrastructure, cultural identity, and minority status have been selected. In sum, urgent policy attention is called for improved access to education and infrastructure facilities, the creation of cultural centers, and specifically for Roma, the recognition of a formal minority status.

Table 12.1 Summary of Short-Term and Most Urgent Policy Recommendations

1. Education

Lack of knowledge of Albanian language	Preschool: tailored and formal Albanian language training taught by Roma teachers
	Primary school: provision of 2–3 hours of class instruction in Romani by a qualified Roma teacher
Frequent mistreatment by teachers in some localities: Roma and Egyptian students are made to sit at the back of classrooms and receive punishment from their teachers more frequently than white Albanian students	Promotion of inclusive and participatory teaching methods and raising teachers' awareness in public and special needs schools: tailored teacher trainings in Roma and Egyptian cultural values and norms to meet the different needs of pupils
	Classes on Roma and Egyptian history and culture for Roma, Egyptian, and Albanian pupils to increase respect for diversity and raise awareness among children about their respective cultural backgrounds and ways of life
Lack of access to education, qualification, and vocational skills as a result of income-poverty	Provision of free access to school services, facilities, and amenities, e.g., schoolbooks, clothes, meals, or the use of education facilities; humanitarian aid in form of food, clothes, or basic amenities for very poor Roma and Egyptian families, conditional upon their children's regular school attendance
	Increased accessibility of secondary and higher or university education through specific scholarships, conditional upon central and local government capacity to establish, administer, and monitor scholarship and grants schemes; this could be done with support of Roma and Egyptian organizations

2. Infrastructure

Lack of access or limited access to basic amenities, e.g., potable water, sanitary facilities, electricity, and heating because of inadequate housing in run-down inner-city areas, urban periphery, and rural areas	Concerted efforts of the government, the private sector, and international partners to expand the public water supply and sanitation and electricity networks to families who are located outside of the respective service networks
	Government efforts to increase and/or improve the infrastructure service delivery to families with formal service connection

3. Cultural Centers

Discrimination based on cultural identity	Establishment of cultural centers to address the eroding family structure of the Roma *fis,* bring far-flung Albanian Roma together, support expressions and sharing of their cultural practices, and strengthen their social capital through instruction in Romani, traditional crafts and customs, music, dance, and history

(*continued*)

Table 12.1 Summary of Short-Term and Most Urgent Policy Recommendations (*Continued*)

Low education qualifications and vocational skills	Creation of cultural centers to provide Albanian language classes for Roma children, and after-school classes with help for homework from bilingual Roma teachers. Provision of adult vocational training aimed at the realities of the local job market, including basic accounting and grant proposal writing, and reading centers to remedy high illiteracy
Lack of community and social cohesion; low value of cultural identity and diversity	Establishment of cultural centers to promote community-based development, in which Roma and Egyptians themselves rebuild their communities with the assistance of local, national, and international partners; this would help to promote interaction and foster cultural, social, and institutional inclusion and social cohesion among Roma, Egyptians and Albanians
4. Minority Status	
Discrimination based on lack of formal minority status	Provision of formal minority status to Roma by the government to meet the European Union accession criteria calling for the respect for, and protection of minorities

APPENDIXES

Working Definitions

Culture—A system of knowledge more or less shared by members of a social group or society. It is a lived experience and is being shaped and changed by people and groups (American Anthropological Association).

Enculturation—Enculturation is the process by which a human being adapts to his/her culture and learns to fulfill the function of his/her status and role.

Enhancing Security—Roma are vulnerable to economic shocks, ill health, natural disasters, and violence. (See No Record of the Case) Helping Roma to cope with risks through the establishment of economic and social security arrangements is an important element of addressing the needs of the communities. In this context, the Needs Assessment (NA) will examine perceptions of vulnerability to risks and coping mechanisms. Security also encompasses improved management of the social risks arising out of a project. It can involve such measures as mitigating the adverse impacts of resettlement; security of property; rule of law; post-conflict reconstruction; increased social cohesion/social integration, and access to the judicial system (World Bank 2002).

Ethnicity—Ethnicity is culturally constructed and can be understood as the cultural heritage (history or peoplehood) of a group of people (Bhavnani 2002).

Egyptians—The Egyptians are a group of people who are often confused with the Roma. They claim their origin is ancient Egypt, do not speak Romani, and distinguish themselves from Roma as a separate ethnic group (ECRI 2000).[112]

---

112. A noted Roma/Gypsy scholar, Carol Silverman, elucidates on the separate identities of Roma and Egyptians.

Facilitating Empowerment—Empowerment is the enhancement of the assets and capabilities of diverse individuals and groups to engage, influence, and/or hold accountable the institutions that affect them. Empowerment can involve such measures as: enhancement of physical or financial assets; strengthening of capabilities in the form of human or social capital; increased voice and participation in the project; increased transparency; and accountability (World Bank 2002).

Gypsies—A term commonly used by non-Roma for Roma groups, as well as other groups historically on the margins of Euro-Atlantic societies; originally indicating the purported Egyptian origins of Roma. It is considered a pejorative term by many Roma (Cahn 2002, p. 164).

Institutions, Rules, and Behavior—Social groups relate to each other in different ways. Some cooperate while others compete. Still others may be in conflict. Social analysis examines both the characteristics of the groups as well as the intra-group relationships. It also examines the norms, values, and behaviors that have been institutionalized through those relationships (World Bank 2002).

Matrilineage—A lineage whose members trace their genealogies through specified female links to a common female ancestor.

National Minority Rights—The Council of Europe established the Framework Convention for the Protection of National Minorities based on universal human rights and anti-racism/anti-discrimination laws. The framework consists of 29 articles that stipulate minority rights with regard to ethnicity, culture, language, and religion. These four pillars are the foundation for asserting identity, voluntary integration, and social cohesion. The foundation must be supported by tolerance, cultural diversity, intercultural dialogue, and the creation of conditions for the effective participation of minorities in cultural, social, and economic life as well as in public affairs, particularly in those areas affecting them (Council of Europe 1995).

"The two groups . . . are self identified as 'Roma' and 'Egyptians.' The main difference between the groups is that Roma usually speak Romani (a language with South Asian origin), but not always (and also learning Albanian as a second language); and the Egyptians speak only Albanian. Most scholars agree that both ethnic groups have the same origin in [northwest] India a thousand years ago, but the Egyptians claim they come from Egypt. In the last ten years the Egyptians in Albania (also those in Kosova and Macedonia) have reached out to the Egyptian government for cultural and political ties, with very limited success. . . . How did these two ethnic groups diverge if their origins are the same? Throughout history, Roma have been the objects of discrimination and there have been various ethnic processes to distance themselves from the stigma of being Roma. So, probably in the Ottoman Empire, which allowed for fluidity of ethnic and linguistic identification (what mattered was religion), the Egyptians assimilated linguistically and developed a separate identity as a way of climbing up the social scale. I know many Egyptians in Macedonia who insist that they are not Roma and that their ancestors came from Egypt. There are some writings by activists and even historians that support this view (Sami Frasheri) and one writer (Kristo Frasheri) claims they are related to the Copts! All this is very unlikely (because the paths of Romani migration into the Balkan[s] did not likely cross Egypt) but what is important is to recognize why they do not want to be Roma, but rather a separate ethnic group."

Participation—Participation refers to the extent to which stakeholders can influence development by contributing to project design, influencing public choices, and holding public institutions accountable for the goods and services they are bound to provide. Participation also refers to the extent to which poor or excluded people, like the Roma, are likely to benefit from access to opportunity (World Bank).

Patrilineage—A lineage whose members embrace the genealogies through specified male links to a common male ancestor.

Poverty—Poverty is multi-dimensional. It is not merely a condition, though it is often measured by criteria such as assets, income levels, or daily caloric intake. Poverty is also a position in society, the product of dynamic interaction and transactions among societal groups and institutions (World Bank 2002).

Promoting Opportunity—Creation of community-based material wealth is vital for the Roma. It can be aided by the generation of employment for Roma youth; the availability of job-training centers; the construction of good roads in the communities; the continuous supply of water and electricity; markets for trading; the establishment of a sufficient educational and public health system; and economic growth in society. In this context, the NA will explore the perceptions of Roma regarding constraints to such economic and social opportunities (World Bank 2002).

Racial Discrimination—Any distinction, exclusion, restriction or preference based on race, color, descent, or national or ethnic origin which has the purpose or effect of nullifying or impairing the recognition, enjoyment or exercise, on an equal footing, of human rights and fundamental freedoms in the political, economic, social, cultural or any other field of public life (International Convention on the Elimination of All Forms of Racial Discrimination). Discrimination can be direct or indirect. The former is overt where one person is treated better than another on the basis of racial or ethnic origin. The latter is where an apparently neutral provision has the effect of putting persons of a certain racial or ethnic origin at a disadvantage (e.g., disallowing headscarves in the workplace) (ERRC 2001).

Racism—Racism is institutionalized power inequalities and systematic discrimination and denial of resources based on the origin of a group of people. In this definition, race is not limited to the biological differences in human beings—in fact there are none—but encompasses groups of people united by their shared heritage (Bhavnani 2002).

Another definition is "a way of thinking which involves the categorization of a group of people as naturally inferior on the basis of stereotypical understandings of perceived social and cultural differences" (Cahn 2002, p. 164).

Roma—Roma are a diverse community of peoples living in Europe, the Americas, Asia and Africa, linked especially by (i) mutual recognition as Roma, (ii) historical origins in India (from which today's Roma are believed to have left no later than the tenth century CEE), (iii) language (many—though not all—Roma are native speakers of the Romani language), and (iv) culture (Cahn 2002, p. 273).

Romani Language—The only Indo-Aryan language spoken exclusively in Europe since the Middle Ages. Phonology and lexicon point to an ancient affinity with the so-called Central Indo-Aryan languages, such as Hindi. An early form of Romani must have been spoken in Asia Minor by the eleventh or twelfth centuries. It absorbed Iranian and Armenian influences, however, the strongest influence was Greek, which has made a significant contribution to Romani. Owing to the Greek influence, early Romani as spoken in the late Byzantine period was already a member of the Balkan linguistic area. With the decline of the Byzantine period, Romani-speaking populations began to emigrate away from the Balkans, settling in central and western Europe during the late fourteenth and fifteenth centuries. This emigration carried with it a split into different dialects, as Romani came into contact with a number of other languages, most notably Turkish, Romanian, Hungarian, Western Slavonic, and German (Cahn 2002, p. 273).

Segmentary Clan (or *Fis*)—A kinship descent system, defining descent categories with reference to more and more remote apical ancestors so that the descent categories form a treelike structure (including successively wider ranges of descendants) (American Anthropological Association).

Social Capital—Social capital refers to the norms and networks that enable collective action. It also refers to the institutions, relationships, and norms that shape the quality and quantity of a society's social interactions. Increasing evidence shows that social cohesion is critical for societies to prosper economically and for development to be sustainable. Social capital is not just the sum of the institutions that underpins a society—it is the glue that holds them together. Social capital reflects new relationships between people and enhances their ability to get things done. Thus, social capital can have vertical and horizontal dimensions. Vertical social capital describes the connections between people that operate through institutions where one person has power over another. Horizontal social capital inheres among peer groups (World Bank 2002).

Social Group—Social group refers to a plurality of individuals who recurrently interact in a position of mutually understood and interlocking social capacity (occupational, gender, etc.) that a person assumes in a particular setting. For socially mobile urban societies, an individual usually negotiates between various less-prescribed and intersecting social identities (American Anthropological Association).

Social Inclusion—Social inclusion is the removal of institutional barriers and the enhancement of incentives to increase the access of diverse individuals and groups to development opportunities under a specific project. Social inclusion can involve such measures as: access to public goods and services generated by the project; access to market opportunities created by the project; access to information; involvement of women in the project (World Bank 2002).

Social Organization—(1) The regularly anticipated and repeated patterns of behavior that are widely observable in social interactions.[113] (2) Social organizations are divided into two

---

113. http://www.umanitoba.ca/anthropology/kintitle.html

groups: informal organizations and formal organizations. Informal organizations are characterized by direct, personal relationships between and among friends. Formal organizations are characterized by indirect, non-personal interactions of their many participants as experienced between members and structured boards and bodies (Hermine De Soto).

Social Structure—The organization of a social group or society seen in terms of structures of positions and roles; social structure is a formal analytic abstraction from the ongoing social relations within communities (American Anthropological Association).

Social System—A system of more or less ordered social relations maintained over time (American Anthropological Association).

Societal Diversity and Gender—People are organized into different social groups based on the status ascribed to them at birth—according to their ethnicity, clan, gender, locality, language, class, or some other marker—or on the status or identity they have achieved or chosen (such as civil servant, laborer, or white collar worker). These social markers are culturally constructed and according to particular cultural traditions they are more or less flexible and changeable (World Bank 2002).

Syncretism—Synthesis of the elements of two or more cultures, particularly religious beliefs and ritual practices (American Anthropological Association).

Questionnaire on Needs Assessment of Roma and Egyptian Communities in Albania

Questionnaire Information

Enumerator code _____ Interview no._____ Date of interview_____

Duration of interview: _____ District _____ Village _____

Location Urban _____ Peri-urban _____ Rural _____

Respondent Information

Initials_____ Sex (M/F) _____ Household head (Y/N) _____

Marital status:_____ Religion _____ Ethnicity_____

Number of members in household _____(including those who may be away from the house
  or outside of Albania)

  Number of elders (over 65) M _____ F _____

  Number of adults (16–65) M_____ F_____

  Number of children (6–15 years) M _____ F _____

  Number of young children (under 6 years) M _____ F _____

Basic information on every family member						
Member Code	Sex Male/Female	Age	Marital Status	Ethnicity	Religion	Does he/she live with the family actually?
Number 1						
Number 2						
Number 3						
Number 4						
Number 5						
Number 6						
Number 7						
Number 8						

Number 9						
Number 10						
Number 11						
Number 12						
Number 13						
Number 14						
Number 15						

SECTION I

❑ **General Information**

1.1.1 What do you think are most difficult problems that you face everyday?

The problems	The most difficult ones	Better or worse than the 1990? Yes/No	Better or worse than 2000? Yes/No
a. Lack of food			
b. Lack of clothing			
c. Bad living conditions			
d. Health problems			
e. Lack of health care			
f. Lack of water			
g. Lack of electricity			
h. Lack of heating			
i. Lack of sewage			
j. Transportation			
k. Other_____			

1.1.2 What do you think are the reasons for your continuous problems?
   a. lack of employment
   b. health
   c. social assistance
   d. education
   e. living conditions
   f. ethnicity
   g. others_____

1.1.3 ENUMERATOR, describe the place the respondent live_____

1.1.4 How many rooms do you live in?
   a. one
   b. two
   c. three
   d. more than three

1.1.5 How many families live in your housing (in the same house/apartment)?
   a. one
   b. two
   c. three
   d. more than three

1.1.6   Where is your toilet?
    a. inside
    b. outside
    c. shared
    d. public
    e. none

1.1.7   To which of the following do you have access in your household?

Items	Do you have access? Yes/No	If yes, number of items you own
a. Telephone		
b. Radio		
c. Clock		
d. Refrigerator		
e. Oven		
f. TV		
g. Car		
h. CD player		
i. Satellite dish		
j. Mobile phone		
k. Washing machine		
m. Sewage system		
n. Bed for each member		
o. Living room furniture		

1.1.8   Who is the owner of the place where you live?
    a. my family
    b. other relatives
    c. municipality
    d. company I work for
    e. rented
    f. other_____

1.1.9   If you pay rent, whom do you pay?
    a. other relatives
    b. municipality
    c. company I work for
    d. other _____

1.1.10 Do you own your own land?
    a. Yes
    b. No

1.1.11 If not, do you rent land?
    a. Yes
    b. No

1.1.12 If yes, for what purpose do use the land?
    a. grow food
    b. other crops
    c. livestock
    d. nothing
    e. other

1.1.13 Was land distributed to you in the 1990s?
    a. Yes
    b. No

1.1.14 If not, do you think land should have been distributed to you?
    a. Yes, my all family was born here
    b. Yes, because I was a member of the former cooperative
    c. No, because my family has never inherited land
    d. No, because the village council decided not to give us land
    e. No, we have arrived after land was distributed
    f. Do not know

1.1.15 From which of the following sources give more money to your household?
    a. regular wages
    b. occasional jobs
    c. self-employment
    d. work for goods
    e. social assistance
    f. pension
    g. investments
    h. remittances from people outside the household
    i. loan
    j. handicraft

1.1.16 How much did your household spend last month?
    a. 5.000–10.000 leke
    b. 10.000–20.000 leke
    c. 20.000–30.000 leke
    d. 30.000–40.000 leke
    e. 40.000–50.000 leke
    f. more than 50.000 leke

1.1.17 We want to ask how many times you have eaten the following items in the last week?

Items	Last week
Meat	
Eggs	
Milk	
Cheese	
Butter	
Rice	
Pasta	
Vegetables	
Fruit	
Bread	
Dessert	
Others_____	

1.1.18 Did you buy your food with the list?
    a. Yes
    b. No

1.1.19 If yes, on how many stores do you have lists?_____

1.1.20 How much money did you spent last month on the following items?

Items	Money spent last month
Food	
Clothing/Shoes	
Housing (electricity, water, etc.)	
Heating	
Transport	
Repaying debts	
Others_____	

1.1.21 Which of the phrases best describes the situation of your family right now?
   a. we do not have enough money to feed our family
   b. we have just enough money to keep us alive
   c. we have money for food but not clothing
   d. we have enough money to meet our needs,
   e. we have enough money to save (if yes, follow with q.1.1.22)

1.1.22 Where do you save your money?
   a. Home
   b. Bank
   c. Do not tell

1.1.23 What are the three major conditions to succeed in life?
   a. good luck
   b. good education
   c. reliable friends with contacts
   d. seriousness and constancy
   e. hard work
   f. support from the state
   g. good professional skills
   h. good health.
   i. traveling or migration
   j. other_____

❑ **Infrastructure**

1.2.1 How do you describe the roads where you live?
   a. excellent
   b. good
   c. so-so
   d. not so good
   e. bad.

1.2.2 With what means do you and your family usually travel?
   a. car
   b. public bus
   c. donkey
   d. horse
   e. foot
   f. bicycle
   g. cart
   h. other_____

1.2.3 Do you have any of the following public services at home?

Items	Do you have access? Yes/No	The average number of hours you have them
a. Drinking water inside the house		
b. Dwelling		
c. Sewage system		
d. Electricity		
e. Telephone		
f. Heating with gas		
g. Heating with coal		
h. Heating with electricity		
i. TV/radio reception		

1.2.4 (If there is no telephone at home) Where is the nearest telephone?
   a. neighbor's house
   b. in the neighborhood
   c. village/commune post-office
   d. next village/neighborhood

1.2.5 Which of the following social services have been provided to you?

Social Services	Does it exist in your place? Yes/No/do not know	Do you use this service? Yes/No/do not know	If No, which is difficulty you face in using it?
a. Assistance for food			
b. Assistance for employment			
c. Social insurance			
d. Health care			
f. Pension			
e. Social assistance			
h. Transport services for disabled persons and elders			
i. Other			

❑   **Education**

1.3.1   What level of school do you have?

Family member	The highest level of education	Number of years of education	Type of school
Member 1			
Member 2			
Member 3			
Member 4			
Member 5			
Member 6			
Member 7			
Member 8			
Member 9			
Member 10			
Member 11			
Member 12			
Member 13			
Member 14			
Member 15			

1.3.2   What justifiable reasons might there be for a boy of your household to not attend school?

Reasons	1. Yes 2. No
a. Lack of decent clothing	
b. Help raising other siblings	
c. He has to work	
d. He has already learned what is necessary	
e. He learns everything at home	
f. School is far away	
g. He does not want to attend	
h. He does not know Albanian very well	
i. Teachers treat him badly	
j. Other students treat him badly	
k. He is married	
l. Wife gave birth	
m. Education makes no differences in life chances	
n. Other	

1.3.3   What justifiable reason might there be for a girl of your household to not attend school?

Reasons	1. Yes 2. No
a. Lack of decent clothing	
b. Help raising other siblings	
c. She has to work	
d. She has already learned what is necessary	
e. She learns everything at home	
f. School is far away	
g. She does not want to attend	
h. She does not know Albanian very well	
i. Teachers treat her badly	
j. Other students treat her badly	
k. She is married	
l. She gave birth	
m. Education makes no differences in life chances	
n. Other	

1.3.4   What is the majority of the children in the class in the school your children attend?
   a. Albanian
   b. Roma
   c. Egyptians
   d. Other_____

1.3.5   Do any of your children attend a special school (for mental problems or lagging development)?
   a. Yes
   b. No

1.3.6   If yes, why?
   a. He/she is mentally ill
   b. He/she is deaf
   c. He/she is mute
   d. He/she is deaf and mute
   e. He/she mentally retarded

1.3.6   What would be the best way to improve education for your child?
   (ONLY FOR ROMA RESPONDENTS)
   a. schools closer to home
   b. Roma teachers
   c. additional language training in Albanian
   d. separate schools for Roma in native language/textbooks

❑   **Employment/Unemployment**

1.4.1   We are going to ask some questions about employment and unemployment.

Family member	What is your present occupation?	What was your last occupation?	When was your last job?	What kind of job did you have before 1990?	What kind of contract do/did you have?
Member 1					
Member 2					
Member 3					
Member 4					
Member 5					
Member 6					
Member 7					
Member 8					
Member 9					
Member 10					
Member 11					
Member 12					
Member 13					
Member 14					
Member 15					

1.4.2   Is it difficult to find a job?
    a. Yes
    b. No
    c. Do not know

1.4.3   If yes, what are the three main reasons for difficulties?
    a. insufficient quantity
    b. overall economic depression in country
    c. ethnic affiliation because you are Roma or Egyptian
    d. poor health status
    e. gender affiliation because you are man or woman
    f. age
    g. bad luck
    h. educational level
    i. skill level
    j. because of your darker skin
    k. other_____

❑   **Migration/Emigration**

1.5.1   Have you ever left your village neighborhood to find work in other villages/towns, cities, and countries?

Family member	Have you ever left the place for more than a month (since 1990)	Where did you go?	What did you do?	For what reasons did you migrate?	Did you send or bring money back home?	How was this money sent?
Member 1						
Member 2						
Member 3						
Member 4						
Member 5						
Member 6						
Member 7						
Member 8						
Member 9						
Member 10						
Member 11						
Member 12						
Member 13						
Member 14						
Member 15						

1.5.2   Do you/anybody from the family like to migrate?
   a. Yes
   b. No
   c. Do not know

1.5.3   What difficulties do you encounter when you migrate?
   a. visa
   b. lack of money
   c. lack of contacts/connections
   d. no one to take care at the family at home
   e. police
   f. language
   g. profession
   h. age
   i. other_____

1.5.4   Who usually migrates in your village/neighborhood?
   a. father
   b. young man
   c. mother
   d. young woman
   e. married couple
   f. family
   g. children

1.5.5   Where do people in your community usually migrate?
    a. other village nearby
    b. Tirana
    c. other town_____
    d. Greece
    e. Italy
    f. other country_____

Section II

❑ Social Capital

2.1.1   For how long has this family been living in this place?
    a. less than 5 years
    b. more than 5 years
    c. more than 10 years

2.1.2   If it is less than 10 years, how do you describe your relationship with your neighbors?
    a. very good
    b. good
    c. average
    d. not good

2.1.3   Are you a member of an organization?
    a. Yes
    b. No

2.1.4   If yes, what is the reason you joined?
    a. Ethnic affiliation
    b. Political affiliation
    c. Gender based associations
    d. Religious associations
    e. Sport associations
    f. Other_____

2.1.5   Have you ever desired to be a member of an organization?
    a. Yes
    b. No

2.1.6   If yes, why did you not become a member?
    a. Because of the ethnic affiliation
    b. Because of the political affiliation
    c. Because of the religious affiliation
    d. Because of gender
    e. Other_____

2.1.7   How many close friends do you have these days? These are people you feel at ease with, can talk to about private matters, or call on for help._____

2.1.8   How many of these close friends are ethnic Albanian?
    a. None
    b. One
    c. Two
    d. Three
    e. More than three

2.1.9   If you suddenly needed to borrow a small amount of money (enough to pay for a week's expenses), are there people beyond your household and close relatives to whom you could turn?
1. Yes
2. No

2.1.10 If you do not have enough money to buy food, what do you do?
a. borrow money from neighbors
b. borrow food from neighbors
c. borrow money/food from your relatives
d. borrow money from employer
e. search the garbage
f. send the children to earn money on the street
g. beg
h. take food from abandoned fields/plots
i. go and buy in the shop on list basis
j. starve.

2.1.11 How much do you trust your neighbors?
a. completely
b. somehow
c. do not trust at all

2.1.12 Generally speaking, would you say that most people can be trusted?
a. Most people can be trusted
b. The people that you know very well can be trusted
c. You need to be careful with most of them
d. Most of people can not be trusted

2.1.13 Do you agree with the following:

	1. Yes 2. No 3. Do not want to answer the question
a. Most people that live in this village/neighborhood are willing to help if you need it	
b. This village/neighborhood, one has to be alert or someone is likely to take advantage of you	

2.1.14 How much do you trust:

	1. A lot 2. Not much 3. None
a. local government officials	
b. central government officials	
c. Roma/Egyptian organizations	

2.1.15 Have you or anyone in your household ever participate in any communal activities, in which people came together to do some work for the benefit of the community?
a. Yes
b. No

2.1.16 If yes, when was the last time?
a. One month ago
b. Three months ago

    c. Six months ago
    d. One year ago
    e. More than one year ago

2.1.17 If there was a problem in this community (water supply, death of member, etc.), how likely is it that people will cooperate to try to solve the problem?
    a. Very likely
    b. Somewhat likely
    c. Neither likely or unlikely
    d. Somewhat likely
    e. Very unlikely

2.1.18 Did you have any reason to approach local leaders for assistance in the last year?
    a. Yes
    b. No

2.1.19 If so, what was the nature of the problem?
    a. conflict with Albanians
    b. conflict with other people of the community
    c. conflict within the family
    d. conflict with the police
    e. lack of income (starvation)
    f. housing problems
    g. employment problems
    h. documents

2.1.20 How many times in the past month have you got together with people to have food or drinks, either at home or in a public place?_____

2.1.21 (IF NOT ZERO) Were any of these people of different:

	1. Yes 2. No
a. ethnic or linguistic background	
b. economic status	
c. social status	
d. religion	

2.1.22 Which of the following groups would you not like to have for neighbors?
    a. Albanians
    b. Roma
    c. Egyptians
    d. other minorities

2.1.23 Which of the following would you rather accept?

	1. Accept 2. Do not accept
a. work with Albanians	
b. your children to have Albanian friends	
c. to live side by side with Albanians	
d. your son to marry an Albanian woman	
e. your daughter to marry an Albanian man	

2.1.24 What are your three main sources of information about what the government is doing (such as agricultural extension, workfare, family planning, etc.)?
   a. relatives/friends/neighbors
   b. community bulletin board
   c. community or local newspaper
   d. national newspaper
   e. radio
   f. television
   g. groups or associations
   h. business or work associates
   i. community leaders
   j. government agent
   k. NGO's

2.1.25 Did you vote in the last election?
   a. Yes
   b. No

2.1.26 Is there any political party you can trust?
   a. Yes
   b. No

2.1.27 Can you name an NGO you would trust?_____

2.1.28 Do you know if there is any Roma/Egyptian organization?
   a. Yes
   b. No

2.1.29 If yes, can you name any Roma/Egyptian NGO that you would trust? _____

2.1.30 What is the best way for people to solve their problems?
   a. everyone should take care of themselves
   b. if people have common problems they should approach them together
   c. it is up to the state to solve problems since we can't do much
   d. other_____

❑ **Violence**

2.2.1 Have problems in your community ever led to violence?
   a. Sometimes
   b. Never

2.2.2 Do you feel safe from crime and violence in your village/neighborhood?
   a. Safe
   b. Somewhat safe
   c. Not safe

2.2.3 Do you feel safe from crime and violence in your home?
   a. Safe
   b. Somewhat safe
   c. Not safe

2.2.4 Has any of your household been the victim of a crime or violence in the last 5 years?
   1. Yes
   2. No

2.2.5 What do you think about the role of police in your village/neighborhood?
   1. Good job
   2. So so
   3. Bad job

❏   **Cultural Identity**

2.3.1   Which of the following do you identify as being Roma/Egyptian?
    a. occupations
    b. nomadic lifestyle
    c. women's dress
    d. marriage customs/ceremony
    e. music
    f. community organization
    g. *fis* affiliation
    h. language
    i. mythology
    j. holidays
    k. religion
    l. other_____

2.3.2   What language do you speak in the home?
    a. Romani
    b. Albanian
    c. Mixed
    d. Other_____

2.3.3   Do you see the Roma/Egyptians as equal as everybody else in the society?
    a. Yes
    b. No

2.3.4   If no, please give reasons? _____

2.3.5   Who do you think has the most power in Albania?
    a. Albanians
    b. Roma
    c. Egyptians
    d. Macedonians
    e. Greeks
    f. Montenegrins
    g. Vlachs
    h. All equal

2.3.6   What do you think is of primary importance for Roma to become equal members of society?

	1. Primary 2. Not primary
a. To have employment for Roma/Egyptians	
b. Roma/Egyptians to participate in the state administration at the local level	
c. To have Roma/Egyptian ministers/MP's	
d. To live together with the majority but not as part of it	
e. To have Roma/Egyptian journalists	
f. To have Roma/Egyptian newspaper	
g. To have a local Roma/Egyptian TV channel	
h. To have a nation-wide Roma/Egyptian TV channel	
i. Roma/Egyptians to be represented everywhere in the state administration	
j. High education	
k. Other_____	

2.3.7 Do you practice any traditional Roma/Egyptian handicrafts like, basket weaving, metal work?
   a. Yes
   b. No

2.3.8 If yes, which one?_____

2.3.9 What *fis* (Roma family group) are you from? (ONLY FOR ROMA RESPONDENTS)
   a. Meckar *fis*
   b. Kurtof *fis*
   c. Cergar *fis*
   d. Karbuxhi *fis*

2.3.10 What are differences between the Roma *fis* you know? (ONLY FOR ROMA RESPONDENTS)
   a. Differences in wealth
   b. Differences in education
   c. Differences in tradition
   d. Differences in religion
   e. Differences in language
   f. Other_____

2.3.11 Which relative is considered most important to the immediate family?
   a. children
   b. mother
   c. father
   d. grandmother
   e. grandfather
   f. aunts (mother's sister)
   g. aunts (father's sister)
   h. uncles (mother's brother)
   i. uncles (father's brother).

2.3.12 Who is the most influential person in your community?
   a. eldest man of your *fis*
   b. eldest man of different *fis*
   c. eldest woman of your *fis*
   d. eldest woman of different *fis*
   e. richest man
   f. richest woman
   g. elected person with the majority votes from the community
   h. most honest person in the community
   i. highest educated person in the community

2.3.13 If your son or daughter gets married, whom does he/she usually marry?
   a. someone from the Roma/Egyptian community
   b. from outside the Roma/Egyptian community
   c. close friends on mother's side
   d. close friends on father's side
   e. member of the *fis*
   f. member of another *fis*.
   g. person from the majority

2.3.14 Who usually makes the arrangements for the marriage?
   a. groom's mother
   b. groom's female relatives
   c. groom's father
   d. groom's male relatives

e. bride's mother
f. bride's female relative
g. bride's father
h. bride's male relatives
i. neighbors
j. close friends of the family

2.3.15 With whom do the newlywed's usually live?
a. with groom's family
b. with bride's family
c. on their own/separate house
d. with another related family
e. with another non-related family.

2.3.16 How common is divorce in your community?
a. Common
b. Neither common nor uncommon
c. Not common

2.3.17 Who usually initiates a divorce?
a. husband
b. wife
c. other_____

2.3.18 What reasons are usually cause for divorce?
a. marital infidelity
b. difficult socioeconomic situation
c. unemployment
d. alcoholism
e. physical abuse
f. psychological abuse
g. abandonment.

2.3.19 In case of divorce, who takes care of the children?
a. mother
b. mother's parents
c. relatives of mother
d. father
e. father's parents
f. relatives of father
g. community members
h. other_____

2.3.20 What are the main holidays you celebrate? OPTIONS *we should ask the Roma leaders for a list to include here.*

2.3.21 Are any of these holidays especially for Roma/Egyptians (other Albanians do not celebrate it)?

2.3.22 List the most important activities that usually occur during the celebration of a holiday? OPTIONS.

2.3.23 Who attends celebrations of holidays?
a. Only members of the *fis*
b. Members of other *fis*
c. Members of the community
d. Persons from the village/neighborhood

2.3.24 Does every community have musicians?
    a. Yes
    b. No

2.3.25 What are the usual instruments?_____

2.3.26 Who teaches Roma/Egyptians to play music?
    a. Parents
    b. Grandparents
    c. Elders of the *fis*
    d. Older musician of the community
    e. School
    f. Other_____

2.3.27 Do you know of any Roma/Egyptian folkdances?
    a. Yes
    b. No

2.3.28 Do you have Roma/Egyptian fairy tales?
    a. Yes
    b. No

2.3.29 Is storytelling (history, legends, myths, poetry, fairy tales) important in your household/
    community?
    a. Important
    b. So so
    c. Not important

2.3.30 If yes, who is the storyteller?
    a. My grandmother/grandfather
    b. The oldest person of the *fis*
    c. The oldest person of another *fis*
    d. Other_____

(BLOCK OF QUESTIONS ONLY FOR ROMA RESPONDENTS)
2.3.31 Are you interested in a cultural/community center where you could participate
    the following?
    a. language (reading, writing) classes
    b. recreational sports
    c. music
    d. vocational training
    e. handicrafts/arts
    f. adult education classes (teaching skills like accounting, sewing, starting a business, etc.)
    g. entertainment (movies, folklore, music, dancing)
    h. hygiene/child rearing classes

2.3.32 If yes, how would you be willing to support the community center?
    a. small fee
    b. volunteer/work in kind
    c. contribute goods/supplies
    d. help in maintenance and cleaning
    e. assist in administration
    f. promotion
    g. other_____

2.3.33 What other needs could a cultural center provide? Please list_____

❏ **Gender**

2.4.1   What are the responsibilities for man/woman in your household?

Responsibilities	Man	Woman
a. earn money		
b. housework		
c. household repair		
d. caring for children		
e. educating the children		
f. caring for other family members		
f. shopping		
h. managing the money		

2.4.2   Do women do the same work as men?
    a. Yes
    b. No

2.4.3. Is it easier or more difficult for women to find work compared to men?
    a. More difficult
    b. The same
    c. Less difficult

2.4.4   What qualities make a "good" man and a "good" woman?

Qualities	"Good" man	"Good" woman
a. Handsome/Beautiful		
b. Hardworking		
c. Honest		
d. Non-alcoholic		
e. Good father/mother		
f. Family responsibility		
g. Intelligent		
h. Educated		

2.4.5   Who controls spending and saving money in your household?
    a. eldest man in family
    b. eldest woman
    c. money-earner
    d. other_____

Section III

❑ **Health**

3.1.1   How do you assess your health?

Family member	How do you assess your health?	Have you ever had a serious illness?	When you are ill, do you seek medical attention?	Do any of you suffer from chronic illness?
Member 1				
Member 2				
Member 3				
Member 4				
Member 5				
Member 6				
Member 7				
Member 8				
Member 9				
Member 10				
Member 11				
Member 12				
Member 13				
Member 14				
Member 15				

3.1.2   What do you think of the medical care you have received?
   a. Good
   b. Average
   c. Bad

3.1.3   Have paid for medical care?
   a. Yes, once
   b. Yes, sometimes
   c. No, never

3.1.4   Do you feel that doctors are less interested in you because you are Roma/Egyptian?
   a. Yes
   b. No

3.1.5   What might be the reasons to not seek medical attention?
   a. It's to far away,
   b. It is too expensive
   c. Roma/Egyptians will not be treated when ask medical care
   d. Other_____

3.1.6   How is the health of your family compared to 5 years ago?
   a. Better
   b. The same
   c. Worse

3.1.7   Do you have enough money to buy medicines?
   a. Yes
   b. No

3.1.8 Do you have Roma/Egyptians who treat you with traditional herbal medicine?
   a. Yes
   b. No

3.1.9 If the health of your family has declined, what do you think are the main reasons?
   a. malnutrition
   b. lack of water
   c. lack of adequate medial care
   d. stress from bad economic situation
   e. bad living conditions

3.1.10 Were there periods during the last year when your family did no have enough to eat?
   a. never
   b. 1 or 2 days during the year
   c. 1 or 2 days every month
   d. constantly.

❑ **Children/Family Planning**

3.2.1 How old were you when your first child was born?_____

3.2.2 At what age do you think your son should get married?_____

3.2.3 At what age do you think your daughter should get married?_____

3.2.4 At what age do you think your son should his first child?_____

3.2.5 At what age do you think your daughter should have her first child?_____

3.2.6 What are your children's life chances in comparison with yours when you were their age?
   a. to find a job
   b. to establish a happy family
   c. to emigrate to a more developed country
   d. to live a healthier life
   e. to provide education to their children
   f. to have honest friends they can trust.

3.2.7 In your tradition, how many children should a family have?
   a. 1
   b. 2
   c. 3
   d. 3–5
   e. 5–7
   f. 7–10
   g. More than 10

3.2.8 This question is about the birth control measures.

Family member	Do you know any kind of birth control?	Do you use any kind of birth control?	If so which is the most common method you use?
Member 1			
Member 2			
Member 3			
Member 4			
Member 5			
Member 6			
Member 7			
Member 8			
Member 9			
Member 10			
Member 11			
Member 12			
Member 13			
Member 14			
Member 15			

3.2.9 Have you ever had an abortion?
    a. Yes
    b. No

3.2.10 If yes, how many? _____ (THIS QUESTION IS FOR WOMEN ONLY)

3.2.11 Who performed these abortions?
    a. Doctor
    b. Nurse
    c. Medical professional
    d. Midwife
    e. Yourself
    f. Other_____

3.2.12 From whom do Roma/Egyptian girls learn about pregnancy and child care?
    a. female relatives
    b. at school
    c. from a health care professional
    d. from other girls
    e. other_____

3.2.13 Who assists Roma/Egyptian mothers while giving birth?
    a. female relatives
    b. neighbors
    c. midwife
    d. doctor
    e. nurse
    f. other_____

3.2.14 Where are Roma/Egyptian babies usually born?
    a. in a hospital
    b. in a clinic

c. at home

d. other_____

3.2.15 What are the responsibilities of male children and female children at home?

Responsibilities	Male children	Female children
a. go to school		
b. do household chores		
c. take care of younger children		
d. earn money		
e. begging		
f. other		

Section IV

❑ **Discrimination**

4.1.1 Have you ever felt discrimination?
  a. Yes, once
  b. Yes, but in few cases
  c. Yes, often
  d. No, never

4.1.2 What form did the discrimination take?
  a. rudeness
  b. denial of services
  c. physical abuse
  d. verbal abuse
  e. violence
  f. other_____

(ENUMERATOR: If it is violence ask what kind?)_____

4.1.3 How do other groups think about you? _____

4.1.4 What do you think of other groups? _____

4.1.5 Have you ever been refused entry into a public place (bar, restaurant, shop, hotel, etc.) because you are Roma/Egyptians?
  a. Yes, once
  b. Yes, sometimes
  c. Yes, often
  d. No, never

4.1.6 Have you ever heard of any cases where Roma/Egyptians were treated unfairly because they were Roma/Egyptians?
  a. Yes, once
  b. Yes, sometimes
  c. Yes, often
  d. No, never

Questions for Non-Roma

4.3.1 How do you feel about Roma/Egyptians? Options 1 to 5.

4.3.2   What three words below best describe Roma/Egyptians in general? Options: honest, hard-working, family-oriented, rich, intelligent, clean, sly, lazy, drunken, stupid, dirty, unemployable, untrustworthy, loud.

4.3.3   Do you personally know any Roma/Egyptians?

4.3.3   A. How do you characterize your acquaintance? Options: distant acquaintances, business associates, acquaintances, close acquaintances, friends, good friends.

4.3.4   Do you feel that the Roma/Egyptian community is in crisis/need of help?

4.3.5   What kind of help should be given the Roma/Egyptians? Options?

4.3.6   What will you do if you fall in love with a Roma/Egyptian person?
    a. Accept
    b. No accept

4.3.7   Which of the following would you accept?

	1. Accept 2. Do not accept
a. work with Roma	
b. work with Egyptians	
c. your children to have Roma friends	
d. your children to have Egyptian friends	
e. to live side by side with Roma	
f. to live side by side with Egyptians	
g. your son to marry a Roma woman	
h. your son to marry an Egyptian woman	
i. your daughter to marry a Roma man	
j. your daughter to marry an Egyptian man	

4.3.8   Do your children play with Roma/Egyptian children?
    a. Accept
    b. No accept

4.3.9   Do you trust your Roma/Egyptian neighbors to take care of your children when you have to leave for an emergency?
    a. Yes
    b. No

Focus Group Discussions

With Women, Men, and Children

There are a number of issues that can be covered by the focus group discussions and the aim is to get specifics, not generalities, about the issues. It is not necessary to assiduously cover each indicator or follow the outline below by the letter; the questions below are merely a guide for the facilitator and are by no means exhaustive. The issues are inter-linked and the discussion may go back and forth between issues. Discussions should flow naturally with only brief interruptions by the facilitator to ask for clarification or guide the discussion back to the desired topics. It is very important not to let the discussion be dominated a small number of participants or spend too much time on one topic.

Carefully choose participants to reflect the desired sex and age (for example, mothers, children, older men). The number of participants should be no less than six and no more than ten. It is best to identify the participants and set a convenient time to have the discussion. Make every attempt to meet in a neutral, enclosed area away from possible interruptions (small children may accompany their mothers).

Introduce yourself and the note-taker then explain the project. Stress that they will not be identified in the report and their opinions will be anonymous. Begin the discussion with an easy, non-emotional question to reduce any tensions and warm up the discussion. A good way is to have every participant present himself/herself and give a short description of his/her family.

Subject indicators: unemployment/underemployment, infrastructure, education, health, migration/emigration, social services, social capital, social organization, culture, handicrafts, gender, children/family planning, security/violence/trafficking, community participation.

Read the definitions of the indicators in the concept paper. Do not use these definitions in the discussions; rather ask questions on each to find out the group's definitions.

Unemployment/Underemployment

Key themes:

1. What kind of work activities do Roma/Egyptians perform?
2. What other activities do Roma/Egyptians do to earn money?
3. What is the most profitable job? Least profitable? Most desired? Least desired?
4. What other occupations might Roma/Egyptians pursue that they are currently not pursuing?
5. How do Roma/Egyptians cope when they are unemployed?
6. What does it mean to be unemployed?
7. Is there a status or stigma attached to be unemployed?
8. How do you maintain your families when you are unemployed?
9. How does employment in the present time compare to the communist period?
10. Is there now more space for Roma/Egyptians to be employed and be rich than during the communist period or the contrary?
11. What difficulties do you have in finding a job?
12. Do you feel that you have more difficulty in find a job because you are Roma/Egyptian (or a woman)?
13. What are so many Roma/Egyptians unemployed?
14. What can be done to change the situation?

Migration/Emigration

Key themes:
1. Do people of your community migrate?
2. Who migrates? Couples, families, men, women?
3. Where do they migrate? Within Albania or to another country?
4. Describe the process of migration, i.e., preparations, method of travel, finding a job.
5. What kind of jobs do people do when they migrate?
6. Do they use skills learned before leaving Albania?
7. Do they learn new skills in the country of migration?
8. Do they practice these new skills when they return?
9. How long do people migrate for?
10. Do any emigrate permanently? If so, describe the process.
11. How often to people migrate?
12. What motivates the frequency?
13. What kinds of things might prevent a person from migrating?
14. What kinds of difficulties might a person encounter while migrating?
15. How do you feel about migration?
16. Would you want your family or close friends to migrate?
17. Do you think that migration is necessary to survive?

Infrastructure

Key themes:

1. Do you have reliable electricity service?
2. If not, how do you cope without electricity?

3. Do you have running water in your house?
4. If not, where do you get your water?
5. Are you satisfied with the supply of water in your community?
6. Is there enough water for irrigation of land, consumption of livestock, and service of households?
7. Are you satisfied with the roads in your area?
8. Do you have telephone service in your house?
9. If not, where is the nearest telephone? Is it a public (post office) or private line?
10. What types of buildings are there in your community? Big, little, brick, wooden, two-story?

Education

Key themes:

1. Do you send your children to school?
2. If yes, why do you think it is necessary and if not, why they are not attending school.
3. Do your children like going to school?
4. Do your children like their teacher, books, and sports?
5. What is the ethnic affiliation of the majority of students in your children's classes?
6. Do you feel that your children have trouble in school because they are Roma/Egyptian? If so, why?
7. How many years of education are necessary?
8. How many years will your children complete?
9. How many years did you complete?
10. Did you or your children repeat a grade? If so, why?
11. If you children have dropped out of school, explain why?
12. What are good reasons for a child to drop out of school?
13. If you child wanted to drop out of school, what would you do?
14. Is education important for a successful life?
15. Is it different for boys and girls?
16. What can be done to increase the educational level of children, i.e., stay in school longer and achieve a higher grade/class level?
17. What do think about Albanian schools?
18. Have you ever thought about separate schools for Roma/Egyptians?
19. Do you think that they would help your children learn and stay in school longer?

Health

Key themes:

1. What do you think of the health services you have received?
2. Do you trust the medical personnel in your community?
3. How often do you see a doctor?
4. What kinds of things prompt you to seek medical care?
5. Would you go for a mild illness (e.g., flu)? Would you only go for a more serious problem (e.g., persistent illness or broken bone)? Or would you go only for a life-threatening problem?

6. What kinds of difficulties do you encounter when trying to get medical care?
7. Does your community have a clinic, hospital, dispensary, or ambulance service?
8. Have you ever (or heard by others) paid money for medical care?
9. Was it obligatory to pay?
10. Does paying money improve medical care?
11. Do you think that Roma/Egyptians are not treated properly because they are Roma/Egyptian?
12. Has this ever happened to you or someone you know? Please explain.
13. Where are Roma/Egyptian children born?
14. Do mothers receive pre-natal care while they are pregnant?
15. How do mothers learn how to take care of their children?
16. Who assists mothers before, during, and after the birth?
17. Is there such a thing as traditional Roma/Egyptian medicine? Please explain.

Children/Family Planning

Key themes:

1. How many children do you have?
2. Ideally, how many children should a family have?
3. Has the ideal number of children changed over time?
4. Which is the best age for a boy to get married? A girl?
5. Are children treated equally within the family?
6. At what age should girls and boys have their first child?
7. Where do girls learn about sex, birth control, and sexually transmitted diseases? And boys?
8. Do you know of any birth control measures?
9. If yes where did you hear of them?
10. Do you use any contraception?
11. Do you think that contraception are useful? Are they harmful?
12. Would you use birth control if you had the opportunity?
13. Are abortions common in your community?
14. Who performs the abortions?
15. What methods are used to in abortions?

Social Services

Key themes:

1. What kind of social services do you know (medical, education, pension, employment, postal, public transportation)?
2. Are any of the services available to you?
3. Do you have access to any of the services?
4. How do you rate the services? Please explain.
5. Are the services the same for everybody or there are differences?
6. If you want to access a service, do you encounter any difficulties?
7. Why do you encounter these difficulties?

8. Do you think that you do not receive a service or receive poor services because you are Roma/Egyptian?
9. How do you think the services might be improved?
10. How do you think your access to the services might be improved?

Social Capital

Key themes:

1. Are there structures (institutions) that help you to solve everyday problems, such as the community, CBOs, NGOs, local government, friends, neighbors?
2. What kind of interaction do you have with the structure?
3. Who or what institution helps you with what issues?
4. To whom are you directed when you need financial aid? Do you go to your familiars or neighbors/members of the community?
5. Do you trust people in your community? Do you interact with them?
6. If your community had a common problem, who do you think would work together to solve the problem?
7. Who would take the initiative or be the leader?
8. If someone in your community had an emergency (e.g., death, accident, fire, etc.), whom would they turn to for help?
9. If someone in your community suffered an economic loss (e.g., job loss, crop failure, theft), whom would they turn to for help?
10. Would anyone be willing and/or able to help in these situations?

Social Organization

Key themes:

1. Do you ever meet with other people?
2. Do you have formal gatherings (e.g., church, collectively decide issues in the community)?
3. Do you get together informally for pleasure?
4. What do you do in the gatherings, formal or informal?
5. How often to you get together?
6. Do you take part in any party, organization or CBO? If yes for what reasons?
7. Have you ever been rejected admission to a party, organization, or CBO?
8. If you are not a member of an organization, do you have contact with any?

Social Inclusion

Key themes:

1. Do you feel that you and the other Albanians are part of one community? Why or why not?
2. Do you feel that you are able to participate freely in community life? Give examples on how you participate or how you are not able to participate.

3. Are you a member of more than one community?
4. Are there people in your community who are left out?
5. Who are they and why are they excluded?
6. Is it possible for those who are excluded to become included?
7. What would need to happen?
8. Who has power in your community?
9. What gives them their power?
10. Are there different levels of power in the community?
11. What does the power allow them to do?
12. Why do others have less power?
13. What is the result of having less power?

Community Participation

Key themes:

1. Do people in your community ever get together to solve common problems?
2. Would you participate in a community action?
3. Do you have a voice in the decisions made in the community? If so, please explain. If not, who does and why don't you?
4. What do you think are the ways the Roma/Egyptian community can contribute in enhancing the capacity of participating in the everyday life of the Albanian society (or interact with the Albanian community, other communities).
5. What do you think you contribution will be that this community participation works?

Culture

Key themes:

1. What makes a Roma/Egyptian a Roma/Egyptian?
2. What are the characteristics of a Roma/Egyptian?
3. What does it mean to be Roma/Egyptian?
4. How do you describe Roma/Egyptian culture?
5. What are the most important parts of the Roma/Egyptian culture?
6. What kind of instruments do Roma/Egyptians play (in cases of folk music)?
7. Do you have myths, stories, histories, or fairy tales? If so, please share them.
8. Are there storytellers?
9. Do you know of any Roma/Egyptian folk dances?
10. Who teaches Roma/Egyptians the stories, music, language, etc.?
11. Do you belong to any specific religion?
12. Is your religion a part of what makes you Roma/Egyptian?
13. Do you believe in other religions?
14. Are others in your community of another religion?
15. Do Roma/Egyptians believe in God? What is the God like?
16. What do you believe will happen when you die?

17. Generally how do you celebrate life events?
18. Do you do anything special in these cases?
19. Do you have holidays that Albanians do not have? If so, what are they? What do you do for the holiday?
20. Can you list the Roma *fises* and tell to which of them do you belong?
21. What are the differences among the *fises*?
22. How do Roma/Egyptian families live?
23. What language do you usually use in the home? In the shops? In the market? In accessing social services?
24. Who is the leader of the Roma/Egyptian community? How is he/she chosen?

Handicrafts

Key themes:

1. What kinds of handicrafts are typical for the Roma/Egyptians?
2. Do you or others in your community practice any handicrafts?
3. How is this skill passed down to you?
4. Do you think that handicrafts are a useful skill that Roma/Egyptians have?
5. Are there people who live based on making/selling handicrafts? Is this their only source of income?
6. How much can one make from handicrafts nowadays?

Gender

Key themes:

1. What kind of work does a woman/man undertake in your family?
2. What kind of responsibilities do women and men have in the community?
3. Can/do women do the same work as men?
4. What are the rights of a woman and of a man in your community?
5. Is divorce common in your community? Who usually initiate it?
6. What are the qualities to make a good woman and a good man?
7. What is the role of the father in regard to the children? The mother?
8. Do women have more or less power/freedom now than before? If so, what caused the change? What is your definition of power?
9. Do some women have more power than others? If so, why?
10. What kind of power do women have?
11. What can they achieve with their power?

Security/Violence/Trafficking

Key themes:

1. How safe do you feel?
2. Do you feel safe from crime and violence?

3. Have you ever heard of cases of violence or discrimination because the persons were Roma/Egyptians?
4. Is the place where you live safe or do you still being out alone after dark?
5. Have you ever had conflicts or feel threatened by other persons?
6. What do you think about the role of the police?
7. Have you ever heard of trafficking cases in your community?
8. Do you think that girls/women are aware of the trafficking?
9. Who teaches them/children how to avoid traffickers?
10. Have you heard cases of children that have been sold to others in order to work abroad or for organ transplants?
11. Have any women/children returned to the community?
12. How were they received? Were they accepted?
13. Do you think that trafficking is a major problem?
14. Are there any people in your community who earn money through prostitution? Is this widespread?
15. Who arranges for the prostitution? Finds the women? The customers?

Questions for Children's Focus Groups

Family

Key themes:

1. Who is your favorite family member (e.g., mother, father, grandmother, sister, etc.)? Why?
2. Do you have any chores in the home? What are they? Which children do which chores?
3. What do you do for fun with your family?
4. Do your grandparents live with you? Aunts, uncles, cousins? Other relatives?

Friends and Play

1. Who do you play with? Are any Albanian or Roma/Egyptians?
2. How many friends do you have?
3. What do you do with your friends?
4. Do you play football or other sports?
5. Where do you play?

School

1. Do you like going to school?
2. What are your favorite subjects? Why?
3. Do you like your textbooks?
4. What language do you speak in school?
5. Where do you learn Albanian?
6. Do you learn about Roma/Egyptian history or culture in school?

Culture, History and Language

1. Can you read or write in Romani? If yes, where did you learn?
2. Do you have any books in Romani? School books?
3. Where do Roma/Egyptians come from?
4. Do you know any stories about Roma/Egyptians?
5. Do you know any fairy tales, myths, or legends about Roma/Egyptians? Can you tell them?
6. Do you know any Roma/Egyptian songs, nursery rhymes, or dances? Will you show us?
7. If so, who teaches you the stories, songs, dances?

Questions for Girls

1. At what age do you want to get married?
2. What kind of man do you want to marry?
3. How many children do you want to have?
4. Where and from whom do you learn about sex and taking care of babies?

Questions for Boys

1. At what age do you want to get married?
2. What kind of woman do you want to marry?
3. How many children do you want to have?
4. Where and from whom do you learn about sex?

Ethnographic Case Studies

Total of 16 studies with:
- 2 Roma men
- 2 Roma women
- 2 Roma boys
- 2 Roma girls
- 2 Egyptian men
- 2 Egyptian women
- 2 Egyptian boys
- 2 Egyptian girls

Ethnographic case studies are one-on-one discussions in which the facilitator tries to capture a detailed picture of the interviewee's life. Questions should be open-ended, yet specific. Remember to use the question words *how, why, when, where, who, what* frequently.

The case studies should attempt to record as much life history, current situation, and hopes for the future. Explore the interviewee's view of their own Roma or Egyptian ethnicity. Find out what they think of relations with the majority and how the situation can be improved. What are the major problems in their life and how can they be alleviated.

Statistical Data, Tables, Graphs, and Flowcharts

Chapter 3. Culture

Music and Dance

Most Roma play music by ear, while most Egyptians read music. A majority of Roma (63 percent) and 51 percent of Egyptian children who play a musical instrument are self-taught, while 17 percent Roma and 27 percent Egyptians are taught by other musicians. Twenty-one percent percent of Roma and 18 percent of Egyptians who play are taught by parents.

Chapter 4. Marriage and Family Planning

Birth Control and Abortion

With an average family size of 6.4, Roma families are larger than Egyptians' whose average family size is 5.2, or Albanians with 4.2 members.

Chapter 5. Income and Living Standards

Introduction

Average annual expenditures per capita for Roma are L48,576 and L59,285 for Egyptians.

State Assistance

Table 5 illustrates that 47 percent of Roma and 65 percent of Egyptian households receive financial assistance through one or more forms of social security. In these households, state assistance constituted 14 percent of the total average Roma households income and 17 percent for Egyptians.

Living Space per Capita

According to a 2001 population and housing census, only 20.2 percent of families countrywide live in homes with surface areas below 40m². In contrast, home surface area per capita is 8.54m² for Roma and 9.49m² for Egyptians.[114]

Main Income Sources

Table D.1. Monthly Income for Roma and Egyptian Households (US$), by Source

Income Source	Roma		Egyptians	
	Income (US$)	Income (%)*	Income (US$)	Income (%)*
Salary/Wages	9.91	7.8	28.84	21.1
Casual Work	27.79	21.9	37.09	27.1
Self-employment*	30.98	24.4	21.76	15.9
Agriculture	1.77	1.4	0.34	0.2
Retirement Benefits	11.29	8.9	15.16	11.1
State Economic Assistance	5.23	4.1	7.92	5.8
Unemployment Benefits	0.79	0.6	0.71	0.5
Formal Business/Private sector	17.89	14.1	11.38	8.3
Money from Relatives in Albania	0.51	0.4	0.40	0.3
Remittances from Relatives abroad	10.26	8.1	4.92	3.6
Handicrafts made at Home	1.43	1.1	1.45	1.1
Other	9.00	7.1	6.72	4.9
Total	126.86	100	136.68	100

Note: Figures in bold indicate the main income sources.
*Includes used clothes, and can/metal collection.
Source: Socioeconomic household questionnaires with Roma and Egyptians for the Needs Assessment (2002/03).

Table D.2. Surface Area of Homes, Total and Per Capita for Roma and Egyptians

Surface Area	Roma			Egyptian		
	% of homes	Average No. of Occupants	Per Capita Surface Area	% of homes	Average No. of Occupants	Per Capita Surface Area
≤ 39 m²	52.9	6.07	3.14	46.1	5.0	3.87
40–69 m²	19.1	6.52	7.54	27.7	5.24	9.45
70–99 m²	13.7	7.02	11.12	16.4	5.62	14.03
100–130 m²	7.3	8	13	5.0	5.37	20.54
> 130m²	7.0	6	40.5	4.7	5.73	30.14

Note: Data should be interpreted with caution. Data are based on statistical averages for 331 Roma and 330 Egyptian families in 11 districts and represent self-evaluations of families.
Source: Socioeconomic questionnaires with Roma and Egyptian families, 2002.

---

114. Based on the above classification of groups, the average space per capita is 3.14m²for Roma families that live in dwellings with surface areas of up to 39m².

Chapter 6. Education

Table D.3. Illiteracy Rate and School Years Completed, by Age Group and Roma *Fis*						
	Age group 7–20			Age group 21–40		
Roma *Fise*	Illiteracy (absolute)	Illiteracy (percentage)	Number of school years completed	Illiteracy (absolute)	Illiteracy (percentage)	Number of school years completed
Meçkar	80	38.8	4.46	22	10.8	6.85
Karbuxh	286	77.9	3.54	164	57.7	5.47
Cergar	38	63.3	3.18	15	51.7	5.36
Bamill	26	86.7	1.25	16	66.7	4.38
Kurtof	1	100	—	1	100	—
Total	**431**	**62.2**	**4.02**	**235**	**39.6**	**6.22**

Source: Socioeconomic household questionnaires with Roma and Egyptians for the Needs Assessment (2002/03).

Decreasing Education Levels

The illiteracy rate for the 21–40-year-olds who attended primary school during the socialist period is 40.1 percent for the Roma (42.7 percent females; 37.2 percent males) and 11.3 percent for the Egyptians (8.4 percent females and 14.0 percent males).[115] However, the illiteracy rate for the 7–20-year-olds, who attend primary school during transition, is 62.2 percent for the Roma (64.7 percent females; 59.5 percent males) and 23.5 percent for the Egyptians (24.6 percent females; 22.3 percent males).

* * * * *

Many 10–12-year-old Roma and Egyptian students, for example, are enrolled in the 1st grade.

---

115. Respondents aged 21–40 attended state schools from 1970–1990, and Roma illiteracy rates and educational levels are comparable from as early as 1970. By 1970, all Roma had been settled in permanent localities, which created the appropriate conditions for the state to enforce mandatory school attendance. Prior to the settlement of Roma, school attendance was unenforceable, so education levels prior to 1970 are not comparable to education levels in later periods.

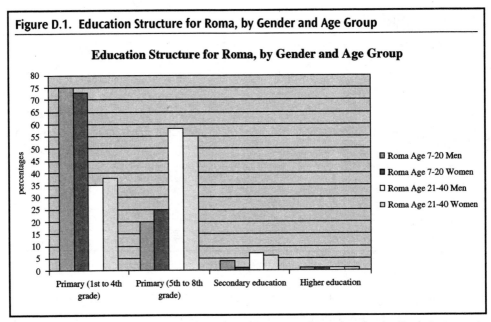

Figure D.1.   **Education Structure for Roma, by Gender and Age Group**

Source: Socioeconomic household questionnaires with Roma and Egyptians for the Needs Assessment (2002/03).

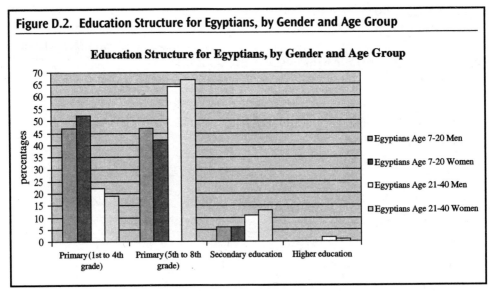

Figure D.2.   **Education Structure for Egyptians, by Gender and Age Group**

Source: Socioeconomic household questionnaires with Roma and Egyptians for the Needs Assessment (2002/03).

Limited access to education facilities

Schools are too far from home for 15 percent of Roma boys, 14 percent of Roma girls, 8 percent of Egyptian boys, and 9 percent of Egyptian girls.

Lack of childcare facilities

Thus, 16 percent of Roma boys and 24 percent of Roma girls, and 9 percent of Egyptian boys and 18 percent of Egyptian girls, help their parents to care for younger brothers and sisters.

Language Difficulties

Some Roma children, specifically 7 percent of boys, and 6 percent of girls, lag behind their Albanian counterparts because they speak little or no Albanian when they begin primary education.

Low perceptions of educational benefits

In fact, 5.2 percent of Roma boys' parents, and 7.1 percent of Roma girls' parents, and 1.8 percent of Egyptian boys' parents, and 1.4 percent of Egyptian girls' parents do not see a link between educational attainment and future opportunities in life.

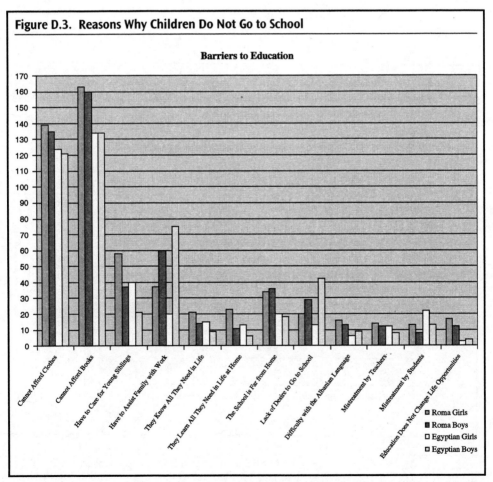

Figure D.3. Reasons Why Children Do Not Go to School

Source: Socioeconomic household questionnaires with Roma and Egyptians for the Needs Assessment (2002/03).

Chapter 7. The Labor Market

Restructuring and Unemployment

Districts	Roma	Egyptians	Total Albanian Population
Shkodra	N/A	70.2	27.99
Fushë Kruja	57.1	57.6	18.00
Tirana	57.1	62.1	25.31
Durrës	59.7	60.3	27.05
Elbasan	53.3	67.3	22.94
Korça	78.5	70.9	21.76
Berat	70.2	64.1	18.26
Fier	69.1	68.8	20.07
Vlora	81.9	53.7	27.23
Gjirokastra	89.7	64.5	23.12
Delvina	76.1	83.3	20.63
Total	67.2	64.3	22.6

Table D.4. Unemployment Rate Among Roma, Egyptians, and Total Population of Albania by Districts[116]

Source: Socioeconomic household questionnaires with Roma and Egyptians for the Needs Assessment, 2002/03; INSTAT, Popullsia e Shqiperise 2001, Tirane 2002

Perceptions Regarding Reasons for Unemployment

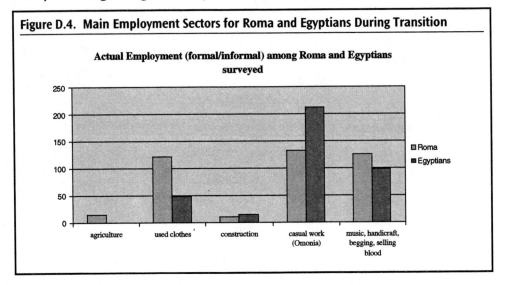

Figure D.4. Main Employment Sectors for Roma and Egyptians During Transition

116. The data for the total population in Albania was taken from the national census in 2001, conducted by INSTAT. The data for the Roma and Egyptians reflect their own perceptions and was derived from the socioeconomic household questionnaires with Roma and Egyptians for the Needs Assessment, 2002/03.

Table D.5. Structural Changes, Effects on Employment, and Impacts on Roma and Egyptians Over Time

Time Period and Social Change	Forms of Employment	Characteristics and Impacts on Livelihoods	Coping Mechanism
Pre-World War II	• Traditional occupations	• Nomadic mode of existence • No formal school attendance, and illiteracy	• Reliance on the *fis*
Socialist Period Structural Change	• Full employment in the public sector • Opportunity to acquire new occupations • Low wages	• Sedentary mode of existence • Formal school attendance, and literacy • Improvements of living conditions for housing, health care, social services • Social capital • Socioeconomic integration	• Functional *fis* structure • Employment in the informal sector
Transition Period Structural Change	• Long-term unemployment, underemployment • Employment in the informal sector and private sector	• Poverty and social exclusion • Decline of living conditions for housing, health care, social services • Decline in education, illiteracy • Socioeconomic disintegration • Weakening of the *fis* • Insecurity and stress	• Migration • Reconstituted forms of social capital • Alternative social organization, creation of associations • Prostitution and trafficking

Source: Socioeconomic household questionnaires with Roma and Egyptians for the Needs Assessment, 2002/03

Chapter 8. Migration

Who Migrates?

Families and Young Men

Figure D.5. International Migration of Egyptians by District

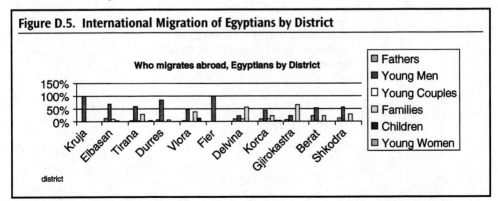

Source: Socioeconomic household questionnaires with Roma and Egyptians for the Needs Assessment (2002/03).

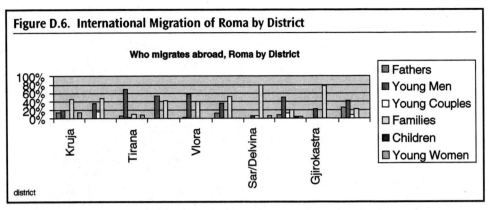

Figure D.6. International Migration of Roma by District

Source: Socioeconomic household questionnaires with Roma and Egyptians for the Needs Assessment (2002/03).

Families with Social Capital

District	International Migration Rate
Berat	high
Delvina/Saranda	high
Durrës	low
Elbasan	high
Fier	medium
Fushë Kruja	low
Gjirokastra	high
Korça	medium
Shkodra	low
Tirana	low
Vlora	medium

Table D.6. International Migration Rates per Districts

Source: "From social exclusion to social inclusion—a Needs Assessment for Roma and Egyptian communities," 2003.

Informal Labor and International Migration

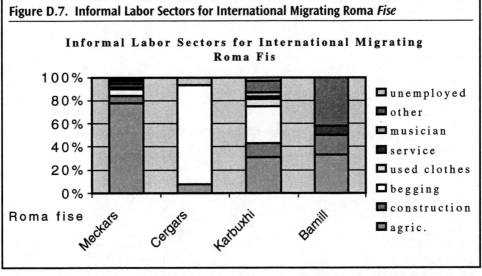

Figure D.7. Informal Labor Sectors for International Migrating Roma *Fise*

Source: Socioeconomic household questionnaires with Roma and Egyptians for the Needs Assessment (2002/03).

Table D.7. Methods of Sending Earnings Home from Abroad (Percent)		
Method	**Roma**	**Egyptians**
Self	82	72
Friends or Acquaintances	15	22
West. Union/Post Service	4	2
Bank	0	4

Source: Socioeconomic household questionnaires with Roma and Egyptians for the Needs Assessment (2002/03).

Child Literacy and Under-education

These children now have, by far, the highest illiteracy rate (87 percent) and the fewest average number of school years completed (1.3) among all Roma *fise.*

Conclusion

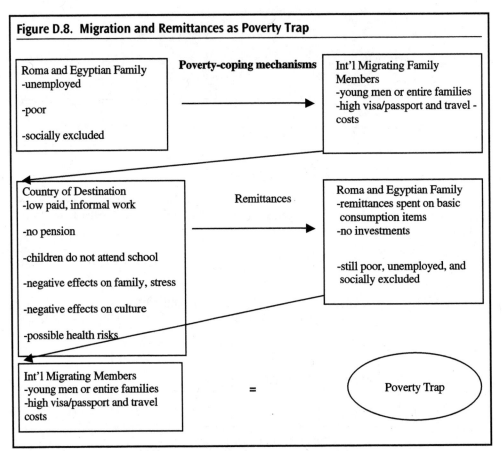

Figure D.8. Migration and Remittances as Poverty Trap

| Roma and Egyptian Family
-unemployed

-poor

-socially excluded | **Poverty-coping mechanisms** | Int'l Migrating Family Members
-young men or entire families
-high visa/passport and travel - costs |

| Country of Destination
-low paid, informal work

-no pension

-children do not attend school

-negative effects on family, stress

-negative effects on culture

-possible health risks | Remittances | Roma and Egyptian Family
-remittances spent on basic consumption items
-no investments

-still poor, unemployed, and socially excluded |

| Int'l Migrating Members
-young men or entire families
-high visa/passport and travel costs | = | Poverty Trap |

Source: "From Social Exclusion to Social Inclusion—A Needs Assessment for Roma and Egyptian Communities," 2003.

Chapter 9. Prostitution and Trafficking

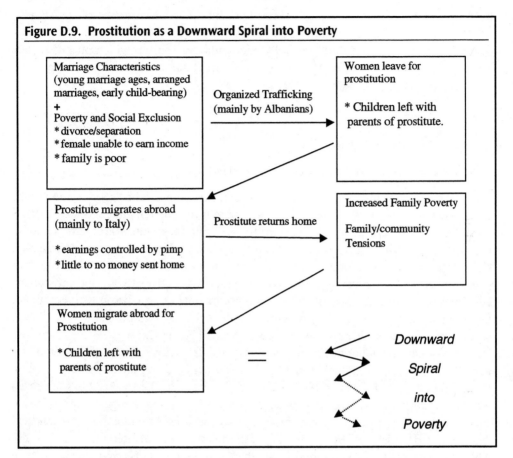

Figure D.9. Prostitution as a Downward Spiral into Poverty

Who Gets Trafficked?

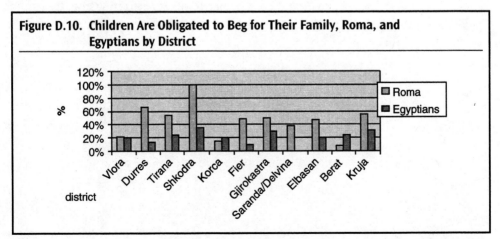

Figure D.10. Children Are Obligated to Beg for Their Family, Roma, and Egyptians by District

Source: Socioeconomic household questionnaires with Roma and Egyptians for the Needs Assessment (2002/03).

Causes, Social and Economic Costs, and Financial Benefits

Karbuxh (78 percent) and Cergar (63 percent) Roma children have extremely high illiteracy rates compared to Meçkar (39 percent) or Egyptian (24 percent) children, who are less commonly trafficked than Karbuxh and Cergar children. The average number of school years completed by Karbuxh (3.5) and Cergar (3.2) children are also low compared to Meçkar (4.5) and Egyptian (5.1) children.

Chapter 10. Social Capital

Trust as Cognitive Social Capital: The Shop Owner

Roma Family A has two children in primary school who both describe good relations with fellow Albanian students and their teacher. Some family members migrate abroad. The family uses the list to feed themselves while bread-winning family members are in international migration. They purchase school supplies for their children "even if" they have to purchase by list. Meanwhile, Roma Families B and C live in the village of Çuka. One son in Family B is 16 years old and in the *second* grade. "We suffer for bread, and not to buy notebooks, pencils, and pens," said his father. Family C does not migrate abroad, because, as explained, family members who would be left behind would not be able to purchase food. "What would my wife and mother eat?" exclaimed the head of Family C.

Family A and neighboring Families B and C live different lives. Without lists, Families B and C were unable to migrate abroad. Moreover, lacking funds to purchase school supplies, their children were unable to attend school. In this example, the 16-year-old son started school only when school supplies were donated to the family by a non-governmental organization. In contrast, Family A used the list to purchase school supplies for their children. They also used the list when bread-winning family members were in international migration. Thus, the wife and mother had food to eat, thanks to the list. In this case, the disparity in financial capital between Family A and Families B and C is small. However, in Family A's example, the list made international migration more likely and also allowed the children to attend school, enabling them to meet short-term needs without detracting from the family's potential to develop and expand human capital.

More Voices of Albania

Chapter 3. Culture

Music and Dance

Ervehe, a Roma informal leader, explained: "Roma have their own music that has been preserved and passed down from generation to generation. Their music has Roma roots. I play the keyboard and harmonica, while others play the clarinet, saxophone, guitar, and others. We have been around to many parts—our grand parents and great grandparents came from Greece and Turkey, and we are very familiar with the music of these countries. Roma music is different from the others."

Folktales

Ali, a Karbuxh Roma leader, stated: "I know our origins are from India. Our grandfather told us folktales when we were little children, through which we were able to learn about our origins. He even told us that the Roma once had a king, and that he was a very fine, charitable, and well-to-do person. He used to go out and meet with other Roma and talk with them."

Matchmaking Customs

Seiti, a Roma from Delvina, explained: "My aunt who lives in Vlora told me about a girl. I myself hadn't seen her in person, but they told me that she was a proper girl, so we agreed to attempt to make the engagement. I went with my father to the girl's house . . . and we asked for her hand in marriage. The girl's family consented and we were engaged. I saw the girl when she brought us *llokums*[117] to entertain us and I liked her. If I had not liked her,

---

117. A gelatinous candy referred to in English as "Turkish delight."

I would have told the girl's father that we would give our final response later. With this, it would have been understood that I had refused. The girl also told her parents that if they liked me, then she would be fine with it. I stayed in Vlora for four or five days, and then we married."

Weddings

A Roma woman explained: "We have a tradition that on Sunday night, when the newly married couple goes to the bedroom, we put a sheet on their bed. On Monday morning, the sheet is displayed to family members. Before, we used to display the bride's gown. When the bride is proven to be a virgin, then a lunch is served . . . because she honored her family and me as her mother-in-law."

On the Fis' Structure

Ilmi, a leader of a large Roma *fis*, stated: "I count my sister's children as *fis*. But when they marry they take another last name and so they leave the *fis*. Only those with the same last name remain in the *fis*. Neither do I count my wife's relatives as *fis*." Ilmi continued: "Our *fis* starts with our grandfather, therefore my grandfather's brothers and sister all count as *fis*. My grandfather's aunt and uncle are also counted. This is how it is everywhere, with all Roma." Meanwhile, Istref also counts within his *fis* "the relatives from the mother's side."

Function of the Roma Fis

Bastri, a Roma leader with high standing in Tirana, explained: "I advise my *fis*. I solve members' problems . . . They come to me because of the respect they have for me, and I convince the two sides, for they listen to my advice. Yesterday, for example, there was a car crash, and four people were injured. I didn't let them kill each other, and I asked them how much it would cost to repair the car. 'L35,000 [US$269],' they told me. Then I told them that within a month, we'll pay for the damage to the car. . . . Our *fis* has many members, more than 5,000. One part of the *fis* is in Korça, whom I advise when they come to me. For example, when a family has a problem with money, we get together and give them a little, depending on what we can. And if someone needs money for an operation, we get together and give it to him. When he gets the money, he pays us back, when he doesn't, it belongs to the past."

The Great Roma ["Barorom"]

"The *fis* generally begins from the grandfather and goes down three or four generations. My grandfather was a respected man. He had a kind of reputation in those days. My grandfather made handicrafts such a baskets and sieves. He had five boys and three girls.

We are members of the Karbuxh *fis*, and most of us come from Turkey. My mother's grandparents were from Folorina [Greece] and Istanbul. Those in Folorina had emigrated there from Istanbul. . . . A small number of Karbuxhinj arrived in Albania during King Zog's time, and when World War II started, others [from Folorina] came too, because they didn't want to be in the middle of a war. When the borders were closed after the war, we were left divided in separate countries. Karbuxhinj [in Albania] settled in Korça, Pogradec, and Elbasan. A few went up to Peqin and Tirana.

My father was the second son in his family. He was married at 13 and had 11 children, 5 boys and 6 girls. Starting at the age of 13, he began working as a horse-dealer. He was an honest horse-dealer. By running an honest business, he gained the people's trust throughout practically all of Albania. Even during the socialist period, my father was a private horse-dealer, but he also worked in the state sector. The head of one cooperative, for example, would order horses from my father. My father would bring horses to him and he would give my father money through the bank. Even veterinarians consulted my father for problems with different horses.

Roma were nomadic until 1965. They were never registered in one city. Most of them hadn't done their military service because they didn't have any documents [proof of residence/identification]. We would go around in tents in those days. For example, an entire *fis* would settle together in one place for six months. . . . We stayed together with relatives from both my mother's and father's side. . . . Starting in 1965–1966, the laws became more stringent and Roma began to be settled in designated areas. My father was settled in Elbasan. In the beginning of the 1970s, my father was elected Council Head, because he had many friends.

My father was very well-to-do, the richest of all Roma, but he also helped the people. He had close friends that were very poor, and my father used his close connections with people from the state to find jobs for his poor friends. People would come to ask him for money to pay for a wedding or an engagement, and my father would help them. There were people who would have a tragedy in the family, such as a death or an illness, and my father would give them money. When there was a dispute between two Roma *fise*, my father would intervene and resolve their dispute. His word had a lot of authority among Roma *fise*.

Whenever a problem arises, we Roma take advice from the entire *fis*. The entire *fis* meets and we look at the problem. If someone wants to take a wife, for example, and if everyone is in agreement, then it is done. But in those days, when there was a special problem, people would come to my father to have it resolved. My father got involved in issues concerning levels as high up as the government. That is, he had a lot of influence.

In the early 1960s, people began to call my father 'Barorom.' In our language, 'Baro' means 'great,' so 'Great Rom.' Our *fis* was the biggest *fis* out of all Karbuxh *fise* and my father had inherited a good name from his father. But he was accepted by the people as Barorom because of his very nature, on his own achievements.

We Roma from Elbasan have gotten along well with the white hand and this comes from tradition. My father had many friends from the white hand. Everywhere in Albania, wherever my father went, he had many friends. We lived together with other Roma *fise*, be it Meçkars, Karbuxhinj, Cergars, or others. In 1975–1976, my father started to be recognized as the 'Barorom' of all Roma *fise* in Albania. Even today, if you were to ask a Roma about my father, he would tell you about him."

The Role of the *Fis* During the Socialist Period: The Gold Coin Market

Astrit, a Roma from Korça, recounts: "I began dealing in the gold coin market on a regular basis during the 1980s. I would buy the coins in my hometown for a lower rate than you would get at the bank. British sterling costs L600 [US$4.62] at the bank, but I would get them for L400 [US$3.08]. I would buy a napoleon coin on the black market for L600 [US$4.62] or L700 [US$5.38], but I would sell them for up to L1,200 [US$9.23] to navy men in Durrës. I would use these coins to purchase items that people from the cities used to ask for, such as brand-name watches, men's shirts and fabrics for dresses, tape recorders, and gold-embroidered scarves from sailors. I found the connection with the navy men through my sister's husband, who lived in Fier. He had a friend in Kavaja, and his friends were good friends with the navy men in Durrës. They trusted my brother-in-law and my brother-in-law trusted me. This is how we made connections. Even if we were caught by the police, we wouldn't tell on each other.

So, I would buy gold coins at lower prices from city folk in Korça, and I would use the coins to buy certain goods from navy men in Durrës, who would bring them illegally from outside the country. Then I would re-sell the goods on the black market in Korça. A large profit was made in each step in this process. Meanwhile, I would get wool dyes in Elbasan with my cousin's mediation. He was good friends with a warehouse owner. I didn't even have enough money to buy a barrel of dye in those days, but the warehouse owner trusted us. He would give us the dyes, and after selling them, we would bring him the money to pay for the dyes . . . We wouldn't deposit our profits in the bank, but would instead keep them in our homes. When the transition period began, I ended up with around L1,000,000 (US$769), which I changed into drachmas."

On the Fis's Decline

One Roma leader explains: "Before the transition, when there was a family celebration or ceremony, all members of our *fis* would come to take part in it. Even the cousins who didn't have our last name would come. We strengthened connections and got to know each other better at these family ceremonies. Whereas now, because families are poor, we aren't able to visit one another like before. I have a lot of cousins in Tirana who I don't know. The uncle of a friend of mine died a little while back. The uncle lived in Tirana, and my friend didn't find out about the death until later."

Chapter 4. Marriage and Family Planning

Marriage at Early Ages

Naim, a Roma *kryeplak* from Elbasan, explained: "Marriages happen at early ages. This is a bad thing, but it's a tradition that we haven't changed because if a [single] girl gets to be 20 years old, we say that she'll be left at home unmarried."

Cultural Norms and Values

Arshin, a Roma from Levan, stated: "A sort of fanaticism exists among us that our own girls have to be a virgin. Therefore, we hasten [to marry her]."

Birth Control and Abortion

Fidaria, a Roma in Bregu i Lumit, explained: "I have had three [abortions] because I don't have any means of supporting them [children]. I did it because of the bad conditions I'm in. I don't have anything to feed them."

Low Education Levels

Fidaria, a Roma in Pojan, explained: "My son is in the 7th grade and my youngest daughter is in the 8th grade. My oldest daughter only completed the 4th grade because she got married young."

✶ ✶ ✶ ✶ ✶

Edlira, an Egyptian mother in Shkodra, explained: "Separations have happened but they were reconciled afterwards. I myself have reconciled some couples."

Changing Attitudes Toward Divorce

Beni, a Roma from the city of Korça, explained: "It was a difficult thing and a dishonor for the woman if she would leave a marriage. This dishonor required that all our mothers and grandmothers endure it . . . they never lifted their head up. But now this practice has become milder, and in many cases, they request the husband for a divorce."

Chapter 5. Income and Living Standards

On State Assistance

The Mayor of Bilisht stated that: "Most of the economic assistance in Bilisht is given to Roma families. During one meeting held at the Municipality, some officials were saying that we should drop this or that Roma family from the state economic program because the family is engaging in the used-clothes market. But to me, state economic assistance does not mean this, because there might be another family that does not sell used clothes, but is still in a better economic situation."

✶ ✶ ✶ ✶ ✶

An official at the State Economic Assistance office in Gjirokastra said that: "Most Roma families have migrated and it is mainly the elderly who have remained here."

✶ ✶ ✶ ✶ ✶

Afërdita, an employee at the Berat city State Economic Assistance office explained that: ". . . An average family cannot get more than L2,700–3,000 monthly. Only large Roma families can get L5,300 monthly. But members of these families also do informal construction work and are able to meet daily expenses."

On the Difficulties of Applying for and Gaining State Economic Assistance

Ylli, a Roma in Gjirokastra, explained: "When the system was overthrown, me and my wife were not able to find our formal employment records. We worked in the artistic enterprise for a long time."

* * * * *

According to Makbule, a Roma woman in Shkodra: "We are all living under very difficult conditions. We have come here from Tirana and Durrës because we could not live there. Here, at least, we can beg in the streets. We live on what people give us. We do not get any state assistance. The [State economic assistance] officers tell us that we are not eligible for it."

Household Expenditures

A Roma in Korça explained that: "The economic difficulties started when we were left without a job. When I was working, I could provide for daily food needs, but now I have a debt of L30,000. So, as soon as I get the assistance, I take it to the grocery store to pay part of my debt."

Food

Fatimi, a Roma in Korça, adds: "I have nothing to cook for breakfast with my children. So we eat whatever is available at home, like bread, sugar, butter, or pasta. Sometimes we eat lunch, sometimes we don't. For supper, we cook pasta or porridge. We buy meat once a month, when we receive state economic assistance."

On a Diet of Poverty

Makbule, a Roma woman from Pojan (Korça), illustrated: "During the week, we eat white beans, cabbage, and potatoes. All these foods make up our main food diet. For supper, we drink a little milk or yogurt and for breakfast tea and cheese. When we don't have these things, we give our children bread with oil and sugar. We buy meat when we have money to afford it. I don't have the money for meat today or tomorrow. It's been two weeks since we haven't had any meat. Eggs cost L14 apiece and we can't afford to buy them."

Old and Dilapidated Housing

Agroni, a Roma man living in a makeshift home near Breg i Lumit said: "We are unemployed and economic assistance has stopped coming. We collect used clothes to sell in the villages. I have three children. We have been staying for two or three years at my mother-in-law's house. My father had his own home, but there were seven of us children in the family, so we had to move out."

On Selling Your House to Invest in the Pyramid Scheme

Meleqe from Korça stated: "My sister-in-law had one room, which she sold. She deposited the money into one of the pyramid companies. Now, she lives with relatives. In Korça, many other Roma have sold their homes. A few of them rent, but can hardly afford it. Others live in huts, mostly along the road to Voskopoja."

Losing Your House by Investing in the Pyramid Scheme

Zenepe, a Roma woman living in a makeshift home by the Lana River in Kombinat (Tirana), talked about her family history: "I was born in Tirana, but my father came here 40 years ago from Bilisht. We are Karbuxhinj. There were six brothers and one sister in my family. My father worked as a cart driver, and my mother cleaned the streets of the city. I finished just four grades of school, while my brothers finished eight grades. We Roma are fanatic, and so my father didn't allow me to continue with school. I married out of love when I was 18 years old, with a Roma man, and one year later I had my first child. I have two children. The oldest is 18, and the other is 13. My husband has been prison in Greece since 1998, so it has been very difficult raising my children. In 1996, I sold my house for L1,500,000 [US$11,550] and I deposited the money in one of the pyramid firms. I was thinking that with the income from this investment, I would be able to buy a bigger house. I lost all the money and ended up on the streets."

* * * * *

Sadete, a Roma woman living in this area, explained: "We were left homeless because we sold our homes and invested our money in the pyramid schemes in 1996. I lost some L2,000,000. My home had two bedrooms and one kitchen. The house that I sold was near here. After I sold the house, we saw an empty spot here, so we built this shack. There are six people in my family, four children and my husband. Right now I am unemployed, but we collect used cans and the children collect scrap iron."

Land Distribution, Subsistence Farming, and Housing

Hasan, an informal Roma leader, stated: "When land was distributed, the Land Distribution Committee asked whether Roma here wanted land or state economic assistance. Since they had never worked the land, they chose state economic assistance. They were given assistance only three times, and after that, the money stopped coming."

* * * * *

Xhavit, a leader of a Roma association, explained: "I had been living in the village of Halil since 1964. Former landowners came over to tell us we shouldn't be there, because it was their land. This is why we moved to Fushë Kruja." Ali, an Egyptian in Fushë Kruja who recently migrated from Kukës, explained: "When land was distributed in 1992, I was given 8,000m² of land. But the former [pre World War II] owner threatened me and told me not to work the land . . . For this reason we had to come here, to Fushë Kruja.

* * * * *

The local leader of a Roma association explained: "In Levan, land distribution was based on the number of family members and the quality of the land." The Levan Roma *kryeplak* added: "People in this village have land. Each family received 0.12 hectare of good quality land per head. Some of us cannot maintain the land, because the maintenance costs are very high, starting from plowing, inputs, and so on. We don't even have irrigation. The villagers here say that they will give away their land, since they cannot afford to keep it. We need some bank credit, because we don't have enough money to invest in our land ourselves. . . ."

Shpresa, a Roma woman from Korça, stated: "I live with my husband and six children. We also have my [divorced] daughter's child living with us. I live just on state economic assistance, which is L5,500 (US$42.50) monthly. My husband is 38 and unemployed. I am completely illiterate, while my husband finished six years of school. What are our problems? We are homeless and don't have enough food. Four people sleep on one sofa, head to feet. The others sleep on the other sofa."

* * * * *

Skënderi, an Egyptian man from Shkodra, stated: "We had one television in our house, but while in migration in Greece, we bought a second one and some clothes."

* * * * *

Explained Selim: "My television was given to me by people who were migrating to the United States and who knew that I was poor." Sadete added: "We have two sofas and a comforter that our neighbor gave us when she bought new ones."

* * * * *

Myrteza, an Egyptian from Korça, described living conditions for his family: "We live in very bad conditions. The house where we used to live partially collapsed, so we came to live in this house. Before, we lived in the old army barracks. My son and his wife sleep outside there, where not even dogs sleep. I take my daughter to sleep with her parents-in-law, because they live a little better than us. There is no water, and no bathroom. We use the public bathroom in the bazaar. The situation gets worse because of the lack of employment. If we had a job, though, we could save some money to fix up the house."

* * * * *

A resident of Pojan (Korça), where Albanian, Roma, and Egyptian families live, explained: "The main problem in our village is drinking water, because there is none. With the overthrow of the former regime, people destroyed the water pipes, so now we have no drinking water. We have gone through periods of eight or nine months with no water at all. The entire village goes and fills up water in neighboring villages."

* * * * *

The head of the "Liria" quarter in Shkodra on the east side of Buna River sees another facet of the problem: "Whoever has money gets water, whoever doesn't have money doesn't get water." We've been living in the same houses since the socialist period, and water was scarce even then. We've even taken water from the Buna River."

* * * * *

"Another problem in our village is the sewage," stated the *kryeplak* of Pojan (Korça). We have built septic tanks, but they need to be cleaned periodically." In Fushë Kruja, one Roma responded: "There's no sewage system here worth mentioning."

* * * * * *

A Roma woman from Fushë Kruja stated: "There are two families living under this one shelter. Altogether there are nine people living in this room, while today my 16-year-old daughter-in-law had a baby. The house is practically falling apart, because we don't have money to repair it. For bathing, we use a basin in the middle of the room."

* * * * *

A Roma mother from Fushë Kruja stated: "How can I send my child to school unclean? I don't have the means to wash him. He washes his feet only once every few months. A teacher at a school in Tirana attended by Roma children explained: "They are not clean, because they have no water in their homes."

Housesitting

Nimete, a Roma woman from Berat, explained: "We have no shelter of our own. Ours was flooded three times this year by the river and now we live in a relative's home, who is a migrant in Greece. But when he comes back, we have no place to live."

Living Space Per Capita

Agimi from Korça explained: "There are 17 of us all living in two rooms. When we go to sleep, we divide up the house into two. Some sleep here, the others sleep there."

Sanitation

The *kryeplak* of Pojan (Korça) commented, "We have built septic tanks but they need to be cleaned periodically."

Electricity

Skënder, a Roma from Pojan (Korça), stated: "The power voltage is 80–90 watts, and only after 10:00 in the evening does it go up."

* * * * *

Avni, an Egyptian from Uznova (Berat), explained: "We were cut off from electricity because we didn't have the money to pay for it. Now we use candle light, because we can't fight the state."

Weak Government Capacity to Provide Health Care Services.

As a doctor from Korça noted. "In Korça, especially during the transition period, you haven't been able to enter the operation room without paying under the table. Doctors also ask for money from the white hand, but the white hand has friends and knows where to turn."

* * * * *

"At a hospital when they see a Roma, they have it in their head that Roma are very wealthy, so they demand a lot of money. The Roma is obliged to give the money, but the people who don't have the money can't. This is the general case for all Albanians, but for Roma they think that we're better off."

Roma and Egyptian Perceptions on Improving Living Conditions and Health Situation

According to a leader of a Roma association in Tirana: "Those families that now live along the Lana River live in shacks, but when they [the local municipality] tear those down, like they say they will, I don't know where they'll go. Former owners have taken the properties and so these families have nowhere to build their shacks on. The government should invest in shelter for them, because they themselves don't have the financial means. We have to think about these families' perspectives."

* * * * *

According to Roma and Egyptians, to improve housing and living conditions, local governments should provide families with shelter or financial assistance for home construction. According to a leader of a Roma association in Tirana: "Those families that now live along the Lana River live in shacks, but when they [the local municipality] tear those down, like they say they will, I don't know where they'll go . . . The government should invest in shelter for them, because they themselves don't have the financial means. . . ."

* * * * *

Makbule, a Roma woman in Berat, illustrated: "I just want some assistance to build a home, because I have three children who are ill. I lived in a shack before, but the river flooded over and took [our home]. Now I'm out on the street. The local government doesn't help us. Floods also took the blankets [the government] gave us, and we've been left in a bad situation. My main problem is housing, because I need to keep my children together. Just one room, that's all I want."

Roma and Egyptians' Perceptions of Health and Health Care Standards

---

Health Problems in Levan (Fier)

"We have cases of mental defects. My own child in fact is mentally disabled. He doesn't develop normally, he was born premature. He's 15 now, but he acts as though he were seven or eight. We also have about three or four cases of meningitis, but this isn't a problem. They are rare cases. And [pointing to a child at his side] this child here used to be normal, but at about 14 or 15, he became paralyzed. There was another one like this who died. There are many crippled children here, about 10 to 15 cases."

Chapter 6. Education

Language Difficulties

Skënder, a Roma leader from Elbasan, stated: "One of the main reasons why our children leave school is that they don't know Albanian well . . . Our children, from age 2–3 and up to 5–6, speak only the Roma language. This is a very delicate issue, because to take a Roma child who doesn't know a single word of Albanian, and to place him side by side with an Albanian child is not fair at all. When the teacher addresses a question to a Roma student, the student responds half in Romani and half in Albanian. His classmates begin to laugh at him, so he leaves school ashamed."

* * * * *

Majlinda, an Albanian teacher in Bilisht, added: "Egyptians seem to be more integrated in every day life because they don't have a language of their own, while the Roma community has its own language. Anybody who begins the 1st grade and has to start learning a new language would have it rather difficult. They are all intelligent children. To overcome this difficulty, I had to learn how to count in their language so that I could teach them the equivalent in Albanian."

* * * *

Nure, a girl from Delvina, is a rare example of the Roma and Egyptian community with high educational qualifications.

Education opportunities and personal initiative

Nure, a 19 year-old young woman from Delvina, identifies herself as Egyptian and Roma. Nure was born in Delvina. Her father identifies as a Roma, and her mother as an Egyptian. Nure's paternal grandparents are Roma from Delvina, who both worked under socialism—the grandfather as a blacksmith, and her grandmother as a collective farm worker picking olives. Her maternal grandparents are Egyptian from Tirana—her grandmother worked as a cleaning person, while her grandfather was a welder. Nure's parents both studied to become teachers. Her mother teaches literature, and English and Albanian languages, and her father is a teacher of history and geography. Her parents met as colleagues teaching at the same school in Peshkopija. Their marriage was not arranged, but based on love.

Nure has an older, and a younger sister. All three sisters are exceptional students and won several school performance awards. They attended an ethnically diverse school in Delvina. The girls shared one room in their parents' home, where they also did their homework. Nure's parents initiated her transfer to a high school in Tirana to improve her chances for entering university. Nure now lives with her maternal Egyptian grandmother in Tirana. She is currently enrolled as a second-semester student of German at the University of Tirana. As in Delvina, Nure continues to be one of the best students in her high school and now university.

Reflecting on her school achievements, Nure clearly acknowledges that her social environment and support of the extended family provided the basis for her motivation at school, and taught her the value of an education. Nure was socialized into the Egyptian culture, i.e., Albanian language, music, and way of life. She is fluent in Albanian and German, but also speaks and reads Greek and Italian. Nure identifies herself as a proud young Egyptian who is conscientious, energetic, open-minded, future- and goal-oriented.

(*continued*)

She aims to become a university teacher. Her short-term goal is to study political science and German at a university in Germany. Based on her school achievements and ambitious and energetic character, Nure was successful in obtaining a scholarship from the Goethe Institute, which will allow her to reach her goal to study abroad. After gaining her university degree abroad, Nure plans to return to Albania to teach at a university. She would like to start a family, marry an Egyptian, and have two children.

Thinking ahead to when she'll be a teacher, Nure would like to help Roma/Egyptian pupils. Remembering her school days in Delvina, where Roma/Evgit children tended to sit at the back of the classroom, and many dropped out of school without a degree, Nure has several ideas on how to address these issues. Nure suggests that schools that initiate additional supportive teaching courses for children who have difficulties attending the morning classes. She also would like to promote the active participation of parents in their children's education.

In order to motivate Roma and Egyptian pupils, Nure considers it crucial to have more Roma and Egyptian teachers in the schools, teaching both Roma/Egyptian and Albanian pupils. Another idea would be to teach Roma children in the Romani language from the first to the 4th grade using Romani school books, while at the same time, also teaching them Albanian with Albanian text books. This model has been successfully applied in Delvina with the Albanian-Greek pupils.

Internal and International Migration

One Roma familiar with Roma education issues explained: "Through international migration, Roma families can somewhat improve their economic situation, but only about 10 percent of their children go to school. The majority . . . are illiterate."

Malnourishment

Majlinda, an Albanian teacher in Bradashesh, stated, "Egyptian students are physically very weak and cannot sit still during lessons. I think this comes from the malnourishment that they've suffered since they were small children."

Language Difficulties

Skënder, a Roma leader from Elbasan, stated: "One of the main reasons why our children leave school is that they don't know Albanian well . . . His classmates begin to laugh at him, so he leaves school ashamed."

Traditional Gender Roles

A primary school principal in Baltëz added: "In our school, there are 70 Roma students from the 1st grade to the 9th grade. Up to the 4th grade, they show some interest in learning. Only a few of them succeed in finishing the 9th grade. Up to the 4th grade, the female-male ratio is almost equal. But starting in the 5th grade, families keep their daughters at home, because they want to marry them off. The school has no Roma girls in grades 5th through 8th. Boys' attendance also goes down because their parents take them to help with work."

* * * * *

In the village of Morava, a Roma girl explained: "I am 11 years old and in the 3rd grade. My mother doesn't like me to go to school, because she thinks I am grown up. She says she is afraid about me being teased by boys. She says 'If rumors spread that boys are teasing you, then the neighbors will think you are not a decent girl.' "

* * * * *

Petrit, an informal leader in Kinostudio (Tirana): "Because of disparities between Albanian children and Roma children in the field of education, a preschool facility was opened in 1996. One of the preschool's aims was to prepare Roma children for public schools. The preschool is open to both Roma and non-Roma children. About 50 children currently attend—25 Roma, 10 Egyptians, and the rest, Albanian. Some Roma children come here in the afternoons to learn. There are about 10 Roma children who stay with their families during the day because they don't have the economic conditions to come to school, so we've created the possibility for them to learn in the afternoon."

Poverty-related Barriers to Education

Selim, a Roma from Çuka (Saranda), said: "My oldest son is 16 years old and now attends the 2nd grade, because we couldn't send him to school any earlier. I told the teacher that we didn't have the money to send the children to school. We hardly earn enough for food, let alone for books, pens, and pencils."

* * * * *

Arben, a 12-year-old Roma boy from Pojan (Korça), explained his reasons for dropping out of school: "My father told me I had to spend my time doing other things, even though I was fond of school. I couldn't do anything about it. As of now, I help my father with trading animals."

* * * * *

A Roma woman from Korça explained: "We go together with our husbands as far as Përmet to sell baskets. We have to pull our children out of school, as we are afraid to leave them at home alone."

* * * * *

An inspector of education in Fier explains: "This law is unenforceable. First, because the fines we delegate for enforcement to the local authorities never get collected. Second, the penalized families are rather poor. In the conditions of not being able to earn their bread, what fine can the state get from them . . . ? A child doesn't go to school to simply fulfill an obligation towards the state, but above all, for his own good. We can apply fines whenever we want, but this will serve for nothing."

A woman in Shkozët stated: "My niece is ending up without any school because in Shkozët, the school is far . . . We're scared to send her to school."

* * * * *

Sonila, a teacher in Bradashesh (Elbasan) explained: "A few years ago, when the new school year started, more then 20 percent of Egyptian girls didn't enroll in the 7th grade, as they were married during the summer holidays."

Safety concerns affect education levels: Xhaviti, a Roma informal leader

"In Levan, only 66 children go to school, while the 250 other children in Levan have never gone to school, or they have dropped out after completing one grade. I think the main reason for this is, first, the distance of school from the community and, second, the events of 1997.

An actual war happened here in 1997, and children were injured. One day, a group of 18 people came down to Levan and shot two Roma from our village. Then the men of the village took up their arms, surrounded the group of 18, and, after a short exchange of fire, shot them all dead. After this, fearing possible revenge, we moved our wives and children to neighboring villages. The people from these villages, who were white, helped us with food. We put up roadblocks everywhere in the village, even near the national road, and didn't allow arms into the village. For months on end, the men were on alert, standing guard day and night, until the situation became normal and the state became strong again. From 1997–1998, none of our children crossed the main road to go to school."

Discrimination by Teachers

A Roma student from Tirana explained that "She [the teacher] gives special treatment to whites. She beats us, but she never beats the white students." A leader of a Roma association in Korça stated: "Our children are looked upon with disdain. Teachers do not treat them well, so they drop out of school."

Chapter 7. Labor

Traditional Occupations

Skënder, a Cergar from Fshati Rom (Fier), illustrates that: "We (as Roma) have been the most advantaged group, because we did business by trading old pans at a time when the other ethnic groups were not allowed to sell even one egg. . . . We have been very privileged. I have been a car-driver, but others worked in handicrafts, horse dealing, or were specialized metal workers, willow workers, or musicians."

Geographical Pockets of Poverty

Kujtim, an informal Roma leader from Gjirokastra, illustrates: "I worked in the handicraft enterprise until the year 1990. I was a master of willow works. All of the women of our community were also working in this enterprise. However, the enterprise was shut down during the transition period, and now I find myself jobless. There are seven people in my family. I cannot go to Greece illegally, as I am not young. This is why unemployment is our main problem. . . ."

Trade in Used Clothes

Bujar, a Roma businessman from Tirana, described his experience in the used-clothes business: "I started dealing in small, informal business in 1985. By 1989, I had purchased furniture for the house and had saved L28,000 [US$3,500]. I had exchanged these savings to US dollars, so I wasn't affected by the devaluation of the *lekë* when the transition started. In 1992, I used the money for business. I went to Romania. I had heard that over there goods were much cheaper than in Albania, where food and clothing was in shortage. That is why I decided to start doing business with these goods. I didn't have acquaintances in Romania, but that's not a problem for us, since we encounter Roma everywhere we go. They help us find and buy goods at reasonable prices. We sold those goods very quickly in the Albanian market, where used clothes were rare. At that time, there were no customs duties or taxes, so all Roma who engaged in this trade got rich very quickly. When I first went to Romania, I only had US$500. I used the money to buy clothes and shirts, two bags in all. I sold them in three days and made L60,000 [US$600]. This encouraged me to go again. Roma who engaged in this type of business from 1990–1994 became wealthy. Then competition with the white hand started. They were more educated and have relations with the customs and tax officers that we Roma do not have. Increasing competition eventually shut us out of the game."

* * * * *

Pranvera, a businesswoman from Rrapishta (Elbasan), explained that compared to three years ago (1999) "income has decreased 5 to 6 times. Previously, we earned L30,000 [US$214] a month, whereas now we earn L5,000 [US$38].

* * * * *

Iris, a young mother from Tirana, described her experience with selling used clothes: "I get the clothes at the market for L300 [US$2.31] and sell them for L500 [US$3.85]. Yesterday I went with my children to the villages, but I got caught by the snow, so I had to return home. I only made L100 [US$0.77], just enough for bread." Fatmira, a Roma woman from Berat, stated: "There are seven in my family, and we are all unemployed. We trade used clothes in-kind in the village and get an onion or beans to feed ourselves. We go with our neighbors and take the children with us. We go as far as Tomorri and Lubesh."

* * * * *

One Roma leader from Driza, stated: "In this village, 70 percent of Roma families that have not migrated internationally are in the used-clothes business. But they owe money to wholesale businessmen. This happens because when the wholesalers give us the bale of clothes, they tell us to sell it and then pay them afterwards. But when we open the bale, we see that it's full of very old clothes—so old that they cannot be sold."

* * * * *

Ervehe, a Roma woman from Korça, stated: "I work together with my husband and son in the used-clothes business. We have been in this business for the last seven or eight years. We buy the clothes from white wholesalers in Tirana, Elbasan, and other cities, who bring them in from Italy or some other place. The clothes are sold by bale. We pay L30,000–32,000 [US$222–237] per bale. We pay for the bales by how much they weigh, but sell the clothes by the piece. With each bale, we can make a profit of L20,000–30,000 [US$148–222], but sometimes we can't even break even. In the summer, we can make a daily turnover of up to L8,000 [US$59]. This is what we do, and how we feed ourselves."

Internal Migration

Jorida, a supervisor at the Office of Economic Assistance in the city of Berat, explained: "The labor market in Berat is small and there are few jobs, and poverty is much greater here than in other cities. Even casual work is difficult to find . . . Unemployed Egyptians have to go and look for jobs in other cities, such as Durrës, Vlora, and sometimes even as far as Saranda. If you wake up at 5 o'clock in the morning, you will see buses full of Egyptians traveling to other cities. They return home in the evenings. Some Egyptians have set up temporary residences [outside Berat] and return home once a week. They can earn up to L1,000 [US$7.69] a day. In these cities, they go to the Omonia square and wait for employers. There are over 50 people here who go . . . for low-skilled work, mainly in construction."

Casual Work and "Omonia" Places

Ndriçim, an unemployed Egyptian from Bradashesh, explained: "Everyday at around 6 or 7 o'clock in the morning I go to the square we call 'Guri i Madh.' There are about 50 of us looking for a job in that square every morning. Many others go to the mechanical plant, or stay home and wait for an employer to call on them. There are even cases in which we work for only three days a month in laying foundation or concrete. Daily wages range from L500–1,000, depending on the difficulty of the job. If I could work for five days a month, I'd be lucky. . . . Most of the people here are low-skilled workers.

Musical Performance

Arian, a young Egyptian from Gjirokastra, explained: "During the summer, we perform every week at weddings. When the wedding season begins, we form a band of four or five friends. We have a bar named 'Musician,' where interested people come and hire the band for weddings or other celebrations. . . . Income from each wedding varies from

L20,000–30,000 per person. . . . With this money we can support ourselves for two or three months. We give the money to our parents, who use it for daily household needs."

Skënder, a Roma from Delvina, explained: "I started playing in bands at weddings when I was 13 or 14. I've played the accordion and the violin. We Roma play music by ear, not by notes. I usually perform at weddings three to four times a month. People hire us and give us an advance of L15,000–20,000, depending on the number of people invited to the wedding. When a girl is married, more people are invited to the wedding, so the pay is higher. The music we play depends on the region where the wedding is held. In the villages where the Greek minority lives, we mostly play Greek music, but we also play authentic Albanian music. In Konispol, they ask us to play Çam music."[118]

Chapter 8. Migration and Remittances

Why Migrate?

A Gjirokastra Roma migrant commented, "There is no work here. The first month, I worked with concrete for two days and earned L30,000. Add L30,000 [from state] assistance, and that's L60,000 to feed yourself and six others."

* * * * *

An Albanian kindergarten teacher in Gjirokastra succinctly explains the role of international migration for Roma and Egyptians: "In Albania, they do not have work. Therefore they have to go abroad. In the private sector, they are not given any jobs, that is to say, discrimination exists."

The Role of Remittances

One Roma from Delvina raised the issue of investment with a small group of local Roma: "I told them that the money they earn over there, they could invest in something here (Albania), but they didn't think much about it." An Egyptian in Shkodra states that commercial investment was impossible due to poor infrastructure: "Look how they have their homes attached to one another. There's no place even to build a new house, let alone a store."

Families with Social Capital

A Roma man from the village of Çuka stated: "I have not gone [abroad] because what would my mother and wife eat?"

---

118. *Çam*: an ethnic group that originated in Greece. They moved to Albania after World War II and now live mainly in southern Albania.

Working and Living Conditions

> **A Roma from Morava (Berat)**
>
> "At the beginning, we earned 4,000 drachmas. During harvesting time, we were paid up to 15–20 drachmas daily, but it was very tiring. We slept in tents, bathed in canals . . . It was very difficult work, but it seemed good to us because we got money out of it. We would stay 2–3 months. If we found other work, we'd stay longer. There were times when we'd be without work for two weeks. . . . we'd borrow money from a friend. There were also Greeks who would help by lending us money. When we came back, we would come back on our own."

Impact on Families and Individuals

An Egyptian mother from Risli recounts: "My son left for Italy two or three months ago. He is unemployed, he doesn't have any documents. . . . I don't sleep at night because of this."

Chapter 9. Prostitution and Trafficking

Entry Points into Prostitution

Jeta, a Roma woman from Kinostudio (Tirana), explained: "He lied to her and told her that he would take her as his wife, but he already had a wife at home. He kept her for a few weeks here, then afterwards, took her to Italy. After one week, she telephoned her mother and told her that he was beating and torturing her."

Families Sell or Rent Girls and Young Women

Gëzim, a Roma in Kinostudio (Tirana), added: "There are those from the white hand that come and tell the parents that they will take the girl to work in Italy. The parents give her out of poverty. They then take them into prostitution."

* * * * *

Eni, a Roma woman from Delvina, explained: "Our parents would tell us to be careful . . . our teacher also would tell us to not talk to strangers when we go out."

* * * * *

Another Roma mother stated: "When the girls go to school, we instruct them to be careful."

Early and Arranged Marriages

A Roma woman from Roskovec explains: "Husbands beat their wives because of the bad economic situation they're in. The wives can't do anything about it, and they have nowhere to go. Therefore they endure [the beating] until the last day comes. Then they go into prostitution."

Family and Community Norms/Values

Generally, many Roma families object to having former prostitutes living in their neighborhoods: "They have come here but don't stay long because we don't accept them because they have gone into prostitution and don't want them to take our children into that life also."

Economic and Social Costs and Benefits

Ana, a Roma woman in Tirana, explained: "The man leaves [his wife] with two or three children and finds another. . . . So she leaves the children at her parents' doorstep and she takes off afterwards."

* * * * *

Selim from Bilisht has returned to Albania after four years in prison in Greece for drugs transportation: "I returned from Greece last year, but now I am jobless and homeless. I had one child, who passed away, and my wife has married another man."

* * * * *

Blendi, a Roma from Levan, responded: "There have been cases in which a prostitute returned home and was accepted by her family, but her brother refused to accept her. There have been cases in which the son of one family learned that his sister returned and he told [his family] 'I won't return from international migration because you have accepted her.' "

Children Who are Rented or Sold by Their Families

Naim, a Roma in a Korça market, explained: "Usually neighbors can take them. They approach the parents and tell them that we will take your child and that nothing will happen to him because he will be under my care. I will take my share and you will take yours. . . . Children start from the ages of eight to twelve."

Children Who are Sent to Work in Nearby Cities and Towns

The head of "Alb Rom" in the district of Durrës commented: "There are as many cases of begging as you want, but here there are no cases of children that are rented out to beg."

Chapter 10. Social Capital

Neighborhood/village Solidarity as Cognitive Social Capital

When asked if neighbors assist community members who are sick, Sajmirë, a Roma in Breg i Lumit, responded: "Yes, the neighborhood helps if someone is sick, and when someone has a problem, somebody goes around the neighborhood and collects something and they give it to him."

Roma or Egyptian Solidarity at the National Level

Eri, a Roma in Shkodra, described the significance of the lack of solidarity between primary *fise*. When asked if he had ever migrated abroad, he explained: "I don't have the visa, nor the money. If I had the visa, I would go with my entire family, because I don't have anywhere to leave my family here, because they aren't our *fis*."

Roma and Egyptian Associations as Structural Social Capital

Zeri, a Roma from Roskovec, reported: "When the association was created, they came and took some lekë and they told us that they would make an association, and that they would help us both with state assistance and with visas . . . There aren't any Roma around who have received any assistance or anything else. . . ."

Selected Albanian Roma and Egyptian NGOs and Contact Information

The following Roma and Egyptian Non-government Organizations assisted in the fulfillment of this project's objectives:

Roma

"Alba Rom." President: Ramazan Elmazi. Address: Lagja NISH Tulla, Durrës.

"Amaro Drom." President: Mr. Skender Veliu. Address: Rruga e Kavajes, Pranë Shtepise Botuese "Naim Frasheri," Kati 3, Tiranë. Tel/Fax: 355-4 249025. Cell phone: 355 68 2039014. email: amarodrom@albaniaonline.net.

Association "Democratic Union of Albanian Roma," President: Mr. Gurali Mejdani. Address: Rruga "Irfan Tomini," P. 9, Shk. 2, Ap. 14, Tiranë. Tel/Fax: 355-42 28630. Cell phone: 355 682047622.

"Disutni Albania." Chairman: Mr. Arben Kosturi. Address: Rruga "Mihal Grameno," Nr. 2, Korçë. Tel: 355 824 4212. Cell phone: 335 69 22 58349. Email: disutnialb@albmail.com.

Association "Roms for Integration." Chairman: Mr. Istref Pellumbi. Address: Rruga e Kavajes, Pallatet e Kafotit C Shk. 1, Nr. 1, Tiranë. Email: integrrom@albmail.com.

"Rromani Baxt." Chairman: Pellumb Fortuna. Address: Rruga "Halit Bega" 28, Tiranë. Tel/Fax: 355 43 68324. Email: afortuna@albaniaonline.net.

Egyptian

"Kabaja." Chairman: Mr. Resul Duro. Tel. 355 8251213, Korçë.

"Nefreta." Chairman: Mr. Behar Sadiku. Address: Rruga "Myrtezim Këlluçi," Tiranë. Cell phone: 355 69 2282875.

"Vellazërimi," Chairman: Mr. Fuat Memeti.

The Patrilineal Kinship Structure of One Roma *Fis*

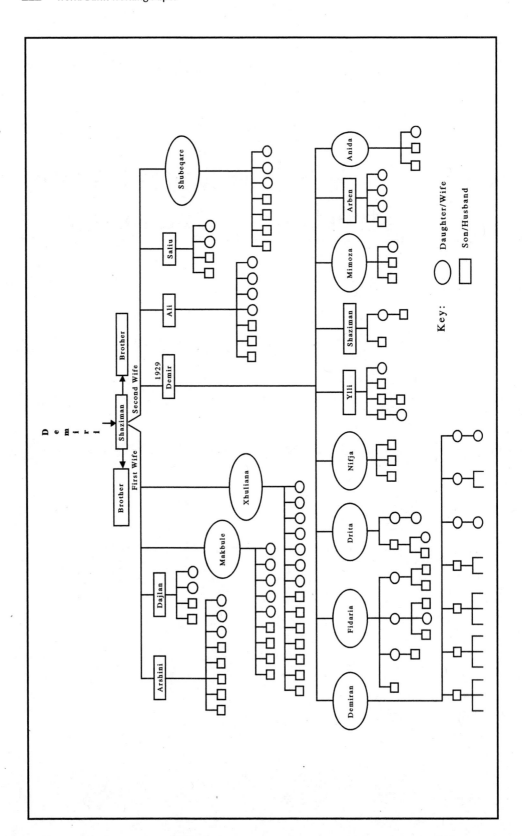

National Minorities in Albania

The Hoxha Period. In Article 42 of the constitution, national minorities were ensured protection with regard to culture, tradition, language, and education. The constitution guaranteed equal development in all spheres of social life, and legally protected minorities from inequality and discrimination. National minorities included Macedonians, Greeks, and Montenegrins but not Roma and Egyptians. Under the forced equality with rest of the Albanian population, they received all the services provided by the state, e.g., education, health, and housing. However, in order to access these services, nomadic populations, including the Roma, were required to settle. By the 1960s, the process of settlement was complete and no nomadic groups remained in Albania (Mara 2002).

The Republic of Albania. In Article 26/Paragraph II, national minorities are guaranteed fundamental human rights and equal protection under the law without discrimination. They are free to express and develop their ethnic, cultural, religious, and linguistic identities and associate in organizations to protect their interests and identities. Furthermore, they may be educated in their mother tongue. Nationality is determined by accepted international norms; at this time, Greeks, Macedonians, and Montenegrins are identified as national minorities. Roma and Egyptians are considered Albanians (ECRI 2002).

European Union Accession Regulations. There are two EU documents that have stipulations regarding human and minority rights that are relevant to the Roma and Egyptians situation. The first are the Copenhagen criteria, established in 1993, to guide countries striving to join the EU towards stable democratic political system and successful economies. These criteria state: "Membership requires that the candidate country has achieved stability of institutions guaranteeing democracy, the rule of law, human rights and respect for and protection of minorities." The second are the Europe Agreements, which were made with each candidate country beginning in 1991, to initiate the legal framework for their integration

223

into the EU. Article 6 states "respect for the democratic principles and human rights established by the Helsinki Final Act and the Charter of Paris for a new Europe." In 1997, the European Commission created Agenda 2000 on the future of the European Community. As a part of this, EU enlargement and the progress of candidate countries were evaluated. It was found that while the integration of minorities in most candidate countries was progressing well, the situation of the Roma in six countries was "cause for concern."[119]

---

119. Quotes and information taken from: European Commission, 2002. *EU Support for Roma Communities in Central and Eastern Europe.* Enlargement Briefing, Brussels. The six countries are Bulgaria, the Czech Republic, Hungary, Poland, Romania, and Slovakia.

"The List"

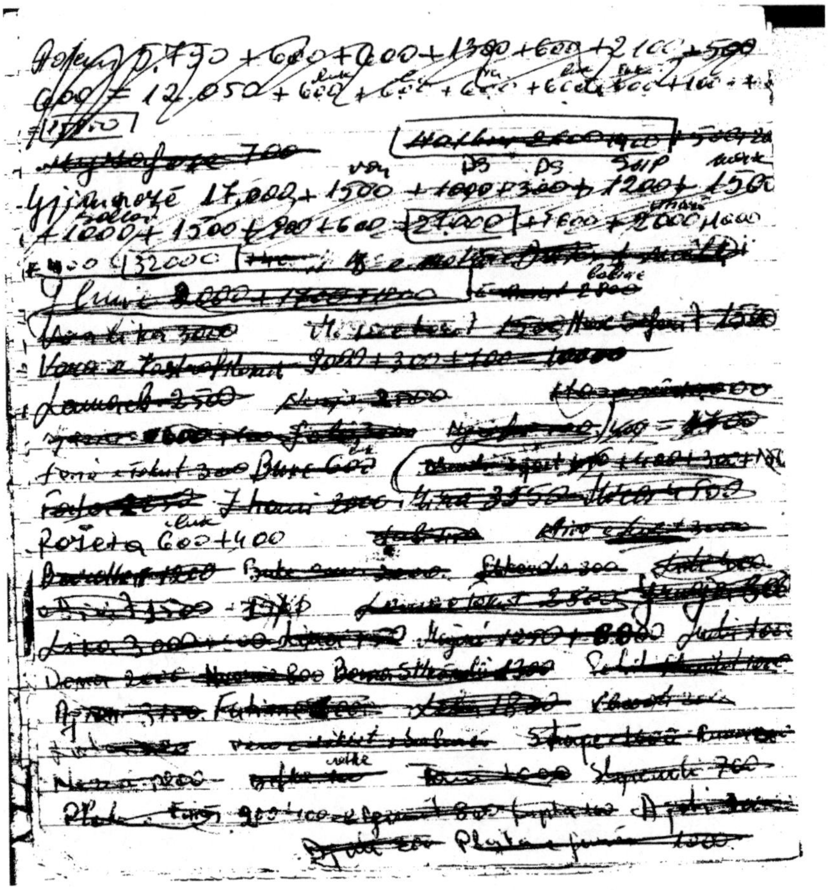
12.050 + 600
17.000 + 1500
Rozeta 600+400

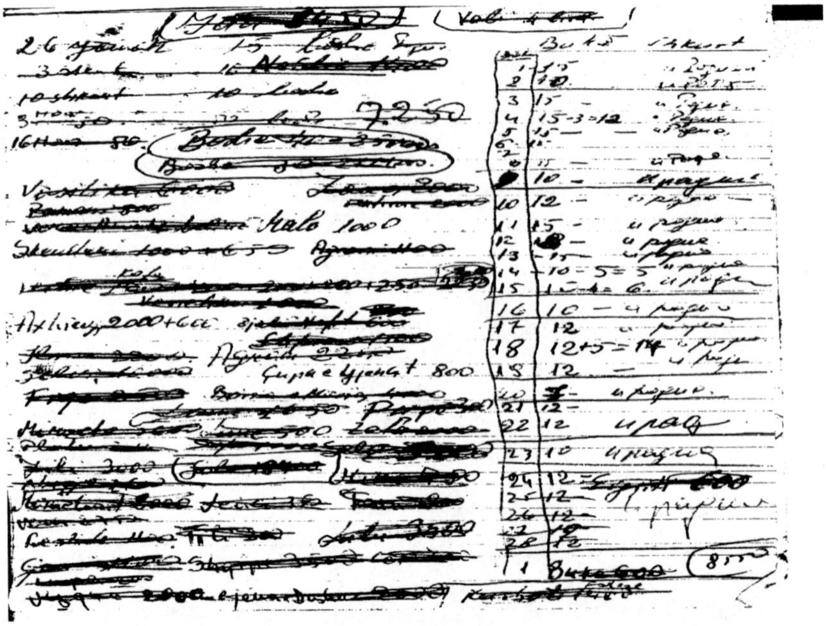
Kalo 1000
Axhiu 2000+600

Community Profiles

1. The District of Shkodra

The district of Shkodra (pop. 185,794; INSTAT 2001) is located in northwestern Albania and borders Montenegro to the north and the Adriatic Sea to the west. Its administrative center, the city of Shkodra (pop. 83,598; INSTAT 2001), is home to historical and cultural monuments. The district's primary economic activity is agriculture, forestry, and fishing. The overall unemployment rate is 28 percent for the district.[120]

Around 60–70 Roma and approximately 1,200 Egyptians reside within the district. Roma are concentrated in a southwest periphery zone, along the Buna River. Egyptians live in the "Liria" quarter of the city, and on both sides of the Buna River. Both Roma and Egyptian communities are extremely poor.

The Roma, comprised of 12–20 families, migrated to Shkodra during the last decade in hopes of better work opportunities. Most families migrated from Fushë Kruja, but some arrived from Tirana, Durrës, Elbasan, Vlora, and Lushnja. Families who migrated from Fushë Kruja had lived in Halilaj until the end of the socialist period. Sources of income include begging and selling used clothes in the city and surrounding villages, and casual employment in construction, pipe-laying, and portage.

Two hundred Egyptians, who make up 30–40 families, live on the west bank of the Buna River near the Roma community. One thousand Egyptians are concentrated on the east bank, in a neighborhood called "Mahalla e Magjypve" (Parruca 2001). Egyptians who live on the west bank have little contact with those on the east bank. Major sources of income include metalwork, musical performance, selling used clothes, and casual work in construction and delivery/portage.

---

120. INSTAT (2002) provided all district unemployment rates listed in this chapter. 2002 unemployment rates are unavailable.

A religious organization has made investments in infrastructure. It currently also provides food assistance to Egyptians and Roma.

School attendance is extremely low among both Roma and Egyptian children. First, families cannot afford to buy books and supplies. Second, parents require children to beg for the family rather than attend school. Third, from 1992–1998, no schools existed in the vicinity of either Roma or Egyptian quarters, so children were unable to attend school during this period.

Today, Roma children attend, although irregularly, a school located near their Roma quarter, which is funded by an international NGO. In 1998, a religious organization built a school that is now attended by 60 Egyptian children on the east side of the river. On the west bank, two NGOs recently organized sewing and literacy courses for women and founded a school that provides literacy courses for children.

2. The District of Kruja

The district of Kruja (pop. 64,357; INSTAT 2001) is located approximately 30 km north of Tirana, the capital city of Albania. Most interviews and surveys within the district were conducted in Fushë Kruja (pop. 18,619; INSTAT 2001), where most Roma and Egyptians live. Unemployment is 19 percent in the district (INSTAT 2002). Major economic activity is based in agriculture and the cement industry, and many families produce hydro-lime, which is sold as building material.

Roma currently in Fushë Kruja have lived in the village of Halilaj since the late 1970s, having migrated there from different regions of the country. In Halilaj, most Roma worked in agriculture. They re-settled in Fushë Kruja during the early years of the transition period in the 1990s.

Several families were given land in Halilaj during this period. However, these families experienced difficulties with the implementation of land distribution laws, because of legal ambiguities or land seizure. In some cases, Albanians with titles to properties that were being occupied by Roma families forced the families to leave.[121]

The Roma community of 800, mostly 150–200 Karbuxhinj families, is concentrated along the town's river. Most homes lack basic infrastructure, such as water supply, sewage hookups, and electricity. These Roma described a high frequency of police violence directed at them.

Sources of income include selling used clothes in Fushë Kruja and surrounding villages, begging and fortune-telling in nearby towns, and casual work as manual laborers.

Most of the 150–200 Roma families do not receive state economic assistance. Some families have been told by the local State Economic Assistance office that they are not eligible for economic assistance in Fushë Kruja because they are still registered as Halilaj residents.

Roma school attendance rates are near zero because families are too poor to purchase books and school supplies.

---

121. For more examples of this practice, see Chapter 5, "Income and Living Standards" and Appendix E, "More Voices of Albania."

Woman-trafficking is extremely common among local Roma. Poor families rent their daughters to Albanian traffickers, or Roma women enter prostitution to support their families.

The Egyptian population of 800 live all over Fushë Kruja. The first Egyptian families arrived in Fushë Kruja in the 1930s. They worked as blacksmiths and tile and brick craftsmen. More families arrived in the 1950s and 1960s. During the early years of the transition period, approximately 13 to 14 additional families, or approximately 70 individuals, migrated to the city from the northeastern districts of Burrel, Peshkopi, and Kukës. Most of these 70 Egyptians are unemployed but also do not receive state economic assistance. Their school attendance rates are low compared to Egyptians in other districts.

Several Egyptian families also live in the historic town of Kruja (pop. 19,400). Major sources of income include production of hydro-lime, casual work in construction and portage, and state economic assistance.

3. The District of Durrës

The district of Durrës (pop. 182,988; INSTAT 2001) is located in western Albania on the Adriatic coast. Its administrative center, the 2,500 year-old city of Durrës (pop. 99,546), is the country's largest port and site of important historical monuments. The district's major economic resources are agriculture, industry, sea and railroad transportation, tourism, and construction. The district's unemployment rate is 27 percent (INSTAT 2002). After Tirana, the city of Durrës is the country's largest target of direct foreign investment, mainly from Italy. Since 1993, migrants from northeastern Albania have settled in the city's outskirts, including some Roma and Egyptians.

Roma have lived in the district since at least the early 1930s. Currently, approximately 1,100 Roma live there. No reliable population estimates for Egyptians were available.

There are Roma communities in Shkozet, in an area called "Kthesa e Ariut," near a former brick manufacturing plant. The majority of Shkozet Roma are Meçkars. These Roma were provided homes and settled near the plant when it opened in 1964. It closed in 1989, but another one was later opened in the city of Durrës, where Roma continued working. High unemployment in Shkozet began when state cooperatives were closed at the beginning of the transition period in the early 1990s. Many families who had worked in socialist agricultural cooperatives were provided with land at the beginning of transition but most have since sold their property. A German organization recently founded a Roma kindergarten which provides children with four years of general education and meals.

Other communities are located in the villages of Xhafzotaj, Fllaka, and Kulla. Some Roma households in Xhafzotaj migrated from other districts following the country's political and social unrest in 1997. They have higher primary school attendance rates than Roma in other localities in the district.

The Roma community in Kthesa e Ariut is mainly comprised of Karbuxhinj Roma, but there are also approximately 20 Cergar households. Cergars were settled and provided homes there in 1968. They had previously lived in Peqin, having moved there from Rrogozhina and Elbasan after the Albanian border's closure in 1946. Some families own and have retained land that was distributed to them by the state in 1992.

Sources of income among Roma within the district include agriculture, selling used clothes, casual work in construction, musical performance, begging, fortune-telling, can and scrap metal collecting, and migrant labor in Italy and Greece.

Both Shkozet and Kthesa e Ariut have high woman- and child-trafficking rates.

The Shkozet-based Roma association, "Alb Rom," directs programs throughout the district in the areas of culture, art, and education.

Most Egyptians of Durrës reside in Këneta, a neighborhood on the outskirts of the city of Durrës, and in another neighborhood near the center of the city. Their main form of employment is casual work and, to a lesser extent, communal services. School attendance is low, especially in that quarter.

4. The District of Tirana

The district of Tirana (pop. 523,150; INSTAT 2001) is located in central Albania, 30 km east of the Adriatic Coast. The city of Tirana (pop. 343,078; INSTAT 2001), the district's administrative center, is the country's capital and largest city. Most residents, including Roma and Egyptians, migrated from surrounding areas during the second half of the 20th century, mostly after 1993. Tirana is the country's largest target of direct foreign investment, as well as its largest economic center. Various branches of the service, construction, and transportation industries are concentrated there. The overall rate of district unemployment is 25 percent (INSTAT 2002).

No reliable population estimates are available for either Roma or Egyptians. However, Roma are mainly concentrated in periphery areas, such as Kinostudio, Bregu i Lumit, Selita, Kombinat, Kodra Kamez, and Yzberisht. Most Roma in Tirana are Karbuxhinj, while a small number of families are Meçkars or Cergars. Although primary *fis* identities exist among Roma in Tirana, most families are organized by extended kinship.

Bregu i Lumit and Kombinat are two of the poorest Roma neighborhoods in the country and have high woman- and child-trafficking rates.

Egyptians live in various mixed neighborhoods in the city of Tirana, mainly in Kinostudio, near the Children's Hospital, and Brraka. Many live in homes with poor infrastructure and have high unemployment rates and low education levels. Unemployment is high, and most with jobs engage in casual work, mainly in construction, or communal services.

Those who live near the Children's Hospital are relatively more prosperous compared to those in Brraka or Kinostudio. Some are musicians or market or street vendors, and some families migrate abroad for short- and long-term periods.

Sources of income include used clothes sales, different forms of casual work, begging, musical performance, and informal work in Greece. A few well-to-do Roma families, who own import-export businesses, live in Tirana.

5. The District of Elbasan

The district of Elbasan (pop. 224,974; INSTAT 2001) is located in central Albania along the banks of the Shkumbin River. Its administrative center is the city of Elbasan (pop. 87,797; INSTAT 2001). Major economic resources include agriculture, forestry, transportation, and the services. The unemployment rate is 23 percent for the district (INSTAT 2002).

Approximately 2,622 Roma and 8,318 Egyptians live within the district.

Most Elbasan Roma are Karbuxhinj. Most Karbuxhinj families migrated to Elbasan from Folorina, Greece, in the mid- to late-1910s. Members of other Roma *fise* recently migrated to Elbasan from Berat. Most live in the outskirts of the city in the "5 Maji" neighborhood of Rrapishta. Some families also live in two other neighborhoods. Approximately 90 Roma live in Cërrik.

Major sources of income include used-clothes sales and casual work. Roma families in Elbasan migrate in large groups for short-term periods to Greece, where they collect used clothes and beg. Because of high poverty and international migration rates, few Roma children in Elbasan attend school.

The Egyptian community is scattered throughout the city of Elbasan, and is one of the poorest in the country. As a source of income, some in Bradashesh sell blood at a local hospital. School attendance is extremely low, since families cannot afford to purchase books, supplies, or clothes for children. Prostitution is extremely common.

Approximately 600 Egyptians live in Bradashesh along the National Road to the north of the city. They also live in Belsh (132), Cërrik (1,750), and in the communes of Gostina (257), Shushica (432), Paper, and Shalës (112).

6. The District of Korça

The district of Korça (pop. 143,499; INSTAT 2001) is located in southeastern Albania and shares a border with Greece and Macedonia. The district is relatively prosperous, with high education levels. Most economic activity is centered in the city of Korça, its administrative center. The city (pop. 55,130; INSTAT 2001) is home to cultural and historical monuments. The district's major economic resources are agriculture, scattered small businesses, and commerce. The district's unemployment rate is 22 percent (INSTAT 2002). Remittances comprise a large portion of family incomes.

Most Roma in Korça are Karbuxhinj who refer to themselves as "Erlinj."[122] They migrated from Turkey to Folorina, Greece, before moving to Korça in the beginning of the 20th century. In the city, Roma families live in dilapidated and overcrowded homes concentrated in the "Kulla e Hirit" neighborhood. Major sources of their income include used clothes sales, casual work, and state economic assistance.

Other Roma families live in different villages throughout the district, such as Maliq, Libonik, Pojan, and Sovjan. Income sources include horse-dealing, agricultural work, used- clothes sales, casual work, and seasonal employment in villages over the Greek border. Some families recently sold land awarded to them in 1992 through state land distribution. In Maliq, unemployment is high because of the bankruptcy of the town's sole major enterprise, a sugar mill (De Soto and others 2001).

Approximately 100 Roma families live in the commune of Pojan. These Roma sold land they had acquired after 1990. According to land registry records, 24 out of 100 Roma families sold 44,000m² of land during the transition period. Families that have retained their land rely heavily on subsistence agriculture. Roma identified running water as a major

---

122. The word "Erli" is a Turkish word that can mean "native inhabitant" or "non-nomadic."

problem in Pojan. According to Pojan's *kryeplak,* residents have experienced several months without running water. When water service is disrupted, residents travel to surrounding villages to collect drinking water. In spite of all, primary school attendance is high compared to attendance levels in other Korça district localities.

Egyptians represent approximately 20 percent of the city's population and live in two neighborhoods, respectively of Muslim and Orthodox Egyptians. Most live in dilapidated and overcrowded houses, while others camp in temporary housing provided by the local municipality. This community is also characterized by high unemployment, low school attendance rates, and prostitution.

7. The District of Fier

The District of Fier (pop. 200,154; INSTAT 2001) is located in western Albania on the Myzeqe plain, and its administrative center is the city of Fier (pop. 56,297; INSTAT 2001). Its major economic resources include agriculture, transportation, and commerce. District unemployment is at 20 percent (INSTAT 2002).

Fier is home to Albania's largest Roma population and a small Egyptian community. Most Roma in Fier are Meçkars, but some belong to the Cergar, Karbuxhinj, or Bamill *fise.* Major sources of income include agriculture and stock farming, migrant labor, casual work, state economic assistance, tin and wickerwork, and begging. Their history of internal migration could not be assessed because relevant data was unavailable. Woman- and child-trafficking are rampant.

It is estimated that 5,200 Roma live in villages throughout the district: in Azotiku, Driza, Mbrostar-Ura, Baltëz, Povelçë, Sektor Seman, Roskovec, and Patos. In the Commune of Levan, 1,400 Roma live in the "1 of May" neighborhood. The Commune is considered the historical capital of Roma in Albania. In Levan, most Roma are Meçkars, except for approximately 10 Bamill families. Roma children have extremely low education levels because of the long distances to schools and safety risks. Many families received land after 1991 but cannot afford maintenance costs.

Most Roma in Driza are Cergars or Bamills who were settled there in 1957. Approximately 400 Roma, however, arrived during the early years of the transition period.

In Roskovec, most Roma are Meçkars. These families were moved from Rrapishta in the 1960s. Households that worked at the local cooperative during the socialist period received 10–15 dynyms[123] of land in 1991, and most still own their land. However, many households cannot afford maintenance costs, and are forced to migrate to Greece to meet daily needs. Their income sources include agriculture and migrant labor in Greece or Italy.

In Baltëz, compared to Roma in other district localities, the Roma are well-off Meçkars. Most families own two dynyms per capita of land. Still, many Roma migrate seasonally and legally to Greece. Baltëz has one school, but few Roma children attend beyond the fourth grade because of migration and early marriage. There is a health clinic in the vil-

---

123. A "dynym" is an area of land comprised of 1,000m². Ten dynyms comprise a hectare.

lage, and a local health specialist explained that contraceptive use was common and, as a result, that family sizes have decreased since 1991.

The Egyptian population in Fier is limited to approximately 15 families. Besides state assistance income, some rely on the traditional occupation of metal-working as a main income source.

8. The District of Vlora

The district of Vlora (pop. 147,267; INSTAT 2001) is located along the Adriatic-Ionian coast. Its administrative center, the city of Vlora (pop. 77,691; INSTAT 2001), is home to one of the country's largest ports. Its major economic resources include agriculture, industry, tourism, transportation, fishing, and commerce. The district unemployment rate is 27 percent (INSTAT 2002).

Approximately 1,100 Roma reside within the district. Meçkar Roma live in the villages of Novosela, Akërni, and Llakatund. Approximately 300 Meçkars live in Novosela, and most have lived there since the 1930s. Major occupations include agriculture and casual construction work. High rates of prostitution were reported, possibly owing to poverty and association with Albanians.

Akërni was founded in 1969 when Albanians and 20 Meçkar families were settled by the state from surrounding villages. A socialist agricultural cooperative was opened in 1976, and families who worked there received six dynyms of land in 1991. However, few families work the land because of high maintenance costs, its poor quality (the land is salted), and a lack of irrigation. Many young Roma males migrate seasonally to Greece. Akërni is the only town in Vlora in which Roma international migration is well-organized and represents a major source of income.

Approximately 250 Roma live in the commune of Llakatund, mostly in Shushica, the commune's administrative center. Shushica was founded after World War II, when a former Italian-owned farm was converted into a socialist agricultural cooperative, and residents of surrounding villages, towns, and districts settled there. In 1991, each resident who worked at the local cooperative during the socialist period received approximately 1,850 square meters of land.

While education levels for Roma in Vlora are much lower than the national average, they are high compared to Roma in other districts.

Though no reliable population estimates were available for Egyptians, most live in the old quarter of the city of Vlora and in surrounding villages, such as Risili. Their major occupation is agriculture. Their education levels are only slightly lower than the national average.

9. The District of Gjirokastra

The district of Gjirokastra (pop. 55,991; INSTAT 2001) is located in southern Albania and shares a border with Greece. Its administrative center, the city of Gjirokastra (pop. 20,630; INSTAT 2001), has many historical and cultural monuments. Major economic resources include agriculture, and services. The district's unemployment rate is 23 percent (INSTAT 2001). A majority of the country's Greek minority lives in this district, and many businesses are Greek-financed.

Approximately 1,200 Bamill Roma live in the Zinxhiraj quarter, located in the periphery of the city. They migrated there in 1944 from northern Greece, and remained there after the Albanian border was closed at the end of World War II (OSCE 2000a). Many families make and sell wicker-based products. Until the transition period, most Roma worked in arts and crafts or city maintenance. An arts and crafts cooperative that opened in 1960 closed in 1992, leaving many Roma unemployed. The Bamills migrate seasonally to Larisa, Greece, where families work in agriculture. Because of international migration, they have low school attendance.

Other Roma families, mainly Meçkars, migrated to the city after 1993 and live near the Zinxhiraj quarter. While their only major source of income is migrant labor in Greece, minor sources of income include used-clothes and wickerwork sales, casual work, and musical performances at weddings.

Most of the district's 4,000 Egyptians live in the Punëtor quarter in the city. Egyptians have lived there for centuries, and are well integrated into the city's cultural traditions. During the socialist period, many Egyptians received university educations. Today, education levels for Egyptians reflect the national average. Major sources of income include small business, migrant labor in Greece, casual work, musical performances at weddings, and state economic assistance. Some Egyptians deny affiliation with the Egyptian community and identify themselves as Albanian.

10. The District of Delvina

The district of Delvina (pop. 10,859; INSTAT 2001) is located in southeast Albania, near Greece. Its administrative center is the city of Delvina (pop. 6,475; INSTAT 2001). Major economic sources are agriculture and livestock. The formerly prominent agro-food industry closed down during the 1990s, resulted in high unemployment, which is 21 percent (INSTAT 2002).

Approximately 300 Cergars and Bamills (70–90 families) and 1,000 Egyptians live in the district. Both Roma and Egyptians report good relations with Albanians.

Most Roma live in the "9 Tetori" neighborhood in the city. Until being settled during the 1950s and 1960s, Roma had lived in surrounding villages. Until the 1980s, most Roma worked on state farms. Approximately 100 live in makeshift housing, while others live in apartments in various city quarters.

Fifteen to twenty Roma families live in the village of Çuka. Most families received land after 1990 and currently lease out their property because of high maintenance costs, receiving L1,500–2,000 monthly per 1,000m².

Characteristics of this community include seasonal international migration to Greece, where they work in agriculture from May through September or October. Some families have emigrated long-term and are now settled in Athens. Major sources of income are migrant labor, sales from sheet metal or wicker-based products, used-clothes sales, casual work in construction, and musical performances at weddings.

Egyptians live in integrated neighborhoods in various parts of the city. Most Egyptians either identified themselves as Albanian or emphasized that there were very few differences between Albanians and Egyptians.

Roma and Egyptian school attendance and history of internal migration in Delvina could not be assessed as relevant data were not available.

11. The District of Berat

The district of Berat (pop. 128,410; INSTAT 2001) is located in southern Albania. Its administrative center, the city of Berat (pop. 44,191; INSTAT 2001), is home to many historical and cultural monuments. Major economic resources include agriculture and industry. District unemployment is 18 percent (INSTAT 2002).

Roma live in the periphery of the city of Berat and in the villages of Uznova, Morava (600), Orizaj, Lapardha, and Agim (300). Roma were settled in Agim in 1962 from Lushnja, Korça, and Goricani. Five Roma families live in the village of Orizaj, among 200 Albanian families, while approximately 30 Karbuxhinj Roma families live in Uznova. Approximately 1,000 Egyptian households live in different neighborhoods—including Vakëf and Kodra e Sulmit—in the city.

A textile factory and a large state farm where many were employed closed down during the 1990s. High unemployment began with the farm closing in 1991. Most of these Roma and Egyptians are still unemployed. Approximately 60 Egyptians work at a local factory that produces purses, and many Egyptians and Roma work in street-sweeping and maintenance. Two foreign-owned Berat textile factories do not employ Roma or Egyptians, possibly because of discrimination.

In the village of Morava, the socioeconomic situation of Roma families is higher than the situation of Roma in other localities in all selected districts. A two-room primary school, health clinic, and semi-paved road were built with the assistance of the local "Amaro Drom" and a Dutch NGO. The history of internal migration for most Roma could not be assessed, as relevant data was unavailable. Almost all households have one or more members working seasonally in Greece. Prostitution is high in Morava, probably because of strong association with Albanians. According to a local Roma nurse, family sizes have fallen slightly during the transition period. Some families benefit from subsistence agriculture, which supplements other forms of informal labor.

A local NGO, in cooperation with international organizations such as Terres des Hommes, Swiss Cooperation, and UNICEF, provides vocational training and after-school classes in general education to underprivileged children in the city. Training for girls includes hairdressing and tailoring, while for boys, plumbing, welding, carpentry, and other skills. Vocations were selected according to local labor market demands. Almost 100 percent of children who take part in this program are Roma or Egyptians. Families of these children are also provided with monthly food assistance.

Conclusion

The Needs Assessment investigated the socioeconomic, cultural, institutional, and historical situation of Roma and Egyptians in several dimensions and identified emerging areas of concern. The study employed both qualitative and quantitative techniques, and is based on a thorough observation of 11 districts with particular concentrations of Roma and Egyptian communities.

This report will contribute to raising awareness of local governments, the private sector, and civil society towards the needs of and major challenges for these communities that have emerged through the structural change of transition. The findings will assist the Government of Albania to develop policies and programs that foster the integration of these communities into Albanian society while retaining their cultural identities.

From Social Exclusion to Social Inclusion

Matrix of Exclusion Manifestations and Recommendations for Inclusion Policies and Actions

Roma and Egyptians have been affected particularly negatively by the social change during transition. For many Roma and Egyptians today, social exclusion has become a part of their daily lives where multiple institutional barriers obstruct their development opportunities in Albania. In the effort to foster social inclusion, tailoring policies for different local problems is key. The following recommendations provide a wide spectrum of possible policies and programs. These could be taken individually, in combination, or in sequence. Implementation is possible at the local, district, or national level. Realization of recommendations could further draw on the support and partnership of a variety of actors that include different government organizations, NGOs, Roma and Egyptian community organizations, the private sector, and international partners.

Dimensions	Identified Manifestations of Sociocultural, Economic, Political, and Institutional Exclusion	Proposed Inclusion Policies and Actions
12. Education		
	Lack of Access to Public Goods and Services	
Particularly acute for Roma	Lack of knowledge of the Albanian language	Pre-school: tailored and formal Albanian language training taught by Roma teachers. Primary School: provision of 2 to 3 hours of class instruction in Romani by a qualified Roma teacher.
Particularly acute for Roma and Egyptians	Frequent mistreatment by teachers in some localities: Roma and Egyptian students are made to sit at the back of classrooms, and receive punishment from their teachers more frequently than white Albanian students	Promotion of inclusive and participatory teaching methods, and raising teachers' awareness in public and special needs schools: tailored teacher trainings in Roma and Egyptian cultural values and norms to meet the different needs of pupils. Classes on Roma and Egyptian history and culture for Roma, Egyptian, and Albanian pupils to increase respect for diversity, and raise awareness among children about their respective cultural backgrounds and ways of life.
	Lack of education and vocational skills due to lack of recognition of the long-term benefits of education and vocational skills in view of limited employment opportunities in the formal sector	Mentoring program for Roma and Egyptian pupils and their parents to convey the need for formal education and training for the post-transitional labor market. Mentors such as students at secondary schools and universities, teachers, trainees, or public and private sector specialists and professionals from all walks of life would act as examples for pupils, sharing their personal educational development, employment, and future aspirations.
Relevant for all Albanians and particularly acute for Roma and Egyptians	Lack of enforcement of the eight-year minimum, compulsory education due to weak government capacity	Activities to strengthen existing and build further capacity of government officials at the central and local level. Support to implement the education law.
	Lack of access to education, qualification, and vocational skills due to income-poverty	Provision of free access to school services, facilities, and amenities, e.g., schoolbooks, clothes, meals, or the use of education facilities; humanitarian aid in form of food, clothes, or basic amenities for very poor Roma and Egyptian families, conditional upon their children's regular school attendance. Increased accessibility of secondary and higher or university education through specific scholarships, conditional upon central and local government capacity to establish, administer, and monitor scholarship and grants schemes. This could be done with support of Roma and Egyptian organizations.

	Lack of educational qualifications, partly due to lack of parental enforcement of school attendance	Public awareness campaigns and measures to make annual grants or scholarships to parents and pupils conditional on past school attendance.
	Lack of vocational skills needed in the formal labor market	Increased and improved formal employment opportunities for all Albanians through a concerted effort between the Government, NGOs, and the private sector to promote vocational training, where qualifications are tailored to the demands of the respective geographical or sectoral labor market.
	Lack of adequate facilities in schools for physically-challenged children; lack of adequate special needs schools and facilities for mentally-challenged children	Creation of facilities and equipment in public schools for physically challenged children. Development of special needs schools and facilities for mentally challenged children. Creation and improvement of these schools and facilities with geographical dispersion across Albania.
13. Health Particularly acute for Roma	Multiple and chronic health problems due to lack of knowledge of basic health care, and medical conditions requiring formal treatment	Awareness campaigns for basic health care and education in basic health care and medical conditions which call for professional attention in health centers, schools, or by medical personnel who travel to different communities.
Particularly acute for Roma and Egyptians	Discrimination by medical personnel through extra charges for treatment or consultations	Clear Government policies to identify, monitor, and act upon the misuse of public service provision, including elimination of illegal payments for medical treatment, and holding offending personnel accountable for respective activities. Partners and project managers with experience in countering offensive practices could assist the Government.
Relevant for all Albanians and particularly acute for Roma and Egyptians	Multiple health problems due to the lack of funds to pay for formal in- and out-patient treatment	Provision of basic medical treatment, such as vaccinations, medical check-ups, and treatment for illnesses free of charge.
	Remote or isolated location and long distances to the nearest health facility	Outreach activities with provision of basic medical services and treatment, and personnel to remote areas.
14. Infrastructure Particularly acute for Roma	Lack of access to basic amenities, e.g., potable water, sanitary facilities, electricity, and heating due to inadequate housing in run-down inner-city areas, urban periphery, and rural areas	Concerted efforts of the Government, the private sector, and international partners to expand the public water supply, and sanitation and electricity networks to families who are located outside of the respective service networks. Government efforts to increase and/or improve the infrastructure service delivery to families with formal service connection.

(continued)

Continued

Dimensions	Identified Manifestations of Sociocultural, Economic, Political, and Institutional Exclusion	Proposed Inclusion Policies and Actions
Particularly acute for Roma and Egyptians	Overcrowded, dilapidated, inadequate housing without basic amenities	Actions to improve housing conditions, and provision of basic amenities, which could include provision of building material and equipment.
Relevant for all Albanians and particularly acute for Roma and Egyptians	Restricted access to potable household-use water, sanitary facilities, electricity, heating, and adequate housing	Concerted efforts of the Government, private sector, and international partners to increase and/or improve the access to public water supply, sanitation, and electricity networks via improved infrastructure service delivery, and network expansions.
15. Social Protection Relevant for all Albanians and particularly acute for Roma and Egyptians	Inability to claim state assistance; e.g., economic assistance ("*ndihmë ekonomike*"), retirement benefits (pensions), unemployment benefits, and disability payments	Welfare reforms addressing general eligibility for social protection, its actual provision, and its reliability, e.g., current requirements that make state economic assistance conditional to the actual presence of the male head-of-household at local social security offices to collect monthly benefits. New policies that allow other designated family members to collect benefits regardless of his or her status as the formal head of the household.
	Lack of long-term unemployment benefits, as state assistance is cut completely after one year without formal employment	Reforms that extend the duration of eligibility for unemployment benefits, and include a time-scaled benefit system, in which benefits would be scaled down over an extended time period, and cut only after this extended time.
16. Information—Public Sector Governance Particularly acute for Roma	Lack of access to information on government policies, decision-making processes, the rule of law, and rights and responsibilities due to language difficulties	Translation of key documents and information material into the Romani language, and broadcasting over local radio stations as public service announcements (PSAs). This could be realized with the support of Roma organizations.
Particularly acute for Roma and Egyptians	Lack of access to information due to illiteracy	Dissemination of key information through community meetings, village councilors, and information centers where Roma would receive support with obtaining and handling documents, such as service contracts, property rights documents, application forms, and notifications.

Relevant for all Albanians and particularly acute for Roma and Egyptians	Lack of access to information due to accommodation in rural and remote areas	Broadcasting of information on government policies, decision-making processes, the rule of law, and rights and responsibilities over local radio stations as public service announcements (PSAs). Joint efforts of the Government, NGOs, community representatives, and international partners to promote vocational training of Roma and Egyptians in the local and national media sector to voice their communities' interests, foster their understanding of governance processes, and promote their participation in decision-making processes.
17. Law and Justice Particularly acute for Roma and Egyptians	Subjective jurisdiction and discrimination	Clear Government policies to address the misuse of public office, and holding offending personnel accountable for respective activities. International partners with experience in countering judicial discrimination could assist the Government.
	Lack of formal marriage registration and denial of citizenship rights for formally unregistered children due to early marriages	Public awareness campaigns by Roma and Egyptian associations to highlight the negative effects of early and unregistered marriages, and unregistered childbirths. Government policies that address unregistered Roma and Egyptian marriages and childbirths and allow citizen status to obtain legal access to public goods and services, including the judiciary, formal employment, and mainstream society.
	Lack of enforcement of alimony and child support due to formally unregistered marriages and child births under the legally non-binding common law	Change of the legal status of some common laws to allow alimony to divorced common-law wives and enforcement of payments. Public awareness campaigns by Roma and Egyptian associations to highlight the negative effects of unregistered marriages, and the legal accountability of husbands for spousal and child support. Information dissemination in cultural centers.
Relevant for all Albanians and particularly acute for Roma and Egyptians	Lack of understanding of judiciary procedures due to unclear laws, rules and regulations, and limited access to lawyers	Improvement of judicial transparency and accountability through dissemination of information on judicial processes and procedures. Promotion of legal advice and counseling in community and/or cultural centers.
	Lack of use of judiciary system due to ambiguous laws, and rules and regulations	Improved legislation with clear definition of rights, rules and responsibilities, such as clear land titing, ownership rights, dispute resolution, and compensation for loss of land following the Government's land distribution in 1992.

(continued)

Continued

Dimensions	Identified Manifestations of Sociocultural, Economic, Political, and Institutional Exclusion	Proposed Inclusion Policies and Actions
Market Opportunities and Employment		
18. Labor market Particularly acute for Roma and Egyptians	Informal sector activities due to decreasing value of existing educational qualification and vocational skills in a labor market with changing demands	Vocational training tailored to sectoral and geographical labor market demands and traditional skills and qualifications, held for instance in cultural centers.
	Informal sector activities due to discrimination	Tax incentives to the private sector or co-payments to social security benefits for Roma and Egyptian private sector employees in extremely poor localities.
	Decline in employment opportunities for traditional professions (e.g., handicrafts, music) due to restructuring of former state-owned enterprises in handicrafts, and the general decline in demand for these products	Development of existing and creation of new local, national and international markets for handicrafts, and organization of trade fairs and exhibitions through collaboration between the Government, the private sector and international partners. Advancement of the existing Roma and Egyptian music market at local, national, and international level, honing in on Roma and Egyptians skilled musical performances.
	Prostitution due to lack of access to formal market and employment opportunities	Vocational training courses for Roma and Egyptian women forced into prostitution -the poverty-coping mechanism of last resort- with a specific focus on divorced women who are particularly vulnerable. Government assistance programs where divorced women become eligible for state economic assistance. Partnership with Roma and Egyptian associations to further encourage divorced women to attend vocational training courses in the preferred training venue, i.e. cultural centers.
Relevant for all groups and particularly acute for Roma and Egyptians	Limited formal employment opportunities, unemployment, long-term unemployment, or under-employment, due to skills mismatch to the post-transition labor market	Vocational training tailored to sectoral and geographical labor market demands. Creation of new employment opportunities through joint efforts of the Government and the private sector, and possible assistance by international partners.

	Dependency on the informal sector, casual work, self-employment, and/or migration with low wages, job insecurity, and high socioeconomic vulnerability due to lack of formal employment opportunities	Concerted efforts of the Government, private sector, and international partners to improve the formal business environment and investment climate that attracts the national or international private sector, increase demand for a steady workforce and supply of employment opportunities with a focus on specific growth sectors and geographical locations with prospective industries, including the creation of viable and sustainable small- and medium-sized enterprises.
Safety and Security of Livelihoods		
19. Social Risks and Vulnerability Particularly acute for Roma and Egyptians	Low school attendance, and illiteracy due to lack of safety measures by local governments for the often long distances to the nearest school, and parents' fear of kidnapping of children, particularly girls	Design and implementation of anti-crime measures by central and local government to foster local protection of citizens and crime victims.
Relevant for all Albanians and particularly acute for Roma and Egyptians	Insecure livelihoods as a result of financial instability of very poor households	Provision of humanitarian aid for food, clothes, and basic amenities conditional to children's school attendance and completion of compulsory education, or to trainees' attendance and completion of vocational training courses.
Social Capital, Voice, and Participation		
20. Social Capital Particularly acute for Roma and Egyptians	Limited voice in policy decision-making processes due to lack of formal or informal associations or networks that facilitate collective action	Joint efforts by the Government and international NGOs to encourage coordination and strengthen cooperation among and between Roma and Egyptians communities, and make funding conditional to such coordination and cooperation.
	Limited participation in policy decision-making processes due to lack of trust in formal or informal associations or networks	Building trust between Roma and Egyptian communities and associations by including both in the planning and implementation of programs for the community as a whole. Increasing trust and rapport between Roma and Egyptian communities and their associations by attaching associations to programs that would benefit both communities.

(continued)

Continued

Dimensions	Identified Manifestations of Sociocultural, Economic, Political, and Institutional Exclusion	Proposed Inclusion Policies and Actions
	Unfocused voice and scattered participation in policy decision-making processes due to lack of good practice of effective interest representation and respective projects	Joint efforts by the Government and international NGOs to promote future national and international links between Roma and Egyptian associations in Albania with related associations in other European countries for exchange of experience and assistance in replication of workable projects tailored to the local context.
Cultural Identity and Diversity		
21. Empowerment—CDD Particularly acute for Roma	Discrimination based on cultural identity	Establishment of cultural centers to address the eroding family structure of the Roma *fis*, bring far-flung Albanian Roma together, support expressions and sharing of their cultural practices, and strengthen their social capital through instruction in Romani, traditional crafts and customs, music, dance, and history.
	Low education qualifications and vocational skills	Creation of cultural centers to provide Albanian language classes for Roma children, and after-school classes with help for homework from bilingual Roma teachers. Provision of adult vocational training aimed at the realities of the local. Job market, including basic accounting and grant proposal writing, and reading centers to remedy high illiteracy.

Relevant for all Albanians and particularly acute for Roma and Egyptians	Lack of community and social cohesion, low value of cultural identity and diversity	Establishment of cultural centers to promote community-based development, in which Roma and Egyptians themselves rebuild their communities with the assistance of local, national, and international partners. This would help to promote interaction and foster cultural, social, and institutional inclusion and social cohesion among Roma, Egyptians, and Albanians.
	Isolation and lack of information, low levels of health care	Establishment of cultural centers to provide counseling and legal advice for marriage and abused women, assist in the formation of informal women's groups to help support women in making decisions that affect their lives, raise awareness of the negative effects of early marriage, and its impact on vocational qualifications. Information on basic health and hygiene, reproductive health, family planning, parenting, particularly for population groups without access to medical facilities due to their remote location.
22. Minority status	Discrimination based on lack of a formal minority status	Government efforts to provide formal minority status to Roma in order to meet the European Union accession criteria calling for the respect for, and protection of minorities.

From Social Exclusion to Social Inclusion—Analytical Framework

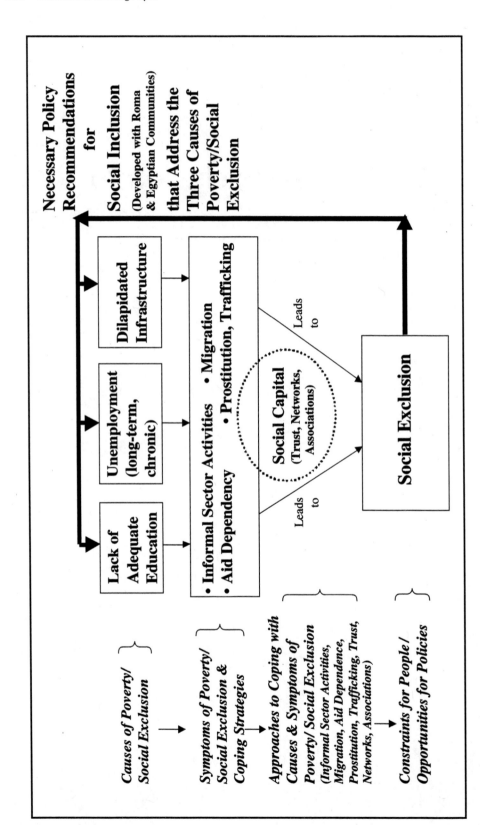

Conference Agenda

"Roma and Egyptians in Albania: From Social Exclusion to Social Inclusion"

October 1st 2003

Agenda

10:00 am–10:10 am	Opening statement-Eugene Scanteie, Country Manager and Head of Mission, World Bank.
10:10 am–10:20 am	Introduction by Hermine De Soto, TTL, World Bank.
10:20 am–10:40 am	Methodology by Ilir Gedeshi–Center for Economic and Social Studies.
10:40 am–11:00 am	Coffee break.
11:00 am–12:30 pm	Presentation of Main Findings and Policy Recommendations
	Hermine De Soto and Sabine Beddies, World Bank.
	Questions
12:30 pm–2:00 pm	Lunch
2:00 pm–3:30 pm	Discussion, Feedback and Dialogue
3:30 pm–3:45 pm	Coffee Break
3:45 pm–5:00 pm	Wrap-up and Next Steps

Summary of the Conference on the Report

"Roma and Egyptian in Albania–from Social Exclusion to Social Inclusion"
Needs Assessment of Roma and Egyptian Communities in Albania

Hermine De Soto, ECSSD, Sabine Beddies, SDV, The World Bank and the Center for
Economic and Social Studies, Tirana

1. Opening of Conference and Introduction by World Bank Country Resident Manager, Mr. Eugene Scanteie

The World Bank's support to Albania's poverty reduction strategy includes operational support to a variety of projects to improve infrastructure, health, and education. In these efforts, it is crucial that it also includes the poorest of the poor, the Roma and Egyptian communities. The report highlights the multi-dimensionality of poverty and social exclusion that Roma and Egyptian communities face in Albania, manifested by low educational and vocational skills, unemployment, dilapidated infrastructure, and several coping mechanisms such as migration, prostitution and trafficking.

Mr. Scanteie, in his opening remarks stressed that the World Bank ought to support the Roma and Egyptian communities in terms of

- Overall policy support in the fields of education, unemployment, social assistance, and recognize the rights of Roma and Egyptians;
- Tailored operational support through upcoming projects (e.g. education, environment and health) as a response to identified priorities; and,
- Facilitating policy dialogue by providing a forum for discussion, and increased voice and participation in decision-making.

2. Background and Context of the Albanian Roma and Egyptian Needs Assessment

A 2002 Qualitative Poverty Assessment in Albania and a policy review of minority groups both identified the Roma and Egyptian[124] communities as the poorest and most marginalized populations in Albania.

In a 2002 report, "Report Submitted by Albania Pursuant to Article 25, Paragraph 1, of the Framework Convention of the Protection of National Minorities," the Government of Albania followed traditional perspectives and considers only those minorities which have their own motherlands that provide them with common characteristics such as religious affiliation, language, culture, customs and traditions, and religious beliefs as national

---

124. Roma and Egyptians consider themselves to be of different ethnic groups. However, "they collectively occupy the place 'Gypsy minority' typical of other Balkan and East European societies. A picture of the dynamic of Albanian attitudes towards disadvantaged minorities is incomplete without attention to both groups" (ERRC 1997, p. 13). Caution needs to be paid when dealing with these terms because many sources refer to Roma and Egyptians as "Roma" or "Gypsy."

minorities. Thus, Greek, Macedonian, and Montenegrin minorities are the only nationally recognized ones. Under this definition, Roma and Aromanians are considered to be only linguistic minorities, not national ones. Since Albanian national census data is only disaggregated according to national minorities, no census data on the Roma exists. According to official records, the ethnic makeup of Albania is: 98 percent Albanian and 2 percent other.

In the framework of the National Strategy for Socio-Economic Development [NSSD (formerly the GPRS)] and on the basis of the Qualitative Poverty Assessment, the Government of Albania requested a Needs Assessment (NA) that would establish a social, economic, and cultural database for the Roma and Egyptian communities and assess how the needs of these communities could be better taken into account as part of the poverty reduction policies and programs of the Government. To accomplish that purpose, the NA studied the Roma and Egyptians and assessed how they are impacted by current poverty reduction and social inclusion efforts and recommended how these communities can be included. The NA would then assist the Government in formulating policies of inclusion that are in accordance with the EU requirements for accession.

The findings of an NA would also help to determine whether a program of capacity-building around cultural centers is warranted, and desirable, for the Roma and Egyptian communities.[125] Simultaneously, the assessment would contribute to raising awareness of the public, NGOs, civil society, and the international donor community on the current situation of social and cultural diversity, "ethnicity," and "minority" status of Roma and Egyptian communities in Albania.

The World Bank agreed to perform this Needs Assessment, which was conducted by the Social Development Unit, ECSSD.

One of the major impediments to developing an effective program to strengthen social and economic development and alleviate poverty for the Roma and Egyptians is the lack of reliable information about them. The NA aims to address this information gap.

Methodology

Focus

The Needs Assessment sought to understand the qualitative aspects of the social and economic situation of the Roma and Egyptians in several dimensions and identify emerging areas of concern. With the participation of the Roma and Egyptians in the process, the assessment addressed the causes, nature, extent, and perceptions of their situation in ten communities. The NA would focus on the following themes:

- Unemployment/Underemployment
- Infrastructure
- Education

---

125. The cultural centers under consideration would be places from which Roma and Egyptians communities could begin to work on issues of community-driven development (CDD), cultural understanding, and social inclusion based on promoting opportunity, facilitating empowerment, and enhancing security.

- Health
- Migration/Emigration
- Social Services
- Social Capital and Social Organization
- Culture (including expressive culture, e.g., language, music, and art)
- Handicrafts
- Gender
- Children/Family Planning
- Security/Violence/Trafficking
- Community Participation and involvement in local decision-making
- Access to Judicial System
- Exclusions Through Stereotypes and Discrimination
- Empowerment Through Roma and Egyptian Participation, Transparency, and Gaining Capital Assets

The NA Study Team. The NA study team consisted primarily of trained researchers and fieldworkers with prior experience and established trust relationships working in Roma and Egyptian communities as well as experience working with World Bank staff. The supervisory staff (World Bank senior staff and the local research manager) and NA study team jointly determined the research design of the NA study, selected the study sample, developed the questionnaire for the interviews, and discussed their design with respective Roma and Egyptian community leaders.

Site Selection. Based on field research undertaken for the Qualitative Poverty Study, and on consultation with Roma and Egyptian community leaders, the NA team selected ten communities as study sites: Fieri, Vlora, Fushë Kruja, Durrës, Shkodra, Delvina, Gjirokastra, Tiranë, Elbasan, and Korçë. For each of these sites, the study collected and analyzed information across a variety of categories such as men, women, children, youth, disabled, and elderly. It was also sensitive to issues of social differentiation, discrimination, age, income, education, occupation, social capital, and culture within each community.

Techniques. The analytic work for the NA included: a desktop review of relevant literature (including official documents on minorities in Albania); Roma and Egyptian community development/participation profiles; and qualitative and quantitative methods (triangulation). The qualitative component included: (a) focus groups with local Roma and Egyptian communities; (b) semi-structured interviews with key stakeholders, and formal and informal male and female leaders in the Roma community and adjoining Albanian community; (c) ethnographic case studies; (d) a quantitative socioeconomic household survey questionnaire. These also identified the perceptions that non-Roma have towards Roma and Egyptian communities through the eyes of the Roma and Egyptians themselves and the perceptions that those non-Roma, who live in close proximity to the Roma and Egyptian communities, have about Roma and Egyptians. In addition, ten community profiles were completed.

This approach further identified the different interests and incentives of those groups that will be most affected by potential changes in the *formal* status of the Roma and Egyptians, i.e., to national minorities, and of those groups that have direct effects on this change by supporting, opposing, or slowing down potential changes.

3. The Organization of the Needs Assessment Report

When the final draft was prepared, it was decided that such a lengthy report should be organized into three parts: Part 1 included the front matter of the aggregate report, and Chapter I, Introduction, Chapter II, Social Exclusion, and Chapter III, Social Inclusion: Recommendations and Policy Implications. Part 2 outlines the findings of the Assessment in nine Chapters: I is Historical Background: The Diversity of Roma and Egyptians; II, Culture; III, on Marriage and Family Planning; IV, Income Living Standards; V, Education; VI, The Labor Market; VII, Migrations and Remittances; VIII, Prostitution and Trafficking; and IX, Social Capital. Part 3 is comprised of Appendixes, including the definitions, study instruments, additional statistical data, and maps, among others, and a bibliography.

4. Background of the Dissemination Conference

This report is based on the day-long October 1, 2003 dissemination conference attended by Roma and Egyptian NGO leaders to discuss the findings and policy recommendations of the Roma and Egyptian Needs Assessment. The participants were informed of the report's findings and subsequently were asked to discuss the report's policy implications and make suggestions and recommendations.

5. Presentation of Report Findings and Policy Recommendations

A brief introduction of each chapter was followed by a thorough presentation of the main findings and results, and concluded with policy recommendations for each chapter.

Prime importance was given to the findings on *education*. High illiteracy rate and low education level, especially among Roma after the transition, were the disturbing findings of the study. Among policy recommendations were: free access to educational facilities, bilingual teachers, mentoring programs, vocational training, and unconditional scholarships for Roma and Egyptian students.

Next, the report delineated *income and living conditions* and how low income was directly related to poor housing conditions, and poor access to public services. Policy recommendations on this matter focused on public works projects, such as the provision of access to water and sanitation facilities as well as electricity and heating, procurement of adequate housing, and construction of health care facilities with rotating healthcare professionals in remote areas. On state assistance programs, report policy recommendations centered on a gradual decrease of the amount paid for the unemployment benefits, instead of the current system and on reforming the "ndihma ekonomike" by recommending that other members of the family be able to receive the benefit if the male household head is not present.

The labor market findings revealed a high rate of unemployment following transition. Poor education, low qualifications, poor social capital, and little or no demand for their traditional skills are among the causes of their unemployment. The policy recommendations were built on the matching of skills to actual employment possibilities through vocational training, the promotion of market opportunities for their traditional handicrafts and skills, and arranging for host country work visas for migrants.

Another important issue was the poor understanding of the legal system. The findings of the study showed that Roma and Egyptians face many difficulties in this area stemming mainly from poor knowledge of the Albanian language and low education level. The policy recommendations stressed the importance of training paralegals to provide advice to the community, translating legal documents—such as contracts—into the Romani language, and dissemination of such information widely to the Roma community through radio and television broadcasts.

The *marriage and family planning* chapter presented interesting evidence related to early marriage and lack of family planning through birth control, and attendant young child bearing ages, unregistered marriages and high divorce rates, and the consequent fallout of an increasing number of single mothers, spousal and family abuse, poverty, and a retreat into prostitution and child trafficking.

Policy recommendations stressed public awareness campaigns aimed at associations, organizations, and national and international NGOs, encouraging the link/cooperation among and between NGOs and community.

6. Participant Discussion and Feedback on Report Findings and Policy Recommendations

Education: Lack of access to education was generally recognized as the most pressing issue both communities are facing. All Roma and Egyptian NGO leaders related illiteracy and low level of education primarily to poverty. "Without education there could be no development, and without development there is no integration," is how the participants viewed the problem.

Implementing the law for a mandatory eight years of education should be applied. In addition, special government policies tailored to the needs of the two communities should be drafted, with input from these two communities participating in policy drafting. This includes giving rise to positive discrimination, where the participants asked that their children be provided with unconditional scholarships (that is, without entering any examination or competition). In accordance with the recommendations and policy implications presented in the report, the participants emphasized the necessity of providing pupils with textbooks and other school supplies, as well as food and proper clothing. Positive reinforcement of other recommendations offered were supplemental training courses in subjects such as the Albanian language, and computer and other vocational skills, among others. The establishment of preschool kindergartens was viewed by all participants as essential in endowing their children with adequate education. This would not only prepare them for when they enter school, but will also attempt to establish an equilibrium between the education level of the children of the two communities and the majority children.

Putting children into school and away from the street is also seen as having a positive impact on preventing child trafficking.

Employment: A second major concern for the participants was employment. As presented in the report, vocational skills training were deemed essential by the participants for lowering the unemployment rate. In addition, they all expressed interest in continuing their traditional skills by developing markets. On the distribution of "ndihma ekonomike," participants agreed with the recommendations of the report that other members of the family be able to get the assistance if the male household head is not available. The same positive response was shown regarding the issuing of collective, or work visas, which would help prevent negative phenomena associated with illegal migration.

Living Conditions: Most Roma and Egyptian live in extremely poor conditions well below the poverty line. Their housing is inadequate, and most of their settlements suffer from poor sanitation and hygiene. The participants asked for a project aimed at improving the hygiene of their community, which currently has very negative effects on their health.

Cultural Centers: All participants were very interested in establishing cultural centers, which were seen as providing assistance to the community for a wide range of concerns. Not only should these centers offer courses on their language, history, traditions and crafts but also in vocational skills, preschool education, legal advice, and assistance and support for abused women. To preserve their cultural heritage, the Roma proffered the idea of establishing a museum which would reflect Roma and Egyptian culture, traditions, history, and values.

Public awareness campaigns are also seen as extremely important. One effective way to raise the awareness of the community would be a weekly TV broadcast on Roma and Egyptians. The conference participates reached a preliminary consensus on following upcoming activities:

Next Steps:
- Write-up of the conference report (see Appendix B), which will be appended to the Needs Assessment report
- Decision meeting for report: *"Roma and Egyptians in Albania—From Social Exclusion to Social Inclusion"*
- Publication of the Needs Assessment
- Translation of the cleared NA report into Albanian
- Use of the Needs Assessment by Roma and Egyptian leaders and NGOs to discuss the implications for poverty alleviation programs and policy development on social inclusion/empowerment with local and national government, policy makers, parliament, white Albanian civil society institutions, the private sector, and the media.
- Financial support (based on the Dutch grant) to Roma and Egyptian associations and NGOs and local leaders to organize, and to actively participate in the dissemination of the key findings and the civil society and policy dialogue;
- Organization of participatory workshops to discuss the findings of the Needs Assessment with a variety of key stakeholders in a policy dialogue, including Roma and Egyptian NGOs and Roma/Egyptian informal and formal leaders, in 11 districts in

Albania (Berat, Delvina, Durrës, Elbasan, Fier, Gjirokastër, Korçë, Krujë, Shkodër, Tiranë, and Vlorë)
- Organization of an international conference with representatives of government, Roma and Egyptian communities, civil society, and the international community, February 2004.

Roma and Egyptian NGO Participants at Conference on "Roma and Egyptians in Albania: From Social Exclusion to Social Inclusion," October 1st 2003

- Beqiri, Ilir, Amaro-Karvani
- Duro, Resul, Head of "Kabaja" Association
- Furtuna, Pellumb, "Romani Baxt" Albania
- Hasantai, Adriatik, Amaro Drom
- Isula, Hasan, Amaro-Dives
- Koka, Shpetim, "Vellazerimi" Association
- Kosturi, Arben, Head of "Disutni-Albania," Korçe.
- Lloshi, Astrit, Secretary of "Kabaja" Association
- Mehmeti, Fuat, "Vellazerimi" Association
- Mejdani, Gurali, Amaro-Dives
- Mile, Dilaver, "22 Marsi" Association
- Noti, Sofi, Foundation "Drejt se ardhmes"
- Pellumbi, Istref, Roma for Integration
- Ruci, Dashamir, Board member
- Sadiku, Behar, "Nefreta" Association
- Shabani, Kujtim, "Disutni-Albania," Korçe.
- Tafa, Arben, "Vellazerimi" Association
- Veliu, Skender, Amaro-Drom

Center for Economic and Social Studies (CESS)

- Jorida Cila, C.E.S.S.
- Ilir Gedeshi, C.E.S.S.

Dissemination Conference Material

1. Press Release: World Bank Conference on Key Findings of the Report from Social Exclusion to Social Inclusion

Tirana, May 28, 2004—The World Bank office in Tirana organized the Conference "From Social Exclusion to Social Inclusion" on Roma and Egyptians. The conference was focused on discussions around key findings with regard to social aspects of Roma and Egyptian communities. The conference took place at Tirana International Hotel premises. Participants at the conference were high level representatives of Albanian Government, UN Agencies, Civil Society, Roma and Egyptian communities, and media.

This report was sponsored and made possible by the partnership between the Government of Albania, the World Bank, UNDP, Soros Foundation, the American Embassy, and the Swiss Agency for Development and Cooperation, and Roma and Egyptian communities across Albania who actively participated since the beginning.

The report investigates the socioeconomic, cultural, institutional, and historical situation of Roma and Egyptian communities in 11 sites across Albania. It presents quantitative and qualitative data on these groups in order to assist the Albanian Government in drafting special programs for these communities. The report also provides insights into social exclusion processes that affect these communities in order to help Government meet some of the EU recommendations on ethnic minorities. The report offers recommendation on concrete actions to facilitate the inclusion of Roma and Egyptians into Albanian society.

This report presents key findings in regard to Roma and Egyptians culture, marriage and family planning, income and living standards, education, labor market, migration and remittances, prostitution and trafficking and social capital.

The report concludes that both groups face social exclusion in different aspects of their lives. These aspects are identified to be related to economic restructuring, unemployment, poverty, weak government capacity, and discrimination. The combination of these factors, their linkages and dynamics increasingly trap their families into poverty, and make the majority of both Roma and Egyptians "outsiders" to Albanian society. In contrast to mainstream society, both groups are denied participation in, and governance of, numerous aspects that affect their lives.

2. Statement of Country Manger, Mr. Nadir Mohammed, at the Conference on Roma and Egyptians

First, I would like to welcome all of you to the Conference on "Roma and Egyptians in Albania: From Social Exclusion to Social Inclusion." Specifically, I would like to welcome representatives from the Government, Parliament, our international development partners, representatives from civil society, and a special welcome to the Roma and Egyptian representatives.

I am very pleased to open this important conference for Roma and Egyptians in Albania. This is a very timely conference, as the country is currently finalizing its second progress report on the implementation of the "National Strategy for Social-Economic Development" NSSED. As you know, the World Bank supports the NSEED with its particular emphasis on poverty reduction and overall economic growth and development.

As there are still vulnerable and poor groups in Albania, such as the Roma and Egyptians, we have organized this conference to first listen to a presentation of the key findings of the Needs Assessment, hear the voices of the Roma and Egyptians community representatives, and then discuss the possible next steps within the context of Albania's poverty reduction strategy.

Background

A recent Qualitative Poverty Assessment in Albania (2002) identified the Roma and Egyptians communities as the poorest and most marginalized populations in Albania. In the framework of the NSSED and on the basis of the Qualitative Poverty Assessment, the Government of Albania had requested a Needs Assessment.

Donor coordination and support

The Needs Assessment is supported by the American Embassy, Soros Foundation, Swiss Development Corporation, UNDP, and the World Bank.

Rational/Objectives of Study

The Needs Assessment investigated the socioeconomic, cultural, institutional, and historical situation of Roma and Egyptians communities in 11 sites across Albania. Its objectives were to:

- Provide quantitative and qualitative data on these groups to assist the Albanian Government in drafting special programs for these communities;
- Provide insights into social exclusion processes that affect these communities to help the Government meet some of the EU recommendations on ethnic minorities; and
- Provide advice on the design of concrete actions that facilitate the inclusion of Roma and Egyptians into Albanian society.

Key Findings

This report presents key findings in regard to Roma and Egyptian culture, marriage and family planning, income and living standards, education, labor market, migration and remittances, prostitution and trafficking and social capital.

Conclusion of report

The report concludes that both groups face social exclusion in different aspects of their lives. These aspects are related to economic restructuring, unemployment, poverty, weak government capacity, and discrimination. The combination of these factors, their linkages and dynamics increasingly trap their families into poverty, and makes the majority of both Roma and Egyptians "outsiders" to Albanian society. In contrast to mainstream society, both groups are denied participation in, and governance of, numerous aspects that affect their lives. Roma and Egyptians conveyed that poverty and discrimination at the institutional and individual level were the primary causes of social exclusion. They suggested that social exclusion could be addressed by creating more jobs and opportunities to attend schools and universities, and by hiring them to work in local and state administrative offices.

Recommendations of report

The study proposes some policy recommendations on how to improve the lives of Roma and Egyptians. Development programs for these communities should not be seen in isolation, but as part of a holistic development approach. Policies can be implemented individually, in combination, or in sequence, at the local, district, or national level, with the support of, and in partnership with, different government organizations, NGOs, Roma and Egyptian community organizations, the private sector, and international partners.

Past World Bank engagement regarding Roma and Egyptian issues

- In 2002/03, World Bank supported an educational exchange program with Albanian Roma leaders and counterparts in Romania

- In 2003, the World Bank has completed the following activities that relate to Roma and Egyptian poverty reduction:
- Needs Assessment with donor support, including a 1-day conference for feedback with all Roma and Egyptian associations in October 2003;
- European Roma conference in Budapest, with Mr. Wolfensohn, and Mr. Soros, and an Albanian Roma delegation as observers, in July 2003;
- In November 2003 the World Bank in cooperation with OSI organized a Young Roma Leaders Study tour in Washington and New York
- Small Grant Program / Competition funded the following activities during the period 2002–2004:
- Roma women of the future
- Integrating Roma and Albanian orphan children into the community
- Experimenting new methods of learning for Roma and Albanian youth
- All children are equal
- Leadership training for Roma Women
- Fostering of Roma children's right and promoting coexistence in harmony with non-roma children

Possible next steps

- Social Services Delivery Project
- Small Grant Program/Competition will be available
- Upcoming work: The World Bank upcoming Country Assistance Strategy will consider the Needs Assessment, including its recommendations, and the outcome of this conference.

I again I would like to thank all participants for their attendance.

Mr. Nadir Mohammed
Country Manager

Bibliography

A. T. 1943. "Magjypët e Shkodrës," *Leka, N. 7,* pp. 230–234.

Beddies, S. 2000. " 'Urban': A Critical Case Study of the Formulation and Operationalism of a Community Initiative," unpublished PhD Dissertation, London School of Economics and Political Science.

Bhavnani, K-K. 2002. "Beyond Durban 2001: The Gender, Race and Development Nexus." *Oral remarks.* Washington, DC: World Bank.

Brunër, G. 1995. "Nemzetisegi kerdes es kisebbsegi konfliktusor Kelet-Europaban." Budapest: Teleki Laszl Alapitvany.

Cahn, C., ed. 2002. "Roma Rights: Race, Justice, and Strategies for Equality." New York: The International Debate Education Association.

COM. 2000. 79 final: "Communication from the Commission: Building an Inclusive Europe," 1 March.

CE (Council of Europe). 1995. "Framework Convention for the Protection of National Minorities." Strasbourg.

Courthiade, M., and J. Duka. "A Social and Historical Profile of the Rroms in Albania."

Dasgupta, P. 2000. "Economic Progress and the Idea of Social Capital." In Dasgupta, P. and Serageldin, I., eds., *Social Capital: a Multifaceted Perspective.* Washington, DC: The World Bank.

De Soto, H., and I. Gedeshi. 2002a. "Dimensions of Romani Poverty in Albania." In *Roma Rights Quarterly Journal of the European Roma Rights Center* 1: 22–30.

———. 2002b. "Migration and Remittances: The Albanian Roma." Unpublished article.

De Soto, H., P. Gordon, I. Gedeshi, and Z. Sinoimeri. 2002. "Poverty in Albania: A Qualitative Assessment." Technical Paper No. 520. Washington, DC: The World Bank.

De Soto, H., S. Beddies, and I. Gedeshi. 2004. "Roma and Egyptians in Albania: From Social Exclusion to Social Inclusion." *Roma Rights Quarterly Journal of the European Roma Rights Center* Fall 2004: 18–42.

Dino, L. 2001. "Egjyptianët dhe romët janë dy etni të ndryshme." *Papirus,* Nëntor.

Dudwick, N., and H. Shahriari. 2000. "Education in Albania: Changing Attitudes and Expectations." Washington, DC: The World Bank.

ECRI (European Commission Against Racism and Intolerance). 2002. "EU Support for Roma Communities in Central and Eastern Europe." Enlargement Briefing, Brussels.

———. 1998. "National Survey on the Experience and Perception of Discrimination and Racism from the Point of View of Potential Victims." *ECRI General Policy Recommendation* No. 4. Strasbourg.

ERRC (European Roma Rights Council). 2001. "Recognizing and Combating Racial Discrimination: A Short Guide." ERRC, Budapest.

———. 1997. "No Record of the Case: Roma in Albania." *Country Report Series* No. 5, June.

Fischer, B. 1999. *Albania at War: 1939–1945.* Purdue University Press.

Fonseca, I. 1995. *Bury Me Standing: The Gypsies and Their Journey.* New York: Alfred A. Knopf.

Grootaert, C., and T. van Bastelae, eds. 2002. "Understanding and Measuring Social Capital. A Multidisciplinary Tool for Practitioners." Washington, DC: The World Bank.

Hasluck, M. 1938. "The Gypsies of Albania," *Journal of the Gypsy Lore Society,* 17(2): 49–61.

INSTAT (Albanian National Institute of Statistics). 2003. *Statistical Yearbook, 1993–2001.* Tirana.

———. 2002. "Popullsia e Shqipërisë në 2001. Rezultatet kryesore të regjistrimit të popullsisë dhe banesave." Tirana.

———. 2001. "Preliminary Results of the Population and Housing Census 2001." Tirana.

Kamberi, S. 2001. "E vërteta mbi egjyptianët e Shqipërisë." *Papirus,* Shkurt, No 2.

Keesing, R. M. 1992. *Cultural Anthropology: A Contemporary Perspective.* Chicago: Holt, Rinehart and Winston.

Koinova, M. 2000. "Minorities in Southeast Europe: Roma of Albania." Center for Documentation and Information on Minorities in Europe—Southeast Europe (CEDIME).

Manoku, Y., S. Zoto, and I. Gedeshi. 2001. "Rreth gjendjes socio-ekonomike të romëve në rrethin e Korçës." *Politika & Shoqëria,* N 2.

Mara, H. 2002. Conversation with the authors, October 14.

Milaj, J. 1943. "Raca shqiptare." Tirana.

OSCE (Organization for Security and Co-Operation). 2000a. "Gjirokastra's Roma: A Profile." In *Special Report* 39, OSCE Presence Office in Albania, Field Office Gjirokastra.

———. 2000b. "Delvina's Roma: A Profile." In *Special Report* 39-1, OSCE Presence Office in Albania, Field Office Gjirokastra.

Qirici, M. T. 2002. "Princi Qyqar, Përralla me motive rome." STEVLA. Tirana.

———. 2001. "Përtej Dashurisë, sipas motiveve të përrallave rome." STEVLA. Tirana.

———. 1999. "Gjylbeharja, Përralla dhe legjenda nga Romët e Shqipërisë." STEVLA. Tirana.

Parruca, A. 2001. "Shkodra, Bastion i qytetërimit shqiptar." *ILAR,* Tirana.

Poulton, H. 1991. "The Balkans: Minorities and States in Conflict." London: Minority Rights Group.

Revenga, A., D. Ringold, and W. M. Tracy. 2002. "Poverty and Ethnicity: A Cross-Country Study of Roma Poverty in Central Europe." Washington, DC: The World Bank.

Ringold, D. 2003. *Roma in an Expanding Europe: Addressing the Poverty Challenge.* World Bank Draft Report. Washington, DC: The World Bank.

———. 2000. "Roma and the Transition in Central and Eastern Europe: Trends and Challenges." Washington, DC: The World Bank.

Sarageldin, I., and C. Grootaert. 2000. "Defining Social Capital: An Integrating World View." Washington, DC: The World Bank.

Shkodra, Z. 1984. "Qyteti shqiptar gjatë Rilindjes Kombëtare." Akademia e Shkencave, Instituti i Historisë, Tiranë.

Silverman, C. 2001. Electronic Letter to authors, May.

———. 1995. "Persecution and Politicization: Roma (Gypsies) of Eastern Europe." *Cultural Survivial Quarterly* (summer).

Swire, J. 1937. "King Zog's Albania."

Taho, B. 2002. "Document on the Situation of Roma in Albania."

UNDP (United Nations Development Program). 2002a. "The Roma in Central and Eastern Europe: Avoiding the Dependency Trap." Bratislava.

———. 2002b. Albanian Human Development Report."

———. 2000. "Raporti i Zhvillimit Njerëzor për Shqipërinë." Tirana.

Unioni "Amaro Drom." 2003. "Zëri i fëmijëve na thërret," Tirana.

Vjetari Statistikor i Shqipërisë, 1992.

World Bank. 2003. "Draft: Social Development in Europe and Central Asia Region: Issues and Directions." Washington, DC: Environmentally and Socially Sustainable Development, Social Development Team, Europe and Central Asia. March.

———. 2002b. "Draft Working Paper: Social Development in Europe and Central Asia Region: Issues and Directions." Washington, DC: Environmentally and Socially Sustainable Development, Social Development Team, Europe and Central Asia, The World Bank.

Materials Used in Desk Review

Ainscow, M., and H. G. Memmenasha. 1998. "The Education of Children with Special Needs: Barriers and Opportunities in Central and Eastern Europe." *UNICEF-ICDC Innocenti Occasional Paper* No. 67, Florence, Italy.

Barany Z. 2002. *The East European Gypsies: Regime Change, Marginality, and Ethnopolitics.* Cambridge: Cambridge University Press.

Bhavnani, K-K. 2002. "Beyond Durban 2001: The Gender, Race and Development Nexus." Oral remarks. Washington DC: The World Bank.

Braham, M. 1993. "The Untouchable: A Survey of the Roma People of Central and Eastern Europe." A Report to the Office of the United Nations High Commissioner for Refugees, Switzerland.

Bugajski, J. 1994. *Ethnic Politics in Eastern Europe.* Armonk, New York: M. E. Sharpe.

Byrne, D. 1999. *Social Exclusion.* Philadelphia: Open University Press.

Cahn, C., ed., 2002. "Roma Rights: Race, Justice, and Strategies for Equality." New York: The International Debate Education Association.

Cahn C. 1997. "Legislating Ruin: Macedonia's Law on Commerce and the Ensuring Police Violence." *Roma Rights* (Newsletter of the European Roma Rights Center), Autumn: 25–34.

Cahn, C., D. Chirico, C. McDonald, V. Mohacsi, T. Peric, and A. Szekely. 1998. "Roma in the Educational Systems of Central and Eastern Europe," *Roma Rights* (Newsletter of the European Roma Rights Center), Summer.

CE (Council of Europe). 1995. "Framework Convention for the Protection of National Minorities." Strasbourg.

Courtiade, M. 1995. "Between Conviviality and Antagonism: The Ambiguous Position of the Romanies in Albania." *Patrin,* No. 3.

Crowe, D. M. 1994. *A History of the Gypsies of Eastern Europe and Russia.* New York: St. Martin's Press.

Dino, L., 2001. "Egjyptianët dhe romët janë dy etni të ndryshme." *Papirus,* Nëntor.

Druker, J. 1997. "Present but Unaccounted for: How Many Roma Live in Central and Eastern Europe? It Depends on Whom You Ask." *Transitions.* September.

EC (European Council). 2002. "EU Support for Roma Communities in Central and Eastern Europe." Enlargement Briefing, Brussels.

ECRE (European Committee on Romani Emanicipation) 2002. Web Page Document. http://www.eu-romani.org/.

ECRI (European Commission Against Racism and Intolerance). 2001. "Second Report on Albania." Council of Europe, Strasbourg.

———. 1998. "National Survey on the Experience and Perception of Discrimination and Racism from the Point of View of Potential Victims." ECRI General Policy Recommendation No. 4, Strasbourg.

EIU (The Economist Intelligence Unit). 2002. "Albania: Country Profile 2002."

ERRC (European Roma Rights Council). 2002a. "Barriers to the Education of Roma in Europe." For the United Nations Special Session on Children.

———. 2002b. "Roma Rights: Extreme Poverty." *Quarterly Journal of the European Roma Rights Center,* No. 1, Budapest.

———. 2002c. "Roma Rights: Fortress Europe." *Quarterly Journal of the European Roma Rights Center,* No. 2, Budapest.

———. 2001a. "Political Participation and Democracy in Europe: A Short Guide for Romani Activists." ERRC, Budapest.

———. 2001b. "Recognizing and Combating Racial Discrimination: A Short Guide." ERRC, Budapest.

———. 2001c. "Roma Rights: Government Programmes on Roma," *Quarterly Journal of the European Roma Rights Center,* No. 2/3, Budapest.

———. 2001d. "State of Impunity: Human Rights Abuse of Roma in Romania." *Country Report Series,* No. 10, Budapest.

———. 2001e. "Roma Rights: Mobilization/Participation." *Quarterly Journal of the European Roma Rights Center,* No. 4, Budapest.

————. 2000a. "Racial Discrimination and Violence Against Roma in Europe." Statement Submitted by the ERRC for the consideration by the UN Committee on the Elimination of Racial Discrimination at its 57th Session, on the occasion of its Thematic Discussion on Roma. August 15–16.

————. 2000b. "Racism: Denial and Acknowledgement." *Quarterly Journal of the European Roma Rights Center,* No. 4, Budapest.

————. 2000c. "Roma Rights: Women's Rights." *Quarterly Journal of the European Roma Rights Center,* No. 1, Budapest.

————. 1998. "A Pleasant Fiction: The Human Rights Situation of Roma in Macedonia." *Country Report Series* No. 7, Budapest.

————. 1997. "No Record of the Case. Roma in Albania." Country Reports series No. 5, available on www.errc.org/publications/reports/albania.pdf.

Fraser, A. 1992. *The Gypsies: The People of Europe.* Oxford: Blackwell.

FSHSHC (Fondacioni Shqiptar i Shoqërisë Civile). 1999. "Marrëdhëniet Ndëretnike dhe Rregullimi Ndërkombëtar i Tyre." FSHSHC, Tiranë.

Gal, K. 2000. "The Council of Europe Framework Convention for the Protection Convention of National Minorities and its Impact on Central and Eastern Europe." Flensburg, Germany: European Center for Minority Issues.

Gheorge, N., and A. Mirga. 1997. "The Roma in the Twenty-First Century: A Policy Paper." Princeton, New Jersey: Project on Ethnic Relations.

Golston, A. J. 2002. "Europe's Gypsy Problem." *Foreign Affairs Journal* 81(2): 146–162.

Hancock, I. 1997a. "The media and the Roma in contemporary Europe: Facts and fictions." Introduction, in Hancock I, ed., 2–3, Princeton, NJ: Project on Ethnic Relations Report.

————. 1997b. "The Struggle for the Second Control of Identity." *Transitions* 4(4): 36–44.

Hasluck, M. 1938. "The Gypsies of Albania." *Journal of the Gypsy Lore Society* 17(2): 49–61.

Hoxha, E. 1983. "Vite të Vegjëlisë: Kujtime për Gjirokastrën." Instituti i Studimeve Marksisite-Leniniste Pranë KQ të PPSh, Tiranë.

Human Rights Watch. 1991. "Destroying Ethnic Identity: The Gypsies of Bulgaria." New York: T. Zang.

IDEA (International Debate Education Association). 2002. "Roma Rights: Race, Justice, and Strategies for Equality." New York.

Iliev, I. 1999. "Some Approaches at Measuring Social Capital among Roma Communities in Bulgaria: Preliminary Notes." Draft Background Paper. Washington, DC: World Bank,

Koinova, M. 2000. "Roma of Albania." CEDIME-SE (Center for Documentation and Information on Minorities in Europe-Southeast Europe), Greek Helsinki Monitor, Athens.

Kolsti, J. 1991. "Albanian Gypsies: The Silent Survivors." In Crowe and Kolsti, eds., *The Gypsies in Eastern Europe.* Armonk. New York: Sharpe.

Lakinska-Popovska, D. 2000a. "Vulnerability of Roma Children in the Dispersed Roma Communities in Skopje." National Centre for Training in Social Development, Skopje, Macedonia.

————. 2000b. "Vulnerability of Roma Children in the Municipality of Shuto Orizari." National Centre for Training in Social Development, Skopje, Macedonia.

Liebich, A. 1992. "Minorities in Eastern Europe: Obstacles to a Reliable Count." *RFE/RL Research Report* 1(20).

Macura, V., and M. Petrovic. 1999. "Housing, Urban Planning and Poverty: Problems Faced by Roma/Gypsy Communities with Particular Reference to Central and Eastern Europe." Strasbourg: Document of the Council of Europe, MG-S-Rom (99) 1.

Mara, H. 2002. Conversation with the authors, October.

Margalit, G. 2002. "Germany and Its Gypsies: A Post-Auschwitz Ordeal." Madison, WI: University of Wisconsin Press.

Marushiakova, E., and P. Vesselina. 2001. "New Ethnic Identities in the Balkans: The Case of the Egyptians." *Philosophy and Sociology* 2(8): 465–477.

Milanovic B. 1998. "Income, Inequality, and Poverty During the Transition from Planned to Market Economy." The World Bank: Washington, DC.

Office for National Statistics. 2001. "Social Capital: A Review of the Literature." London: United Kingdom.

Orsos, H., E. Bohn, K. Fleck, and A. Imre. 2000. "Evaluation of the Effectiveness of Alternative Secondary School Models for the Education of Roma Children." Prepared for the World Bank, ECA Human Development Department, Washington DC.

OSCE, 2000c. "Report on the Situation of Roma and Sinti in the OSCE Area." OSCE High Commissioner on National Minorities, The Hague.

Pavis, R. 1998. "Roma/Gypsies Issues in Eastern Europe." Draft PDG Grant Narrative Summary. Washington DC: World Bank.

Project on Ethnic Relations. 1996. "The Media and the Roma in Contemporary Europe: Facts and Fictions." Conference Report, Prague.

Poulton, H. 1991. "The Balkans: Minorities and States in Conflict." Minority Rights Group, London.

Qirici, M. 2002. "Princi Qyqar, Përralla me motive rome." Tirana.

Reyniers, A. 1995. "Gypsy Populations and their Movements Within Central and Eastern Europe and Towards some OECD Countries." International Migration and Labour Market Policies Occasional Papers, No. 1. OECD, Paris.

Shkurti, M. 2001. "The OSCE and the Issue of Security of Roma in the OSCE Area." European University Centre for Peace Studies.

Silverman, C. 2001. Electronic Letter to authors of the concept paper.

———. 1996a. "Music and power: Gender and performance among Roma (Gypsies) of Skopje, Macedonia." *The World of Music, Journal of the International Institute of Traditional Music* 38 (1): 1–15.

———. 1996b. "Music and marginality: Roma (Gypsies) of Bulgaria and Macedonia." In M. Slobin, ed., *Returning Culture: Musical Changes in Central-Eastern Europe.* Durham, N.C.: Duke University Press.

———. 1996c. "State, Market and Gender Relationships Among Bulgarian Roma, 1970s–1980s." *East European Anthropology Review* 14(2): 4–15.

———. 1995a. "Prosecution and Politicization: Roma (Gypsies) of Eastern Europe." *Cultural Survival* 19 (2):43–49.

———. 1995b. "Roma of Shuto Orizari, Macedonia: Class, Politics, and Community." In D. Kideckel, ed., *East-Central European communities: The Struggle for Balance in Turbulent Times.*" Boulder, CO: Westview Press.

———. 1989. "Reconstructing folklore: Media and cultural policy in Eastern Europe." *Communication* 11(2): 141–160.

———. 1988. "Negotiating Gypsiness: Strategy in Context." *Journal of American Folklore* 101 (401): 261–275.

———. 1982. "Everyday Drama: Impression Management of Urban Gypsies." *Urban Anthropology* 11 (3–4): 377–398.

Stewart, M. 1997. "The Time of the Gypsies." Boulder, CO: Westview Press.

Tanaka, B. J., A. Gheorge, and H. Heuss. 1998. "Toward a Pakiv European Roma Fund: Income Generating Programmes for Roma in Central and Eastern Europe." Report commissioned by the Council of Europe and Freudenberg Foundation. MG-S-ROM (98) 10. Strasbourg: Council of Europe.

UNDP. 2000. "Raporti i Zhvillimit Njerëzor për Shqipërinë."

———. 2002a. "The Albanian Response to the Millennium Development Goals." Human Development Promotion Center, Tirana, Albania.

———. 2002b. "Common Country Assessment, Albania." Albanian Center for Economic Research, Tirana, Albania.

UNDP-RSC/ILO. 2002. "Towards Diversity with a Human Face: Roma Issues in Central and Eastern Europe." Bratislava.

UN-HCHR. 1991. The Committee on the Elimination of Racial Discrimination. Fact Sheet No.12.

UNICEF. 1999. "Women in Transition." Regional Monitoring Reports, No. 6. UNICEF International Child Development Centre, Florence.

U.S. Department of State. 2002. "Albania: Country Report on Human Rights Practices 2001." Bureau of Democracy, Human Rights and Labor, Department of State, Washington, DC.

———. 1995. "Country Reports on Human Rights Practices for 1994." Washington, DC: U.S. Government Printing Office, February.

World Bank. 2002a. "Poverty and Welfare of Roma in Slovak Republic." World Bank: Bratislava.

———. 2002b. "Roma and Transition in Central and Eastern Europe—Trends and Challenges." Washington DC.

———. 2002c. "Slovak Republik Living Standards, Employment and Labor Market Study." Report No. 23976, Washington DC.

———. 2002d. "Social Analysis Sourcebook: Incorporating Social Dimensions into Bank-Supported Projects." Social Development Department, Washington DC.

———. 2001a. "Child Welfare Reform Project." Report No. 21012-BUL. Washington DC.

———. 2001b. "Hungary Long-Term Poverty, Social Protection, and the Labor Market." Report No. 20645-HU. Washington DC.

Zoon, I. 2001a. "On the Margins: Roma and Public Services in Romania, Bulgaria and Macedonia, with a supplement on housing in the Czech Republic." New York: Open Society Institute.

———. 2001b. "On the Margins: Slovakia, Roma and Public Services in Slovakia." New York: Open Society Institute.

IBRD 33359

ALBANIA

SERBIA AND
MONTENEGRO

FYR
MACEDONIA

GREECE

Adriatic
Sea

ALBANIA

- ○ SELECTED CITIES AND TOWNS
- ◉ DISTRICT CAPITALS
- ✪ NATIONAL CAPITAL
- ∿ RIVERS
- — MAIN ROADS
- — RAILROADS
- — DISTRICT BOUNDARIES
- —··— INTERNATIONAL BOUNDARIES

Maja Jezercë
(2693 m)

North Albanian Alps
MALSI E
MADHE
Valbona
TROPOJË
Bajram
Curri
Han i Hoti
Koplik
Fierzë
Drin
HAS
Krumë
To
Prizren
Lake
Scutari
SHKODËR
PUKË
Shkodër
(Scutari)
Koman
Pukë
Fush
Arrëz
Kalimash
Kukës
42°N
KUKËS
LEZHË
MIRDITË
Zall-Rec
Shëngjin
Drinit Bay
Rubik
Kurbneshi
Drin i Zi
Lezhë
Kërshen
Peshkopi
Shkopet
Lake
Ulzës
Fushë Kuqe
Laç
Ulëz
Burrel
DIBRA
Rodonit Bay
LAÇ
Mamurasi
Krujë
MAT
Lalëzit
Bay
KRUJË
Fushë
Krujë
Bulqizë
DURRËS
TIRANË
(TIRANA)
BULQIZË
Durrës
Vorë
Shijak
Durrësit
Bay
Ibë
TIRANË
Krrabë
Librazhd
To
Struga
Kavajë
PEQIN
Elbasan
LIBRAZHD
KAVAJË
Peqin
Vidhës
Perrenjas
Lake
Ohrid
41°N
Cërrik
ELBASAN
LUSHNJË
POGRADEC
Lake
Prespa
Karavastasë
Bay
Lushnjë
Kajan
Gramsh
Pogradec
FIER
KUÇOVË
GRAMSH
Little
Lake Prespa
Fier
Marinzë
Kuçovë
Patos
Berat
Maliq
DEVOLL
Kafaraj
Ballsh
BERAT
KORÇË
Korçë
Bilisht
MALLA-
KASTER
Vjosë
SKRAPAR
Selenice
Vlorës
Bay
Vlorë
TEPELENË
Çorovodë
Krahës
Mavrovë
Tepelenë
PËRMET
Ersekë
Kelcyrë
KOLONJË
Përmet
Vjosë
GREECE
VLORË
GJIROKASTËR
Pindus
Mountains
40°N
40°N
Gjirokastër
DELVINË
Delvinë
To
Ioanina
Sarandë
Kakavija
GREECE
SARANDË

To
Podgorica

Buna

0   10   20   30   40 Kilometers
0   10   20   30 Miles

19°E   20°E   21°E

This map was produced by the Map Design Unit of The World Bank.
The boundaries, colors, denominations and any other information
shown on this map do not imply, on the part of The World Bank
Group, any judgment on the legal status of any territory, or any
endorsement or acceptance of such boundaries.

SEPTEMBER 2004